THE CENTER WILL HOLD

A Collection of Essays
in Honor of
MURIEL HARRIS

THE CENTER WILL HOLD

Critical Perspectives on Writing Center Scholarship

Edited by

MICHAEL A. PEMBERTON
JOYCE KINKEAD

UTAH STATE UNIVERSITY PRESS

Logan, Utah

2003

Cover design by Barbara Yale-Read
Manufactured in The United States of America

Library of Congress Cataloging-in-Publication Data

The center will hold : critical perspectives on writing center scholarship / edited by
Michael A. Pemberton, Joyce Kinkead.
     p. cm.
Includes bibliographical references and index.
  ISBN 0-87421-570-6 (pbk.)
  1. English Language—Rhetoric—Study and teaching. 2. Report writing—Study and teaching
(Higher) 3. Interdisciplinary approach in education 4. Writing centers. I. Pemberton, Michael A. II.
Kinkead, Joyce A., 1954-
  PE1404.C46 2003
  808'.042'0711—dc21
                           2003012585

CONTENTS

ACKNOWLEDGMENTS

We teach more by what we are than by what we teach.

WILL DURANT

Whenever we talk about writing centers, we almost always refer to the *community* of writing centers, indicative of the close-knit ties among those who direct and staff these campus units. The community concept is especially important since, as writing center directors typically remark, "there is only one of us on any campus." Thus, reaching out, listening to others, and asking for advice are common, as are conference reunions over breakfast.

Both of us have benefitted from the generosity and expertise of our colleagues over the years, which have contributed to our own professional development. While neither one of us was attending conferences as early as Muriel Harris was in the 1970s, she, in particular, has been our most faithful supporter, sharer of knowledge, and role model. Mickey hosted the Writing Centers Association conference in Purdue in 1984, the event that was to result in the formation of the NCTE-sanctioned National Writing Centers Association, an organization that has been a mooring to both of us. To say that she has enriched our professional and personal lives would be an understatement. For us, Mickey is the very model of a writing center director, aptly named "exemplar" by the CCCC Awards Committee in 2000.

Other colleagues have been instrumental as well, especially through the NWCA (re-named International Writing Centers Association) meetings and conferences: Pamela Farrell Childers, Mildred Steele, Bonnie Sunstein, Jay Jacoby, Harvey Kail, Nancy Grimm, Byron Stay, Eric Hobson, Jon Olson, Paula Gillespie, Leigh Ryan, Brad Hughes, and others far too numerous to name.

For this manuscript, we called on Marina Hall for assistance with editing. Likewise, we are grateful to the reviewers of the volume who offered advice on revisions. Michael Spooner, Director of the Utah State University Press, is a stellar editor, colleague, and friend. We would also like to express our sincere gratitude and appreciation to Janice Neuleib, Joan Mullin, Julie Neff-Lippman, Irene Lurkis Clark, Jeanette Harris, Lady Falls Brown, Lori Baker, Ed Lotto, Barry Maid, Jeanne Simpson, Stephen Adkison, and Margaret Johnson for their support of this project from its earliest stages.

At our own campuses, we wish to thank the following. For Joyce at Utah State University: Andrea Peterson, Director of the Writing Center; Jeffrey Smitten, Head of English; Stan L. Albrecht, Executive Vice President and Provost; and Laura Marks, also of the Provost's office. For Michael at Georgia Southern University: Larry Burton, Chair of the Writing and Linguistics Department; Bettye Stewart in the University Writing Center; and Janice Walker, Suellynn Duffey, and Angela Crow— great associates all.

We offer this book to the writing center community as a tribute to our exemplary colleague, Mickey Harris.

October, 2003
Statesboro, Georgia
Logan, Utah

INTRODUCTION[1]
Benchmarks in Writing Center Scholarship

Michael A. Pemberton
Joyce Kinkead

The "graying of the professoriate" has been a topic of interest for the past decade as higher education literature has pondered the demographics of an aging population of faculty members. With the retirements—anticipated and accomplished—it behooves us to move the stories about writing center histories into the archives in a more formal manner. One would like to say that it will be helpful for those who follow the pioneers to understand how we got here from there so they can enjoy the "wisdom of the past." Would that it had been all wisdom.

Fortunately, a good deal of the wisdom that has accumulated can be attributed to one writing center figure, Muriel Harris. When the Conference on College Composition and Communication honored Muriel Harris with its Exemplar Award at the 2000 convention, the organization merely affirmed what those working in the writing center profession have known for years: Muriel Harris has made profound contributions to our field in innumerable ways. When she published the first issue of the *Writing Lab Newsletter* in April 1977, she helped establish the basis of a new professional community and provided it with an important mechanism for cohesion. While writing centers had been in existence for a great many years before this—at the University of Iowa, for example, under the guidance of Lou Kelly—it was not until the creation of the *Newsletter* that writing center directors and staff had a national forum for regular publication and professional contact. Over the course of the next 25 years, Muriel Harris and the *Newsletter* have become two of the writing center community's most valuable resources. Together, they have confirmed writing center studies as a legitimate area of scholarly inquiry, given shape to a new field of study that has become increasingly sophisticated theoretically, educated hundreds of writing center professionals, and helped us to envision the nature of writing centers and the direction of writing center scholarship in the millennium to come.

Had the *Writing Lab Newsletter* been Muriel Harris's only contribution to the field, it would have been noteworthy in itself; yet Professor Harris's contributions have gone far beyond this. Her regular publications in professional journals such as *College English* and *College Composition and Communication*, her innumerable book chapters, and a number of full-length texts—most notably *Tutoring Writing: A Sourcebook for Writing Labs* (1982), *Teaching One-to-One: The Writing Conference* (1986), and *The Prentice Hall Reference Guide to Grammar and Usage* (2003)—not only have kept writing center scholarship in the eye of the larger composition community, but they also have spoken about the work we do with theoretical incisiveness, invoking current research into collaborative learning, situated discourse communities, networks of power and authority, and technological literacy. In all these ways and more, Muriel Harris continues to be one of the most forward-thinking and visionary members of the writing center community she helped to found nearly a quarter of a century ago.

In honor of Muriel Harris, then, this text provides a critical perspective on current issues in the writing center field that have emerged, in part, as a result of Harris's research, scholarship, teaching, and service to the field. For the last thirty years, Harris has been working to expand the writing center community, to help define it, and to identify shared principles with others who work in the larger area of composition studies. For the most part this work has been successful. We, as writing center professionals, have convened at conferences, founded forums for publication, and established national and regional organizations. But we now face the critical question "What next?" as we prepare ourselves for the demands of the coming century and the institutional, demographic, and financial changes that it is likely to bring. It is an appropriate point to reflect on the past and envision the future and, in doing so, to acknowledge the contributions that Muriel Harris has made to the present state of the writing center "world."

We offer this text, then, as both an overview of Muriel Harris's continuing legacy and as a general framework for the writing center research that is yet to come. The contributors to this volume offer explicit recognition of the role that Muriel Harris has played in the field's development and to the development of their own research agendas, but they also see that history as only a starting point from which to provide reflective, descriptive, and predictive looks at the field which Dr. Harris has helped to shape.

Though it is hardly possible, even in a substantial book such as this, to enumerate the multiple ways, great and small, Muriel Harris has influenced writing center scholarship and practice, we would nevertheless like to suggest several that we feel are among the most pervasive and significant. Identifying these areas will serve a dual purpose for us here, giving us the opportunity not only to review (and honor) Harris's contributions to the field, but to introduce, in turn, each of the chapters that builds on those contributions.

COMMUNITY-BUILDING AND THE WRITING LAB NEWSLETTER

Almost from the start of the writing centers movement, Muriel Harris has been a presence—a presence for the good. The 1977 panel of writing center directors and tutors at the Conference on College Composition and Communication (CCCC)—a panel which included Harris—was a continuing response to the CCCC 1973 report on the learning skills center, which was itself a response to the change in climate and student profile on college campuses that resulted from open admissions. "Skills" center sessions had been on the NCTE and CCCC programs in 1971, evoking some fear from conference attendees that the mechanized programs used in centers might replace writing teachers. Attendees disagreed with one another strenuously about how best to meet the needs of students. The pedagogical debates targeted mass-produced audiotapes and argued for humanistic and humane interventions such as the one-to-one tutorial. At the end of this volatile session, Harris took out pen and pad, invited participants to write their names and addresses, and, using that list, mailed out the first issue of the *Writing Lab Newsletter* (*WLN*), produced on a Sears typewriter at her kitchen table. In this issue and those that followed, Harris sought to explain, through illustrative contributions by practitioners, the rationale and mission of writing labs and writing centers, calming the fears of those who thought such places focused exclusively on the "mechanical aspects of writing." By editing the primary organ of communication for the writing center/lab community, she, in effect, set the agenda for its development.

But this was not the *Newsletter*'s only, or even necessarily its most important function for the nascent writing center "interest group." In the opening chapter of this collection, Michael Pemberton offers an historical overview of the *Writing Lab Newsletter*'s development from what began, in essence, as an informal bulletin and mailing list into one of the field's primary venues for publication and research. Pemberton approaches this task both as an archival account—detailing the physical and editorial changes in the *Newsletter* over the years—and as a sociohistorical investigation, connecting developments in the *Newsletter* to similar developments in the writing center field. He also makes the case for how the *WLN* served the political agenda of the community.

Organization is key to Muriel Harris's lasting influence on the writing center movement. In addition to establishing the *WLN* so that directors could be in contact with one another, Harris moved to organize special interest groups of writing lab directors at the 1979 and 1980 CCCC sessions that became annual events coupled with materials exchange. Certainly 1979 proved a benchmark year in which a group of directors in the east central region of the country gathered for a spring meeting; out of this gathering the National Writing Centers Association evolved. A number of voices joined Harris's in promoting the writing center agenda. Mildred Steele of Central College in Pella, Iowa, spearheaded a resolution on the professional status of writing lab professionals that was approved at the 1981 CCCC; Jay Jacoby authored a second version of this resolution for the 1987 CCCC. *Resolution*, in fact, characterized Harris's work and those who worked in partnership with her.

Even in these early days, Harris went to great lengths to provide forums for discussions, including hosting the 1983 conference of the Writing Centers Association at Purdue with its theme of "New Directions, New Connections." At that meeting, the members of the inaugural executive committee of the new National Writing Centers Association were nominated. By the fall meeting of the NCTE, the association had approval and staged its first official meeting with the charter board in action to author professional statements, provide support to those in the field, and establish a secretariat.

BUILDING A RESEARCH AND SCHOLARSHIP AGENDA

But the *Newsletter* would not remain the only venue available for the publication of writing center work. Dissemination of essays about writing center practice and policies soon found outlets in new periodicals devoted to the increasingly important issues of tutoring, basic writing, and pedagogy: *Journal of Basic Writing* (1979); *WPA: Writing Program Administration* (1979); *The Writing Center Journal* (1980). Books also followed: Hawkins and Brooks's *Improving Writing Skills* (1981), Harris's *Tutoring Writing* (1982), Steward and Croft's *The Writing Laboratory* (1982), Jackie Goldsby's *Peer Tutoring in Basic Writing: A Tutor's Journal* (1981) from the Bay Area Writing Project.

Harris's edited volume proved a seminal reference book for writing center professionals, and Harris's formidable role in the establishment and acceptance of writing centers in the profession includes an enviable scholarly track record that has been sustained over her entire career. In addition to highlighting best practices, she has been the model of Ernest Boyer's scholarship of service as well as a fine researcher. Her research agenda over the years has covered a wide range of topics in the field of writing center studies, among them close analyses of conversation in writing conferences, issues central to teacher training, models for integrating writing centers with WAC and ESL programs, applications of computer technology for instructional delivery, critical components of writing center administration, and pedagogical theory. The breadth and depth of her scholarship has touched virtually every aspect of writing center inquiry, and the body of her work has become a touchstone of excellence for those who hope to follow in her footsteps.

Early in her academic career, as the director of the newly-formed Writing Lab at Purdue University, Muriel Harris, like many of us, was a scholar in search of a professional identity. While the "process approach" had gained tremendous momentum in rhetoric/composition studies by the late 1970s, writing centers were still deeply influenced by a current-traditional paradigm that valorized grammatical correctness over process and invested in an institutional model that relegated them to the domain of remediation. The influence of this current-traditional model on Harris's emerging view of writing centers can be seen in some of her earliest publications, which focused primarily on grammar and spelling pedagogy: "The Big Five: Individualizing Improvement in Spelling" (1977), "Contradictory Perceptions of Rules of Writing" (1979), and "Mending the Fragmented Free Modifier" (1981). Yet it is also clear that this narrow view of writing and the constricting paradigm that imposed it did not suit her vision of what a writing center could and *should* be. She began to explore alternative models and found herself writing frequently about the writing center's instructional *mission* in articles like "Beyond Freshmen Composition: Other Uses of the Writing Lab" (with Kathleen Blake Yancey, 1980), "Process and Product: Dominant Models for Writing Centers" (1981), "Growing

Pains: The Coming of Age of Writing Centers" (1982), and "Writing Labs: Why Bother?" (1983). She confirmed her role as a leader in the field, asking questions, challenging assumptions, creating new instructional and institutional goals, and indicating new research directions to a growing cadre of like-minded professionals.

As Harris reflected on the possibilities for writing centers as vital sites for teaching, learning, and research, her publications mirrored her thoughts. In "Evaluation: The Process for Revision" (1978), she aligned herself firmly with the process movement, and in "Individualized Diagnosis: Searching for Causes, Not Symptoms of Writing Deficiencies" (1978), she also aligned herself with Mina Shaughnessy's view that "basic writers" made "errors" for a reason, not because they were merely slothful or intellectually inadequate. The best way to discover these causes, in Harris's view, was to engage students in dialogue about their writing—to see them as individuals with the ability to use language in powerful ways given the opportunity—in short, to have one-to-one conferences with them in writing centers. Through much of the 1980s, then, Harris promoted the value of the writing center and writing center conferences as powerful learning environments where students could reap valuable cognitive benefits from talking about their writing and receiving feedback from interested peers. Drawing on the work of Linda Flower and John Hayes (1980, 1981), Harris often framed her arguments in cognitive terms, referring to rhetorical strategies, mental processes, and cognitive models in articles such as "Strategies, Options, Flexibility, and the Composing Process" (1982), "Modeling: A Process Method of Teaching" (1983), "Diagnosing Writing Process Problems: A Pedagogical Application of Speaking-Aloud Protocol Analyses" (1985), and "Simultaneous and Successive Cognitive Processing and Writing Skills: Relationships Between Proficiencies" (with Mary Wachs, 1986).

The need for continued research on writing centers remains a driving force in our field, and as we have elevated our professional standing not just institutionally, but academically as well, it has become incumbent upon us to produce research and scholarship that meets the highest standards of intellectual rigor. It must pass muster theoretically, methodologically, and professionally. But we now have to ask, what should that research look like? Where should its focus be? What theories should it draw from, and how should it situate itself in relation to the larger area of composition studies? Nancy Grimm confronts several of these questions in her chapter, making a strong case for the importance and value of research as one part of a writing center's overall instructional mission and offering several goals such research might pursue. She argues that by making research a "featured character" of the service we provide to students and our institutions (just as Muriel Harris has done), we will add significant value to both our teaching and service missions.

But research *into* our teaching and service missions has long posed special problems for writing centers, particularly because they are not often geared to quantifiable results or easy correspondences between student conferences and retention and/or improved grades. The "proof" of writing center effectiveness, though a necessity in times of tight budgets and strident calls for accountability, has often relied on anecdotal evidence or research studies with shaky methodologies. Neal Lerner reviews the work that has been conducted on "Writing Center Assessment" in his chapter, and he lays out a clear agenda for how we should improve the quality of such research in the future.

TEACHING, TUTORING, AND COLLABORATING

Research is not the only featured player in the writing center world or in Muriel Harris's life. Pedagogy, too, holds an important place, and nowhere is this more evident than in her guide for tutors, *Teaching One-to-One: The Writing Conference* (1985). Part theory, part history, part training manual, this text was used to prepare a whole generation of writing center tutors and directors, and also set the tone for how scholars and practitioners *talked about* writing centers for years to come. The power of such a text to inscribe a discourse community and construct a "master narrative" for a field is the subject of Harvey Kail's chapter. Kail investigates the materials we have used to train tutors, the "manuals" of various sorts that embody a kind of writing center *bildungsroman* at the same time that they impart tutorial strategies. Because they offer a narrative blend of tutorial instruction, writing center history, and theory, Kail claims that these manuals also embody "plots" that construct a tutor's mission in metaphorical terms. We must understand these narratives, he says, and be willing to question some of the value systems that are implicit in such metaphors, including Harris's.

Harris's focus on pedagogy is also strongly apparent in the pages of the *WLN*. Articles about teaching and tutoring appear in virtually every issue of the *Newsletter,* and these articles are among the most frequently used resources for tutor training courses and workshops. Harris knows that many of her readers measure their true success in terms of the students they assist and the developing writers they help to grow, and the *Newsletter* has always been strongly supportive of this perspective. But this is not to say that pedagogy is an uncontested battleground in the *WLN* or that its readers have all achieved a comfortable consensus about their role as practitioners. We often struggle with questions about *what sort of teachers we are*. As Harris states in her 1995 piece on "Why Writers Need Writing Tutors:"

> Tutorial instruction . . . introduces into the educational setting a middle person, the tutor, who inhabits a world somewhere between student and teacher. . . . Students readily view a tutor as someone to help them surmount the hurdles others have set up for them, and as a result students respond differently to tutors than to teachers. (27-28)

But this odd positioning has naturally raised many questions about power, responsibility, expectations, and tutorial strategy. We are expected to help, but not help too much or in the wrong way. We are expected to be authorities, but we're not supposed to be authoritative. Where once the dictum "the student should do the work, not the tutor" held sway, we have recently been challenged by "critiques of pure tutoring" that urge us to reclaim our authority in the name of good teaching and professional status. Harris has long been an active voice in this discussion, and she has encouraged readers to carry on the debate in the pages of the *Newsletter*. Peter Carino, in his chapter, helps to frame this debate, offering a historical perspective on the idea of "authority" as it has developed in writing center scholarship, teasing out its multiple meanings in our professional discourse, and problematizing the simple belief that the tutor who helps the most is the one who directs the least.

A key term in Carino's overview is "collaboration," a pedagogical and professional practice we could all be said to embrace and a teaching strategy that Muriel Harris has supported for her whole professional life. But "collaboration," like "authority," is a term with multiple meanings and multiple implications for writing centers. If writing centers are truly collaborative—in theory as well as in practice—what does that imply about the way we should be structured, institutionally as well as pedagogically? Michele Eodice, like Carino, believes that collaboration is, indeed, at the heart of what we do in writing centers, but she wonders whether we are collaborative *enough*. Should we be satisfied to consider collaboration *only* as a feature of the tutor/student interaction, or should it, in fact, be central to the way we teach, work with, administer, and interact with others?

This question is critically important to future writing center directors, a group that is the focus of Rebecca Jackson, Carrie Leverenz, and Joe Law's chapter on graduate courses in writing center theory, practice, and administration. The authors remind us that "writing center pedagogy" is no longer limited to a focus on student/tutor interactions and the techniques we can use to help students become better writers. It now encompasses the training and coursework we provide to those who will be our professional descendants. Just as Kail explores the metaphorical construction of individual training manuals, Jackson et al. assess the extent to which several graduate-level writing center courses across the country are places where the formation of writing center disciplinary identities takes place.

WRITING CENTER ADMINISTRATION

In recent years, Harris's research has begun to move away from (but not completely abandon) the particulars of cognition and effective conferencing strategies and move toward a consideration of the political/administrative agendas that shape a writing center's position in larger institutional contexts. In part, this shift reflects Harris's current status as the *de facto* spokesperson for writing center issues and concerns on a national level, but it is also, in many ways, the result of twenty-five years of experience fighting battles—and watching others fight battles—with administrators and faculty who believed writing centers were little more than remedial services or sites for institutionalized plagiarism. Her 1991 article in the *Writing Center Journal*, "Solutions and Trade-Offs in Writing Center Administration" (which won that year's Outstanding Scholarship Award from the NWCA), revealed her awareness of the serious difficulties faced by many writing center professionals. She asked readers to consider how they would respond to situations like these, situations that were all too familiar to many in her audience:

> You, as director, are being reviewed for promotion and tenure by people who don't particularly value or understand what writing centers are all about. (71)

> The administration wants to cut the lab's budget because of general financial needs, and a good place to start, they think, is a student service like the writing center. (74)

By raising these questions, Harris challenged her readers to think seriously about their academic status and to recognize the professional victimization to which many of them were being subjected. She confronted these issues head-on, but showed a deep sensitivity to the institutional vulnerabilities under which many of her colleagues worked.

A number of the articles Harris has published since 1999 have addressed additional complexities which attend a writing center administrator's professional life. In book chapters and journal articles such as "Diverse Research Methodologies at Work for Diverse Audiences: Shaping the Writing Center to the Institution" (1999), "Preparing to Sit at the Head Table: Maintaining Writing Center Viability in the Twenty-First Century" (2000), and "Writing Center Administration: Making Local, Institutional Knowledge in our Writing Centers" (forthcoming), Harris has continued to study and reflect on the ways in which writing centers can integrate themselves more fully into campus communities, ensuring not only their continued intellectual growth but also their economic survival.

As she has become a stronger voice in the discipline, she has become an even stronger advocate for writing centers institutionally. She has taken administrators to task for failure to communicate, failure to support the writing center that provides a cornucopia of benefits in cost-effective ways to a higher education institution. Jo Koster takes up this banner in her chapter and challenges writing center administrators to draw on their rhetorical powers to market those benefits as the center meets its multiple missions of serving the larger institution.

WRITING CENTER SPACES (REAL AND VIRTUAL)

Harris has long been interested in writing center "spaces" and the characteristics that constitute an "ideal" center in design as well as practice. As early as 1985, in her article "Theory and Reality: The Ideal Writing Center(s)," Harris began to dream of what a writing center could be, given time, money, training opportunities, and the support of an enlightened administration. She recognized that many of these dreams were likely to remain dreams—for her, at least—given the realities of life in an institution where every unit competes for limited funds and believes its own needs are the most important. When she described the Purdue Writing Lab for *Writing Centers in Context* (1993a), she sounded uncharacteristically forlorn when talking about the future:

We are still seriously overcrowded in both rooms, but given the accompanying overcrowding in the rest of the building, there is little hope at present for further expansion. We dream of additional space for more tutoring tables and computers as well as space for more appropriate equipment for ESL students to practice speaking skills, but this is little more than wishful thinking. (6)

Despite these limitations, Harris's own writing center is marked by its welcoming coffeepot, homey couch, and comforting plants. The importance of place and the implicit messages spaces leave with students are explored in Hadfield et al.'s chapter on architecture, design, and learning. This chapter focuses on how writing center directors can enter the conversation of designers to achieve spaces that enhance learning.

But Harris, quite typically, could not stay forlorn about her own situation for long. If she could not escape the restrictive physical limitations of her own writing center space, then she determined to move beyond it by expanding into the virtual world of the Internet, a prospect that was only just beginning to open at the time *Writing Centers in Context* was published.

Certainly no review of Muriel Harris's contribution to the writing center field would be complete without a mention of her work on Online Writing Labs (OWLs). The Purdue University Online Writing Lab, whose creation she spearheaded, has become the de facto standard against which other OWLs are measured. Though Harris has long evidenced an interest in computers—her article "Computers Across the Curriculum" (with Madelon Cheek) appeared in the second issue of *Computers and Composition* in 1985—it took the full-scale development of the Internet before her interest in online writing center work came to fruition. Ten years after her first computer-focused article, Harris published three pieces about OWLs in 1995. The first (with Michael Pemberton), "Online Writing Labs (OWLs): A Taxonomy of Options and Issues," offered a detailed framework to help others who might be thinking about designing OWLs; the second, "Hatching an OWL (Online Writing Lab)," described how her own OWL was designed and grew; and the third, "From the (Writing) Center to the Edge: Moving Writers Along the Internet," considered how e-mail, MOOs, Gophers, and the World Wide Web could enhance a writing center's operations. The OWL at Purdue University was one of the nation's first, but it has since spawned well over a hundred more at colleges, universities, two-year colleges, and high schools across the country.

The expansion of the Internet as a resource for educators also enabled the development of professional listservs, virtual "spaces" where professionals, novices, teachers, and other interested parties can connect, share information, get and be mentored, and coalesce into a mutually-supportive community. The listserv that has come to fulfill those functions in the writing center community is WCenter, founded by Lady Falls Brown at Texas Technological University in 1991. WCenter has, in some ways, taken on the community-building role begun by the *Newsletter*, and it has adopted much the same tone—chatty and friendly sometimes, serious and intellectually engaged at others. James Inman and Donna Sewell investigate some of the important ways in which mentoring and training takes place on WCenter. What techniques for online mentoring appear to be most constructive? they wonder. What are the implications for future mentoring in electronic spaces? How, they ask, can online discourse best fulfill the vision that Muriel Harris has set forth for responsible, ethical mentoring and the development of an active, productive community of scholars?

And so we end where we began—with Muriel Harris. This is unsurprising, of course, because Muriel Harris remains at the forefront of writing center scholarship and practice—researching, designing, developing, and publishing. She has mentored us with her advice[2] and kept our spirits up with her unflagging (and wonderfully twisted) sense of humor.

She has left us a remarkable legacy, and it isn't over yet.

APPENDIX
Muriel Harris's Publications, 1977-2002

1. BOOKS AUTHORED

Prentice Hall Reference Guide to Grammar and Usage. (Fifth Edition) Upper Saddle River, New Jersey: Prentice Hall, in press.

Prentice Hall Reference Guide to Grammar and Usage. (Fourth Edition) Upper Saddle River, New Jersey: Prentice Hall, 2000.

The Writer's FAQs: A Pocket Handbook. Upper Saddle River, New Jersey: Prentice Hall, 2000.

Prentice Hall Reference Guide to Grammar and Usage. (Third Edition) Upper Saddle River, New Jersey: Prentice Hall, 1997.

Prentice Hall Reference Guide to Grammar and Usage. (Second Edition) Englewood Cliffs, New Jersey: Prentice Hall, 1994.

Prentice Hall Reference Guide to Grammar and Usage. Englewood Cliffs, New Jersey: Prentice Hall, 1991.

Practicing Grammar and Usage. Englewood Cliffs, New Jersey: Prentice Hall, 1991.

Teaching One-to-One: The Writing Conference. Urbana, Illinois: National Council of Teachers of English, 1986.

Making Paragraphs Work (With Thomas Gaston). New York: Holt, Rinehart, and Winston, 1985.

Practice for a Purpose. Boston: Houghton Mifflin, 1984.

2. BOOKS EDITED

The Writing Lab Directory. West Lafayette, Indiana: Purdue University Department of English, 1984.

Proceedings of the Writing Centers Association Fifth Annual Conference. West Lafayette, Indiana: Purdue University, 1983.

Tutoring Writing: A Sourcebook for Writing Labs. Glenview, Illinois: Scott, Foresman and Company, 1982.

3. JOURNAL FOUNDED AND EDITED

Writing Lab Newsletter (founded in 1977; editor 1977 to present)

4. BOOK CHAPTERS

"Writing Center Administration: Making Local, Institutional Knowledge in our Writing Centers." In *Writing Center Research: Extending the Conversation.* Ed. Paula Gillespie, Alice Gillam, Lady Falls Brown, and Byron Stay. Mahwah, NJ: Lawrence Erlbaum, 2002.

"Writing Centers, the Internet, Listservs, OWLs, and MOOs." (Contribution to book by Pamela B. Childers). *Secondary School Writing Centers in the 21st Century.* Boynton/Cook. Forthcoming.

"'What Would You Like to Work on Today?': The Writing Center as a Site for Teacher Training." *Preparing College Teachers of Writing: Histories, Theories, Programs, and Practices.* Eds. Betty Pytlik and Sarah Liggett. Oxford UP, 2002. 194–207.

"Fill 'er Up, Pass the Band-Aids, Center the Margin, and Praise the Lord: Mixing Metaphors in the Writing Lab." (with Katherine M. Fischer) *The Politics of Writing Centers.* Ed. Jane Nelson and Kathy Evertz. Portsmouth, NH: Heinemann, 2001. 23–36.

"Talk to Me: Engaging Reluctant Writers." *A Tutor's Guide: Helping Writers One-to-One.* Ed. Ben Rafoth. Portsmouth, NH: Boynton/Cook, 2000. 24–34.

"Making Up Tomorrow's Agenda and Shopping Lists Today: Preparing for Future Technologies in Writing Centers." *Taking Flight with OWLS: Research into Technology Use in Writing Centers.* Ed. James Inman and Donna Sewell. Mahwah, NJ: Lawrence Erlbaum Associates, 2000. 193–202.

"Whenever I hear. . . . [#97]" *Comp Tales.* Eds. Richard H. Haswell and Min-Zhan Lu. New York: Longman, 2000. 120–121.

"Diverse Research Methodologies at Work for Diverse Audiences: Shaping the Writing Center to the Institution." *The Writing Program Administrator as Researcher.* Ed. Shirley K. Rose and Irwin Weiser. Portsmouth, NH: Boynton/Cook Heinemann, 1999. 1–17.

"Selecting and Training Undergraduate and Graduate Staffs in a Writing Lab." *Administrative Problem Solving for Writing Programs and Writing Centers.* Ed. Linda Myer Breslin. Urbana, IL: National Council of Teachers of English, 1999. 14–29.

"A Writing Center without a WAC Program: The De facto WAC Center/Writing Center." *The Interdisciplinary Partnership: Writing Centers and Writing Across the Curriculum Programs.* Ed. Jacob Blumner and Robert Barnett. Westport, CT: Greenwood, 1999. 89–103.

"A Discussion on Collaborative Design Methods for Collaborative Online Spaces." (Co-author: Stuart Blythe, with Suzanne Pollert and Amy Stellmach). *Weaving Knowledge Together: Writing Centers and Collaboration.* Ed. Carol Haviland and Thia Wolf. Emmitsburg, MD: NWCA Press, 1998. 81–105.

"Writing Center Theory." *Theorizing Composition: A Critical Sourcebook of Theory and Scholarship in Contemporary Composition Studies.* Ed. Mary Lynch Kennedy. Westport, CT: Greenwood Press, 1998. 364–371.

"Managing Services in the Writing Center: Scheduling, Record-Keeping, Forms." *The Writing Center Resource Manual.* Ed. Bobbie Silk. Emmitsburg, MD: NWCA Press, 1998. III. 2. 1–9.

"A Multi-function OWL (Online Writing Lab): Using Computers to Expand the Role of Writing Centers in Communication across the Curriculum." *Electronic*

Communication Across the Curriculum. Ed. Donna Reiss, Art Young, and Dickie Selfe. Urbana, IL: NCTE, 1998. 3–16.

"When Writers Write About Writing." *Teaching Writing Creatively.* Ed. David Starkey. Portsmouth, NH: Boynton/Cook, 1998. 58–70.

"Cultural Conflicts in the Writing Center: Expectations and Assumptions of ESL Students." *Writing in Multicultural Settings.* Ed. Carol Severino, Juan C. Guerra, and Johnella E. Butler. New York: MLA, 1997. 220–233.

"Presenting Writing Center Scholarship: Issues in Educating Review and Search Committees." *Academic Advancement in Composition Studies: Scholarship, Publication, Promotion, Tenure.* Ed. Richard Gebhardt and Barbara Gebhardt. Mahwah, NJ: Lawrence Erlbaum,1997. 87–102.

"Working with Individual Differences in the Writing Tutorial." *Most Excellent Differences: Essays on Using Type Theory in the English Classroom.* Ed. Thomas Thompson. Gainesville: CAPT, 1996. 90–100.

"Individualized Instruction in Writing Centers: Attending to Writers' Cross-Cultural Differences." *Intersections: Theory-Practice in the Writing Center.* Ed. Joan Mullin and Ray Wallace. Urbana, IL: NCTE: 1994. 96–110.

"A Multi-service Writing Lab in a Multiversity: The Purdue University Writing Lab." *Writing Centers in Context.* Ed. Jeanette Harris and Joyce Kinkead. Urbana, IL: NCTE, 1993. 1–27.

"Don't Believe Everything You're Taught—Matching Writing Processes and Personal Preferences." *The Subject is Writing.* Ed. Wendy Bishop. Upper Montclair, NJ: Boynton/Cook, 1993. 189–201.

"The Writing Center and Tutoring in the WAC Program." *Writing Across the Curriculum: A Guide to Developing Programs.* Ed. Susan McLeod and Margot Soven. Newbury Park, CA: Sage, 1992. 154–174.

"Teacher/Student Talk: The Collaborative Conference." *Perspectives on Talk and Learning.* Ed. Susan Hynds and Donald Rubin. Urbana, Illinois: National Council of Teachers of English, 1990. 149–161.

"A Writing Profile: How I Write." *Writers on Writing,* Vol II. Ed. Tom Waldrep. New York: Random House, 1988. 101–109.

"Diagnosing Writing Process Problems: A Pedagogical Application of Speaking-Aloud Protocol Analyses." *When a Writer Can't Write: Research in Writer's Block and Other Writing Process Problems.* Ed. Mike Rose. New York: Guildford Press, 1985. 166–181.

"Process and Product: Dominant Models for Writing Centers." *"Improving Writing Skills."* Ed. Thom Hawkins and Phyllis Brooks. *New Directions for College Learning Assistance.* San Francisco: Jossey-Bass, 1981. 3. 1–8.

"Review of Current Research." *The Composing Process,* Working Papers, No. 1. Ed. David Ewing. Center for Interdisciplinary Studies in Composition. West Lafayette,Indiana: Purdue University School of Humanities, Social Studies, and Education, 1980. 1–18.

"The Overgraded Paper: Another Case of More is Less." *How to Handle the Paper Load: Classroom Practices in Teaching English, 1979–1980.* Ed. Gene Stanford. Urbana, Illinois: National Council of Teachers of English, 1979. 91–94.

"The Big Five: Individualizing Improvement in Spelling." *Classroom Practices in Teaching English, 1977–1978: Teaching the Basics—Really!* Ed. Ouida Clapp. Urbana, Illinois: National Council of Teachers of English, 1977. 104–107.

5. PAMPHLETS

Writing Centers. SLATE Starter Sheet. Urbana, Illinois: National Council of Teachers of English, 1988.

6. ENCYCLOPEDIA ENTRIES

"Writing Centers." *Encyclopedia of English Studies and Language Arts.* Ed. Alan Purves. New York: Scholastic, 1994. 1293–1295.

7. JOURNAL ARTICLES

A. Refereed Journals

"Writing Centers: Resources for Students and Instructors." *Successful Professor* (online journal). In press.

"Centering in on Professional Choices." *College Composition and Communication* 52:3 (2001): 429–440.

"Preparing to Sit at the Head Table: Maintaining Writing Center Viability in the Twenty-First Century." *Writing Center Journal* 20.2 (Spring/Summer, 2000): 13–21.

"Response to: "Two Comments on 'Situating Teacher Practice.'" *College English* 59.8 (1997): 956–960.

"Response to: 'Open Admissions and the Construction of Writing Center History: A Tale of Three Models.'" *Writing Center Journal* 17.2 (Spring 1997): 134–140.

"From the (Writing) Center to the Edge: Moving Writers Along the Internet." *The Clearing House* 69.1 (1995): 21–23.

"Online Writing Labs (OWLs): A Taxonomy of Options and Issues." (With Michael Pemberton) *Computers and Composition* 12.2 (1995): 145–159.

"Talking in the Middle: Why Writers Need Writing Tutors." *College English* 57.1 (1995): 27–42.

• Reprinted in *The Writing Teacher's Sourcebook.* 4th ed. Eds. Edward P.J. Corbett, Nancy Myers, and Gary Tate. Oxford: Oxford UP, 2000.

• Reprinted in *Teaching in Progress: Theories, Practices, Scenarios.* New York: Longman, 1996. 139–151.

"Tutoring ESL Students: Issues and Options." (With Tony Silva) *College Composition and Communication* 44.2 (1993): 525–537.

- Reprinted in *Background Readings for Instructors Using the Bedford Guide*, Ed. T. R. Johnson. Boston: Bedford Books of St. Martin's, 1999.
- Reprinted in *Teaching with the Bedford Guide for College Writers*. Ed. X.J. Kennedy, Dorothy Kennedy, and Sylvia A. Halladay. Vol.2: Background Readings. Ed. Shirley Morahan. Boston: Bedford Books of St. Martin's, 1996.
- Reprinted in Robert J. Connors and Cheryl Glenn. *The St. Martin's Guide to Teaching Writing*, 3rd ed. Boston: St. Martin's, 1995.

"Collaboration Is Not Collaboration Is Not Collaboration: Writing Center Tutorials vs. Peer Response Groups." *College Composition and Communication* 43 (1992): 369–383.

- Reprinted in *The Allyn & Bacon Guide to Writing Center Theory and Practice*. Eds. Robert Barnett and Jacob Blumner. Boston: Allyn & Bacon, 2000.

"Solutions and Trade-Offs in Writing Center Administration." *Writing Center Journal* 12.1 (1991): 63–79.

"What's Up and What's In: Trends and Traditions in Writing Centers." *Writing Center Journal* 11.1 (1990): 15–25.

"Explaining Grammatical Concepts." (With Katherine Rowan) *Journal of Basic Writing* 8.2 (1989): 21–41.

- Reprinted in *Sourcebook for Writing Teachers*. New York:Allyn & Bacon, 1996.

"Composing Behaviors of One-and Multi-draft Writers." *College English* 51 (1989): 174–191.

- To be reprinted in Glen Blalock. *Background Readings*. 6th ed. Boston: St. Martin's, forthcoming.
- To be reprinted in *Concepts in Composition: Theory and Practice in the Teaching of Writing*, Ed. Irene Clark. Mahwah, NJ: Lawrence Erlbaum. 2002.
- Reprinted in *The Subject of Writing is Writing*. Ed. Lisa McClure. Chicago: NTC, 1999.
- Translated into Norwegian and selected for inclusion in *Skriveteori*. Ed. Eva Bjorkvold and Sylvi Penne. Oslo: J. W. Cappelens. 1998.
- Reprinted in Glen Blalock. *Background Readings for Instructors Using the Bedford Handbook 5th Edition*. Boston: Bedford, 1997.
- Reprinted in Glenn Blalock. *Background Readings*. 2nd ed. Boston: St Martin's, 1994.

"Peer Tutoring: How Tutors Learn." *Teaching English in the Two-Year College* 15.1 (1988): 28–33.

"Ins and Outs of Conferencing." *Writing Instructor* 6.2 (1987): 87–96.

"Training Teachers for the Writing Lab: A Multi-dimensional Perspective." (With Ronald Adams, Robert Child, and Kathleen Henriott) *Writing Center Journal* 7.2 (1987): 3–19.

"Simultaneous and Successive Cognitive Processing and Writing Skills: Relationships Between Proficiencies." (With Mary Wachs) *Written Communication* 3.4 (1986): 449–470.

"Simultaneous and Successive Processing in University Students: Their Contribution to Academic Performance." (With Mary Wachs) *Journal of Psychoeducational Assessment* 4(1986): 103–112.

"Visualization and Spelling Competence. " *Journal of Remedial and Developmental Education* 9.2 (1985): 2–5.

"Theory and Reality: The Ideal Writing Center(s)." *Writing Center Journal* 5.2 (1985): 4–9.

"Writing Labs: Why Bother?" *The English Quarterly* 16.2 (1983): 6–13.

"Modeling: A Process Method of Teaching." *College English* 45 (1983): 74–84.

"A Grab-Bag of Diagnostic Techniques." *Teaching English in the Two-Year College* 9 (1983): 111–115.

"Supplementary Writing Instruction for Engineering Students." *Engineering Education* 73 (1983): 311–313.

"Strategies, Options, Flexibility, and the Composing Process." *The English Quarterly* 15 (1982): 51–61.

"An Introduction to the Basics of Writing Labs." *Journal of Teaching Writing* 1.1 (1982): 109–113.

"Growing Pains: The Coming of Age of Writing Centers." *The Writing Center Journal* 2.1. (1982): 1–8.

"The View from the Writing Lab: Another Way to Evaluate a Composition Program." *WPA:Writing Program Administration Journal* 5 (1981): 13–19.

"Mending the Fragmented Free Modifier." *College Composition and Communication* 32 (1981): 175–182.
  •Reprinted in *Rhetoric and Composition: A Sourcebook for Teachers of Writing*. Ed. Richard Graves. New ed. Upper Montclair, New Jersey: Boynton-Cook, 1984. 245–251.

"Beyond Freshman Composition: Other Uses of the Writing Lab." (With Kathleen Blake Yancey) *The Writing Center Journal* 1.1. (1980): 43–49.

"The Roles a Tutor Plays: Effective Tutoring Techniques." *English Journal* 69 (1980): 62–65.

"Audience Feedback in the Pre-Writing Stage." *English in the Two-Year College* 12.2 (1980): 7–8.

"(Muriel Harris Responds)." *College English* 41 (1979): 342–345.
  •Reprinted in *Tutoring Writing: A Sourcebook for Writing Labs*. Ed. Muriel Harris. Glenview, Illinois: Scott, Foresman, and Co., 1982. 62–65.

"Contradictory Perceptions of Rules of Writing." *College Composition and Communication* 30 (1979): 218–220.

"Individualized Diagnosis: Searching for Causes, Not Symptoms of Writing Deficiencies." *College English* 40 (1978): 318–323.
  •Reprinted in *Tutoring Writing: A Sourcebook for Writing Labs*. Ed. Muriel Harris. Glenview, Illinois: Scott, Foresman, and Co., 1982. 53–59.

"Evaluation: The Process for Revision." *Journal of Basic Writing* 1.4 (1978) 82–90.
  •Reprinted in *Critical Issues in Writing*. Ed. Annette Allen and Richard Donovan. New York: NETWORKS, 1980: 30–34.

"Using Persuasion to Plan a Moon Walk." *Exercise Exchange* 21.2 (1977): 40–45.
•Reprinted in *Writing Exercises from Exercise Exchange*. Ed. Charles R. Duke. Urbana, Illinois: National Council of Teachers of English, 1984. 2: 141–143.
"Making the Writing Lab an Instructor's Resource Room." *College Composition and Communication* 28 (1977): 376–378.
"Structuring the Supplementary Writing Lab." *ERIC Clearinghouse on Reading and Communication Skills*. ERIC ED (1976).

B. Unrefereed Journals

"Hatching an OWL (Online Writing Lab)." *Association of Computers in Writing Newsletter* 9.4 (Winter 1995–1996): 12–14.
"Working One-to-One with Writers: The Necessity of Tutorial Collaboration." *Alabama English* 2.2 (1990): 13–18.
"A User's Guide to Writing Centers." *Composition Chronicle* 1.9 (1989): 4–7.
"An Interdisciplinary Program Linking Computers and Writing Instruction." (With Madelon Cheek) *Collegiate Microcomputer* 3.3 (1985): 213–218.
"Encouraging Mature, Not Premature Editing." *Connecticut English Journal* 15.2 (1984): 67–69.
"Computers Across the Curriculum." (With Madelon Cheek) *Computers and Composition* 1.2 (1984): 3–5.
"Publish—or Perish Intellectually." *Iowa English Bulletin* 30.2 (1981): 14–15.
"Tutorial vs. Self-Instruction in Purdue's Writing Lab." *National Association of Remedial/Developmental Studies in Post Secondary Education* 3.1–2 (1979): 2.
"Structuring the Supplementary Writing Lab." *Arizona English Bulletin* 19.2 (1977): 26–29.

C. Interview

"Interview with Muriel Harris." Interviewer: Joan Mullin. *Composition Studies* 23.1 (Spring 1995): 37–53.

8. BOOK REVIEWS

Review: "Situating Teacher Practice: A Review of *Teaching Students to Write*, 2nd ed., by Beth Neman (New York: Oxford UP, 1995); *How English Teachers Get Taught: Methods of Teaching the Methods Class* by Peter Smagorinsky and Melissa Whiting (Urbana: NCTE, 1995); and *Writing Center Perspectives*. Eds. Byron Stay, Christina Murphy, and Eric Hobson (Emmitsburg: NWCA, 1995)." College English 59.1 (1997): 83–88.
Review of *The Writing Center: New Directions*. Eds. Ray Wallace and Jeanne Simpson (New York: Garland, 1991). *College Composition and Communication* 43.1 (1992): 98–101.
Review of *Understanding Persuasion*, by Raymond S. Ross and Mark G. Ross (Englewood Cliffs, New Jersey: Prentice-Hall, 1981). *Rhetoric Society Quarterly* 12 (1982): 203–205.

1

THE WRITING LAB NEWSLETTER AS HISTORY
Tracing the Growth of a Scholarly Community

MICHAEL A. PEMBERTON

In her May 2001 review of five recently published writing center books for *College English,* Jeanette Harris begins by noting how remarkable it is to see so many such texts published in a single year. "For a long time," she says, "the writing center community considered it a good year if more than two books focusing on writing centers made their way into print. . . . In fact, for a while it looked as if the term *writing center scholarship* might be an oxymoron" (662). Harris's observation, just pointed enough to make many writing center professionals wince, is not so much a lament over the dearth of reputable scholarship as a tacit recognition of the relatively short history writing center studies have as a specialized area of inquiry. For the first few decades of the community's existence as a community, most writing center directors were more interested in surviving annual funding uncertainties than conducting directed research or pursuing publication, and there was often very little institutional support for writing center research even if a director were so inclined. Writing center work was generally looked upon as a service function, geared toward remediation, and not worthy of much regard academically or institutionally.

There was not much support to be found in a network of colleagues with similar interests, either, largely because such a network did not yet exist. Though a great many colleges, universities, and high schools contained writing centers or learning centers—some of them with histories that extended back to the 1930s or earlier—contact among these centers was very limited. As late as the mid-1970s, there were no formal writing center organizations, no publications with writing centers as their focus, and relatively few opportunities for tutors and directors to gather together and discuss issues of mutual concern.

By the late 1970s, however, the number of people interested in writing center work had reached a critical mass. At a pivotal panel presentation at the 1977 Conference on College Composition and Communication (CCCC) in St. Louis, Muriel Harris, Mary Croft, Janice Neuleib, and Joyce Steward met to present papers and lead a discussion on writing lab theory and administration.

> [T]heir audience was so large that many had to listen from the hallway. . . . [P]articipants recognized that their vigorous exchange of ideas could help them in the development of their own writing lab programs and that they needed a means of continuing their useful exchange. The enthusiasm of their discoveries ran the Writing Lab session head-on into the next presentation. Harris remembers that as participants for the next presentation tried to push their way into the room, she suggested that a newsletter would be the best way to continue their collaboration. She also realized that they needed each other's addresses and passed around a sheet of paper [to collect them]. (Ballard and Anderson 1989, 7)

Even with a critical mass, a group has no power, no clout without an organ to communicate its platform and mission. Harris' innate sense of the need for such an instrument led to the creation of *The Writing Lab Newsletter (WLN)*, a manifesto through which writing center personnel could find a voice. Robert Connors once described the newsletter as a *kaffeklatsch* for its informal, welcoming nature; underlying that coziness was a political action instrument that led to the increased professionalism of the writing center community.

LAUNCHING A MOVEMENT

Muriel Harris—beginning assistant professor at Purdue University, faculty wife, Renaissance scholar, director of a brand-new "experimental" writing lab (all markers of a fairly powerless position)—voluntarily produced the first issue of *The Writing Lab Newsletter* and distributed it to the 49 people on the original mailing list in April 1977. No one at the time, least of all Harris, could have predicted what the eventual results of that initial effort would be—that the *WLN* would continue regular publication for over 25 years, eventually attract more than 1000 subscribers, become the principal means of communication among writing center tutors and directors, help to found a growing writing center community, and usher in an new era of writing center professionalism, scholarship, research, and theory.

With the prophetic words "WE ARE LAUNCHED!", volume 1.1 of the *WLN* proclaimed that a new specialization within the growing rhetoric/composition community had been established, and over the course of the next quarter century, the *WLN* has given voice to its members' concerns, interests, ideas, and fears, chronicling the growth of the developing writing center field on a monthly basis. The *Newsletter* and the community have evolved together, interdependently, and the changes that have taken place in one have quite often been reflected by or been a reflection *of* changes that have taken place in the other. For this reason, then, the *WLN*—perhaps more than any other resource—provides a unique window into the evolutionary process that has made the writing center community what it is today.

ETHOS AND THE PHATIC SHIFT

When Robert Connors wrote a review called "Journals in Composition Studies" for *College English* in 1984, *The Writing Lab Newsletter* was singled out for special attention, partly because it represented the recent emergence of a new constituency within composition studies—writing center specialists—and partly because of the unique ethos it embodied:

> As Lisa Ede has pointed out to me, most of the content of newsletters is phatic communication, a sort of "Hey, I'm out here too and we're all facing the same kinds of problems" halloo from some colleague previously unknown. *The Writing Lab Newsletter* illustrates this, remaining today what it has been since its inception—a classic and admirably useful newsletter without pretense to scholarly importance. . . . *WLN* acts like a bulletin-board for writing lab administrators, keeping them in touch, announcing who's had a baby or lost a relative, offering help at home and handy-dandy tips. Though *WLN* remains a very specialized publication, useful only to writing lab administrators and tutors, it serves its special purpose well. It is, in addition, the most personalized and informal of all the journals covered here, strongly imbued with the character of its editor, Muriel Harris. It is the only writing journal that makes its readers feel like friends. (359)

Some aspects of this description, notably the "bulletin-board" function and friendly ethos, are as true of the *WLN* today as they were in 1984. But the nature of the bulletin board and its ethos have changed somewhat over time, due largely to the changing face of the profession and the subtle evolution of the *WLN* itself. The *Newsletter*'s communicative stance slowly became less personal and more professional, shifting away from birth announcements and brief requests for help, and moving toward calls for proposals, conference announcements, and job advertisements. All these forms of communication work to build and maintain community within a field, but they make different assumptions about the nature of the community and the best mechanisms for maintaining cohesion.

Tracking the points where the first type of phatic communication (personal/direct address) began to fade away in favor of the second (professional/indirect address) is difficult, given that the personal has never disappeared completely from the *WLN*. Many current articles use personal address or take the form of personal anecdotes. Harris's introductory editor's column in each issue, for instance, is always very personal, addressing readers directly and making friendly appeals from time to time. Still, it is possible to identify two of the regular features in the *Newsletter*'s earliest issues—features with purely personal phatic functions—that have either completely vanished or that no longer appear with any regularity. These are (1) lists of new subscribers' mailing addresses and (2) "letters to the editor" that make suggestions or requests.

Sharing names and addresses was, perhaps, the *WLN*'s most important function in its early years. Growing directly out of the CCCC session that gave the newsletter its start, the publication of address lists reflected how critical it was for members of the nascent community to know who they were, individually, and where they were all located. As Harris proclaimed at the start of volume 1, issue 1:

> Here is the first issue of THE WRITING LAB NEWSLETTER proposed at the CCCC's, and our first order of business is to have each other's names. Enclosed is an initial list, but as you spread the word and encourage other lab people to join us, supplementary lists will be included in future newsletters. (1)[1]

These supplemental lists appeared in every issue for the next three years, but before long they became an impractical burden on the *Newsletter*'s very limited printing space. In September 1981, because of the "stack of manuscripts waiting to appear" and because during the previous summer over 50 people had joined the newsletter group, Harris announced it would no longer be possible to continue listing the names and addresses of all the new members in the Newsletter (6.1, 1).[2]

The mailing list at that point exceeded 1000 subscribers, and the one-time "small community" of writing center specialists was no longer quite so small anymore. The *Newsletter* was clearly achieving its intended goals: to create and build community and to provide a place for scholarly output.

In a similar fashion, one of the *Newsletter*'s earliest staple features— short letters and announcements from members of the newsletter group—was gradually crowded out by longer, more substantive articles and extended reports on professional meetings. In volume 2.5 (January 1978), for example, short pieces of correspondence almost completely fill the issue. Paul Bator (Wayne State) asks to hear from people with experience in basic writing and/or proficiency testing, Ken Bruffee (Brooklyn College) provides a short bibliography on training peer tutors, and a new "Editor's Mailbag" prints four short letters announcing, among other things, new writing labs at Brigham Young University and Southern Methodist University; another of the letters asks whether the *Newsletter* might consider publishing job announcements for qualified "lab people" (3). A mere two years later, lengthy program descriptions and professional announcements take up a majority of the publication's available space. Short letters from readers linger for a long time; at least one is printed in every issue through November 1986 (11.3). After that date, they appear only sporadically, the next one not showing up until June 1987 (11.10).

Still, despite its increasingly professional tone, Harris believes that the core ethos of the *Newsletter* has remained essentially unchanged. It continues to be personal, practical, and accessible, providing an important mechanism for new tutors and directors to enter the writing center community and immediately feel a part of it. "The *Newsletter* is still a way for people to keep in touch, new people in particular," she says. "A lot of people express gratitude for the *Newsletter*'s role in doing this—they don't read listservs or go to conferences. I still try to keep it open to people at all levels of expertise. . . .I think of it as a conversation rather than a publication with a head editor. The *Newsletter* is a community for keeping people in by mentoring them" (Harris 2001).

BUILDING A COMMUNITY OF PROFESSIONALS

Besides publishing information about its subscribers and generating a sense of community through the concrete act of identifying them by name, the *Newsletter* also functioned, then as today, as a news service, publicizing conferences and professional meetings that would allow the community to gather face to face. Unsurprisingly, the first conferences announced in the *WLN* were not focused on writing centers *per se.* Volume 1.1 included an announcement for "SET IT WRITE—A Conference on the Teaching of Writing" at Illinois State, and volume 1.2 publicized the sixth annual Wyoming Conference on Freshman and Sophomore English. The March 1978 (2.7) issue did forecast an upcoming "Special Interest Session on Writing Labs at the CCCC's" (1), but the first actual writing center conference announced in the *WLN* was the Ohio Writing Labs Conference, hosted by the English department at Youngstown State University, Nancy McCracken coordinating (January 1979, 3.5). In later issues, conference announcements and calls for manuscripts appeared frequently, eventually being given their own section in March 1981 (5.7).

In keeping with the philosophy that "if it's not written, it didn't happen," early issues of the *Newsletter* documented "conference reports" from CCCC and other meetings, and these reports are striking, not only for what has changed but for what has remained the same. Consider the following list of "the most important areas discussed" in a special CCCC session on "The Writing Lab as Supplement to Freshman English" by James S. Hill:

> 1. continuity of instruction in the classroom and lab, 2. the use of grammatical exercises in the lab as opposed to composition, 3. general expense of operating a lab, 4. accountability to the English Department, 5. the importance of effective communication between the lab and classroom, 6. the psychological implications of the lab as a place of learning rather than for "bad" students, 7. referral procedures—drop in or appointment, 8. the lab as one hour credit in addition to the classroom, 9. the importance of having a rhetorician in the English Department who can oversee and organize the format of the lab, and 10. the use of teaching assistants in the lab. (May 1978, 2.9:1)

These early conference reports also display a fair amount of drumbeating and revivalist enthusiasm, promoting both the strength of the community and the growth of the profession. Harris was particularly adept at displaying this sense of excitement. In her report on the 1979 CCCC, she begins by saying:

Writing labs are thriving and, while still in a state of growth, have already become one of the major areas of concentration in the field of composition. In the 1979 CCCC's program, writing labs were listed as one of the seven major topics dealt with in multiple conferences sessions. In addition to the five sessions on writing labs so adeptly coordinated by Janice Neuleib (Illinois State University), there was also the Special Interest Session on Writing Labs which attracted over 150 people! From all this, I have a strong sense not only of the continued growth of labs but also of the establishment of labs as integral parts of composition programs. (May 1979, 3.9:1)

For writing center specialists, many of whom were "at the periphery of the academic structure" with "less pay, less job security, and no access to tenure" (Harris, 3.9:1), the existence of a vital, thriving organization that shared professional interests while working to address these inequalities was an exciting prospect indeed.

Job announcements gave concrete evidence to the growing sense of professionalism. The first such advertisement to appear in the *WLN* was for a full-time, tenure track, assistant professor position directing the writing lab (half time) at Central Connecticut College. The February 1980 (4.6) issue published four such job announcements—though not all were specifically for writing lab specialists—and subsequent issues regularly included job ads, gradually focusing more and more on writing center director and tutorial positions.

ORGANIZING THE COMMUNITY FOR ACTION

As the newsletter group grew, so did the impetus to establish more formal, independent, professional organizations, and the *WLN* was an important mechanism for publicizing these groups as they coalesced, established charters, and held conferences. The early 1980s were especially active in this regard. The April 1981 (5.8) issue announced the upcoming third annual conference of the Writing Centers Association (later to become the East Central WCA) as well as the formation of the Southeastern WCA with Gary Olson as president.[3] In September 1982 (7.7), the Rocky Mountain WCA announced its first conference, and in November 1982 the National Writing Centers Association (NWCA) was recognized by NCTE and awarded assembly status (first announced in a short note in issue 7.4, December 1982). January 1983 (7.5) saw notices for the first Midwest WCA conference; the initial meeting of the Texas Association of Writing Center Directors, organized by Jeanette Harris; and a "Calendar of Writing Lab Conferences" that listed six regional events scheduled between February and May. In the September 1983 (8.1) issue, NWCA's first president, Nancy McCracken, explained how the national organization had grown out of the WCA: East Central, an article that was followed on the next page by a "News from the Regions" column, listing contact information for the five existing regionals (WCA: East Central, Southeast WCA, Rocky Mountain WCA, Midwest WCA, and Texas WCA) and two regionals that were "in progress" (Mid-Atlantic WCA and New England WCA). A call for the first meeting of the newly-formed Pacific Coast WCA appeared less than a year later (June 1984, 8.10).

The dramatic growth of writing center professional organizations, in some ways, begged important questions that had to be addressed before the organizations could claim to represent a "community" or achieve some sort of epistemological coherence: Just what, exactly, did it mean to work in a writing center or to be a "writing center professional"? What was the profession's theoretical grounding? What were the principles of its pedagogy? What should the goals of the discipline be, professionally and academically, and what were the best methods for working to achieve them? These questions entailed not only matters of self-definition and practice but also status and respect. The only way to elevate the status of writing center professionals in an academic community was (and is) to imbue it with its own epistemological principles, theoretical foundations, and research agendas.

The newsletter provided space for important discussions in and about the profession in contrast to *CCC* and *College English*, which shut out such explorations. In the early 1980s, the *WLN* published a number minor "manifestos," statements of principle or critiques of the field that were intended largely to serve as a "wake up call" to those who might otherwise have been content to see a professional literature filled with little more than Connors's "handy dandy tips" for tutoring. Beginning with Judith Fishman's "The Writing Center—What Is Its Center?" in September 1980 (5.1), a number of writers—Stephen North, Angela Scanzello, William Stull, Maureen Ryan, Patricia Murray, and Linda Bannister among them—reflected on the need for writing center people to do more than just organize; they had to earn credibility and be willing to flex their professional credentials in order to gain the respect they deserved.

Fishman's article confronted some of the harsh realities of writing center work. Too often, she said, center folk felt they could not afford the luxury of defining who they were and what they did because working in a writing center meant a constant struggle for survival. "Many of us are uncentered, unstable, and vulnerable in our own institutions. . . .We live on the periphery, many without faculty status, without a tenure track position" (2). Given these pressures and the constant demands to demonstrate successful results for student learning, claimed Fishman, too many center directors lapsed into the easy out of grammar exercises, programmed instruction, and similar activities that allowed for easily-quantifiable outcomes testing. She challenged her audience to think differently: "We are a part of a larger whole and a larger effort," she states, "to effect change in the way in which our students are educated" (4). Her argument was, in effect, a declaration of independence and a rallying cry for defensible borders. Not only must writing center professionals make efforts to protect themselves institutionally, but they also must promote a student-centered, collaborative, process-oriented environment in the center itself, driving their own pedagogies rather than being driven by those which might be more administratively convenient.

One year later, Steve North made similar points in "Us 'n' Howie: The Shape of Our Ignorance," but he was far less diplomatic than Fishman. In a strikingly acerbic style, North said:

> I'm here to tell you that the PROBLEM, in capital letters, is that we don't know the fundamentals. That when it comes to teaching writing in individualized ways, one to one, *we don't know what we are doing.* . . . Teaching writing in writing centers is expensive, hard work. If we are to survive, we must do it very, very well—better than anyone else. For that to happen, we must know everything we can about what we do and how we do it; we have to be able to measure our success, and on our terms. (September 1981, 6.1:5–6)

Other writers took up these calls with equal fervor in later issues of the *WLN*, though their tone was somewhat less strident. Angela Scanzello, in "The Writing Center in an Identity Crisis" (December 1981, 6.4), admitted the difficulty of defining just what a writing center is, but argued that it "can no longer be limited to a 'place' where underachievers may be taught to write better by using programmed materials with the help of tutors" (8). William Stull, writing about "The Writing Lab's Three Constituencies" in the January 1982 (6.5) issue, extolled the progress writing centers had made since the 1970s, but charged his audience to think of themselves as professionals with professional status. "[W]e need to cultivate our hard-won self-respect. . . . We must, if we are to earn lasting respect from our students and colleagues—and from ourselves" (3).

The central message conveyed in these early manifestos was this: respect for writing centers and the people who work in them will only come if they are well-read, well-trained, and willing to wage war on the battleground of theory for the pedagogies they believe are the most effective. The readers of the *Newsletter* heard these cries and responded to them, some by pursuing advanced degrees, others by marshalling the results of current research in defense of their pedagogies, still others by sharing their experiences at conferences and in print.

In both direct and indirect ways, then, through address lists, job advertisements, calls for proposals, conference announcements, event calendars, conference reports, minutes from the meetings of regional and national organizations, and published manifestos, *The Writing Lab Newsletter* was instrumental in the continuing growth and development of the writing center profession. It facilitated communication and organization among its members, built a network of academics and professionals with similar interests, and provided a forum for discussions that helped to build both a professional identity for writing center specialists and agendas for future action.

BUILDING A COMMUNITY OF SCHOLARS

Yet the existence of a professional community in and of itself is no guarantee of increased respect or enhanced status in an academic institution. The only way for writing centers to escape the stigma of their second-class "service function" in educational institutions is to enhance their intellectual credentials, to conduct research and apply theory in ways that other academics will recognize and value. Unfortunately, *The Writing Lab Newsletter*, particularly in its earliest incarnation, was suitable only for the promotion of a growing research agenda, not its publication or dissemination. Its five- to ten-page format was not long enough to publish traditional academic articles with detailed research findings or extended theoretical arguments. The low print quality and lack of a peer review process also dissuaded many academics from seeing it as an outlet for serious research; few promotion and tenure committees were likely to regard it very highly.

Working in its favor, however, was the fact that early on there were almost no alternative outlets for writing center scholarship. The *Writing Center Journal* (*WCJ*) did not publish its first issue until 1980, and neither

College English nor *College Composition and Communication* saw writing center research as an area of much interest to its readership. Writing center scholars could very well feel marginalized and shut out by the major composition journals, and when *WCJ* did appear, it may well have given other editors the opportunity to shunt writing center essays to a less central journal. In point of fact, very few people at that time had any clear sense of what writing center scholarship was or what writing center theory might be. The *WLN*, then, provided an essential role as a forum for discussing these issues, once again grappling with matters of definition and attempting to reconcile sometimes conflicting perspectives about where the field was going and what it should be trying to accomplish. Later, as the profile and ethos of the *Newsletter* became more professional and conformed more closely to the traditional norms of academic publishing, academics were more likely to see it as a legitimate (and status-enhancing) venue for publication.

The development has been a gradual one, though. The first actual "article" in the *WLN* was Lorraine Perkins's "An Approach to Organization" in the December 1977 (2.4) issue. Though little more than a description of how to discuss the concepts of "topic" and "thesis" in a half-hour "interview," it was the lengthiest article that had appeared in *WLN* to date. James Hill's March 1978 (2.7) article, "The Writing Lab: An Anecdote," was the first to include a narrative retelling of a tutorial session, and Jane Optiz's summary of her Writing Workshop's first semester of operation at Saint John's University (May 1978, 2.9) was the first published statistical account of student usage patterns for a writing center. A few months later, Tilly Eggers's article on "Evaluation and Instruction" in the December 1979 (4.4) issue became the first to cite work by well-known rhetoricians and linguists (James Moffett, James Britton, Frank Smith, and Kenneth Goodman), invoking them in support of the tutorial approach used in her writing center at the University of Wyoming. In each of these articles, it is possible to see some initial probings toward research models and methods—pedagogical theory, case study, statistical analysis, application of previous research—but they are clearly just probings at this point, not rigorous work firmly grounded in well-established paradigms of investigation. This lack of rigor was partly due to the fact that "writing center research" had yet to be defined, but it was also due to the *WLN*'s ethos which did not really invite the publication of traditional, serious-minded, rigorous scholarship. Not until Janice Neuleib's "Proving We Did It" appeared in March 1980 (4.7) did any articles even include bibliographic references.

The early 1980s, however, were a transformative period for the *Newsletter* in terms of the kind and quality of scholarship it began to publish. The November 1980 (5.3) issue saw the publication of John Sadlon's comparison group study on "The Effect of a Skills Center Upon the Writing Improvement of Freshmen Composition Students," a relatively short piece that nevertheless followed the conventions of experimental reports: description of purpose, description of methods and procedures, review of previous research, presentation of results, and summative conclusion. The borrowed paradigm brought with it a sense of rigor and legitimacy that many readers found appealing. At the very least, it demonstrated that writing center specialists could conduct and present research using investigative models that had already been sanctioned by the academy.

Without question, writing centers were searching for a theoretical firmament that would, among other things, provide them with a coherent agenda for research. Writers in the *WLN* regularly began to demand that tutors and directors be conversant with current theory, and in their published pieces they sometimes incorporated theories from other disciplines, sometimes drew directly from recent work in composition studies. Thomas Dukes's "The Writing Lab as Crisis Center: Suggestions for the Interview" (May 1981, 5.9), for example, considered how crisis intervention theory might impact writing center practice; Steve North's "Us `n Howie: The Shape of Our Ignorance" (September 1981, 6.1) argued that writing center professionals had to become more conversant with the work of composition theorists such as Janet Emig, Sondra Perl, Nancy Sommers, Richard Beach, Linda Flower and John Hayes, and Mina Shaughnessy; and Mary King in her April 1982 (6.8) "A Writing Lab Profile" stated firmly that

> The writing center professional, then, needs training in composition theory and in linguistics; otherwise she/he may bring to student writing an interpretive and prescriptive habit of reading, accompanied by an overemphasis on error. . . . Some knowledge about information processing and reading reinforces the teacher's commitment to reading student papers for ideas, as does learning theory, especially Piaget's theories of cognitive development. Piaget emphasized the importance of social interaction in learning, providing the basis for the teaching style needed in a writing center. (7)

One pivotal article that responded to these calls was Janice Neuleib's December 1984 (9.4) piece on "Research in the Writing Center: What to Do and Where to Go to Become Research Oriented." Beginning with her own frustrations with experimental pre-treatment, post-treatment designs that just didn't seem to work in a writing center environment, Neuleib sought alternative designs and methodologies that would. In the course of this article, she offered readers a number of models that could work well for writing center research—case studies, protocol analyses, surveys, rhetorical studies, computer-assisted instruction, and multivariate statistical analyses—and, citing Harris's work in particular, she concluded that "we are often doing research in composition by what we do daily in writing centers. We just don't remember that it is research" (12).

Over the years, writing center professionals have taken North's, King's, and Neuleib's admonitions to heart, and this is nowhere more evident than in the articles that have appeared in the *Newsletter*. Even a cursory review of some of the articles under "Theories" in *The Writing Lab Newsletter Index* indicates the increasing attention to research and the importance of theory to writing center work. Early articles such as Tilly Eggers's "Evaluation and Instruction" (December 1979, 4.4) and Mary King's "Teaching for Cognitive Growth" (March 1983, 7.7) highlighted the practical contributions of theory to tutoring practice; later articles such as Mick Kennedy's "Expressionism and Social Constructionism in the Writing Center: How Do They Benefit Students?" (November 1997, 22.3) and James Upton's "Brain-Compatible Learning: The Writing Center Connection" (June 1999, 23.10) seem to have a much stronger focus on theory as theory. It is also true that articles which foreground theory have become much more commonplace in recent issues of the *Newsletter*. Of the 132 articles included in the "Theories" section of the *WLN* Index, nearly 50% of them (64) have been published in the last seven years.[4] Harris herself notes that one of the biggest changes in the content of the *Newsletter* is that "people have gotten more sophisticated and thoughtful. The depth of the articles has increased dramatically, and this is especially evident in those written by tutors. The knowledge base is more complete, and the quality of the writing has greatly increased" (interview, 2001).

CONTRIBUTIONS AND IMPACTS

It would be hard to overstate the contribution that *The Writing Lab Newsletter* has made to the field of writing center scholarship, and it's a contribution that continues to this day. Beginning with a small group of people sharing similar interests after a single conference panel twenty-five years ago, the *Newsletter* and its readers have been important, driving forces behind what is now one of rhetoric and composition's most active and vibrant special interest groups. At the CCCC conference in Denver, Colorado (2001), for example, more than thirty panels on writing centers were listed in the conference program—one of the most prominent areas of interest at the entire conference. Most major publishers and many university presses displayed books on writing center research and practice, and the annual WCenter breakfast drew nearly a hundred attendees. The National Writing Centers Association has been renamed the International Writing Centers Association (IWCA), with an executive board that includes representatives from ten regional WCAs, three publications, a listserv, and a website. Annual scholarship awards are given for best article and best book about writing centers, and the IWCA regularly awards grants to writing center professionals and graduate students conducting original research.

Through it all, the *Newsletter* has been there—connecting, promoting, publicizing, supporting, enhancing, stimulating, provoking, and publishing. It has sought to professionalize the field by elevating it to the realm of theory while, at the same time, making sure it never forgets that pedagogy lies at the heart of what it does. It has embraced the field's diversity and given voice to its many concerns, but it has always insisted that there are some principles we can all agree upon: the care we have for our students, the value of collaborative learning, the importance of an ethical pedagogy, the joy of teaching. It has demanded the best work from the most experienced scholars, and it has welcomed the newest discoveries of the least experienced tutors. In fact, the *Newsletter,* through its "Tutors Column" has provided a publication outlet for undergraduate and graduate students, allowing them to become active members of the writing center community. It has not only grown with and recorded the shape of the emerging writing center field over the last 25 years, but it has also been a motivating force, a primary agent of that growth.

Of course, in saying the *Newsletter* has made this contribution, I am also saying that Muriel Harris has done so. As the *Newsletter*'s only editor and one of the most visible and productive scholars in the field of writing center research, theory, and practice, Muriel Harris has helped determine the shape of writing center studies. Those of us who are fully invested in this discipline and all its possibilities owe her a tremendous debt. Unsurprisingly, Mickey doesn't see it that way. In reflecting on her experience as editor of the *WLN*, Mickey says in typically self-effacing fashion:

> It's been a very positive experience. I get to read a lot of incredibly good writing, I stay in contact with people, and I think I've helped some people realize they are authors with interesting things to say. I hope that the *Newsletter* has helped to establish the writing center community—the regionals, the annual breakfast, the *WLN* is a part of that. I feel attached to the community and still want to be a part of it; I want the *Newsletter* to remain that way, too. I'm grateful to be a part of it. (interview, 2001)

It is not unreasonable to say, however, despite Mickey's protestations of modesty, that in a fundamental way, the *Writing Lab Newsletter* created the essential network that would allow a group of diverse scholars with similar interests and institutional positions to become a genuine academic community. This community used the periodical to develop its own sense of self and to set in place agendas for research and political action. It is difficult to imagine how the writing center profession would have evolved were it not for this voice and the leadership of its editor, Muriel Harris.

APPENDIX 1
A *Chronology of Format Changes in the* Writing Lab Newsletter, *1977–2003*

While issues of format may not initially seem of importance, the information that follows about the concrete ways the *WLN* evolved demonstrates in graphic and tangible ways the growth and professionalization of the writing center community at large.

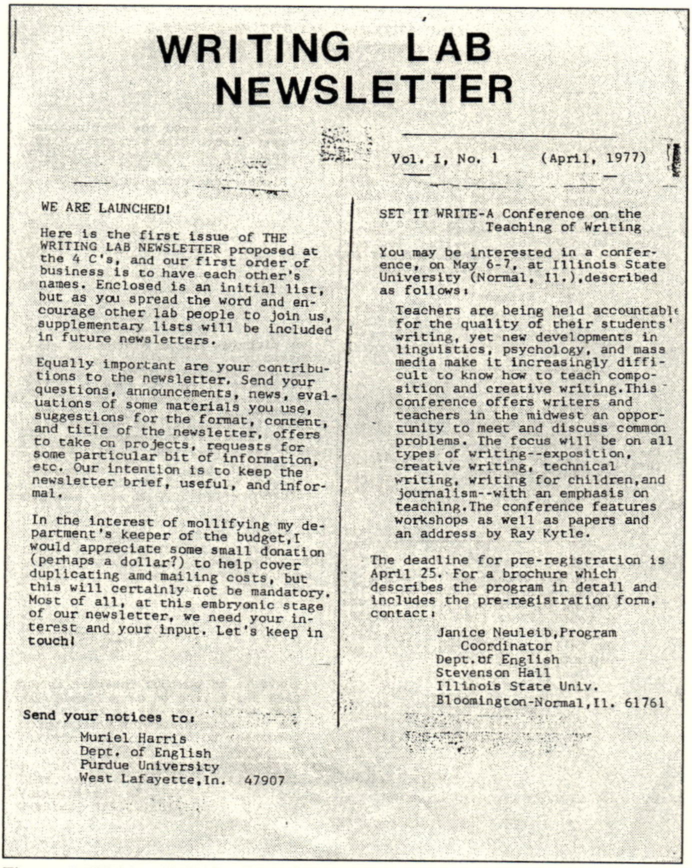

WRITING LAB NEWSLETTER

Vol. I, No. 1   (April, 1977)

WE ARE LAUNCHED!

Here is the first issue of THE WRITING LAB NEWSLETTER proposed at the 4 C's, and our first order of business is to have each other's names. Enclosed is an initial list, but as you spread the word and encourage other lab people to join us, supplementary lists will be included in future newsletters.

Equally important are your contributions to the newsletter. Send your questions, announcements, news, evaluations of some materials you use, suggestions for the format, content, and title of the newsletter, offers to take on projects, requests for some particular bit of information, etc. Our intention is to keep the newsletter brief, useful, and informal.

In the interest of mollifying my department's keeper of the budget, I would appreciate some small donation (perhaps a dollar?) to help cover duplicating amd mailing costs, but this will certainly not be mandatory. Most of all, at this embryonic stage of our newsletter, we need your interest and your input. Let's keep in touch!

Send your notices to:
   Muriel Harris
   Dept. of English
   Purdue University
   West Lafayette,In.   47907

SET IT WRITE-A Conference on the Teaching of Writing

You may be interested in a conference, on May 6-7, at Illinois State University (Normal, Il.),described as follows:

Teachers are being held accountable for the quality of their students' writing, yet new developments in linguistics, psychology, and mass media make it increasingly difficult to know how to teach composition and creative writing.This conference offers writers and teachers in the midwest an opportunity to meet and discuss common problems. The focus will be on all types of writing--exposition, creative writing, technical writing, writing for children,and journalism--with an emphasis on teaching.The conference features workshops as well as papers and an address by Ray Kytle.

The deadline for pre-registration is April 25. For a brochure which describes the program in detail and includes the pre-registration form, contact:

   Janice Neuleib,Program
      Coordinator
   Dept.of English
   Stevenson Hall
   Illinois State Univ.
   Bloomington-Normal,Il. 61761

Figure 1. *Writing Lab Newsletter,* Volume 1, Number 1

The first issue of *The Writing Lab Newsletter* was, by nearly all measures, a primitive production. Columns typed on a standard typewriter were cut with scissors and affixed to a sheet of typing paper with Scotch tape.

Ruled lines between the columns were crooked, the lettering in the masthead was crude and off-center, and dark tape shadows appeared throughout. It was amateurish and unimpressive. But it was a beginning.

By issue 1.2 (June 1977), the tape shadows had mostly disappeared, but the format remained otherwise unchanged until issue 2.2 (October 1977), when a small decorative picture of a fruit basket was added to the upper left corner. In issue 2.4 (December 1977), this graphic was replaced by a border of holly along the top edge, and in subsequent issues, pictures of plants decorated the title header in annual cycles through issue 9.10 (June 1985). It was early in this period that "Harris's daughter, Rebecca, fresh from her journalism classes at Indiana University, initiated the *Newsletter*'s first technical innovations when she showed her mother that rubber cement and border tape produced a more attractive paste-up" (Ballard and Anderson 1989, 7).

The total number of pages fluctuated during the first three years, ranging between five and ten, depending on the number of new submissions and the number of people who joined the newsletter group. In May 1980 (4.9), the length stabilized (more or less) at ten pages until March 1984 (8.7) when it jumped to twelve, and March 1985 when it jumped again to fourteen.

The first issue of the fall 1985 academic year (10.1, September) introduced some significant changes, reflecting what Harris referred to as "an on-going search for a more readable format" (1). A new title header appeared—a hand-drawn pencil enclosing the words "Writing Lab Newsletter," running headers appeared in the upper corners of each page, and ornate borders between articles disappeared in favor of cleaner, straighter lines. A heavier bond paper also gave the *Newsletter* a more substantial feel and a heftier aesthetic appearance. The use of thicker, more durable paper may have been prompted by the fact—later confirmed by a formal reader survey—that "[a]s many as 20 to 30 readers commonly share[d] a single copy of an issue which [was] passed from lab directors to department chairs to deans" (Ballard and Anderson 1989, 8).

Two and a half years later, thanks to a Macintosh desktop publishing system provided by Purdue's Dean of Academic Services, the *Newsletter* printed its first entirely computer-formatted issue in January 1988 (12.5). Accompanying this technological shift was the introduction of its first table of contents ("...inside..."), a title for the editor's monthly introduction to the issue ("...from the editor..."), justified columns, running page numbers in the bottom corners, a more sophisticated and easily readable serif typeface, and wider margins overall. The hand-drawn pencil in the masthead was updated with a computer-generated version and, overall, the whole publication underwent a major facelift. It was now slick, clean, and professional looking, exchanging its second-hand, hand-crafted apparel for a business suit and spats.

The next major change in format occurred in September 1988 (13.1), shortly after the results of a reader survey were collected and tallied. Harris's "...from the editor..." message in the June 1988 (12.10) issue notes that

> I've found from browsing through those surveys that some things about the newsletter format will have to change. For example, despite the small (very small) minority of us who like publications on colored paper (to brighten up our mailboxes, identify current issues more easily, and locate older issues in files), the vast majority of this group does a lot of duplicating of articles from the newsletter, and copying machines are apparently unable to cope with colored paper. And I didn't realize how those staples at the sides of issues were snapping people's fingernails and their patience when prying open pages to read and to copy (sorry). So, no more side staples. (1–2)

The first issue of volume 13 (September 1988) was indeed missing the familiar staple in the corner, a staple that represented, in some ways, the last vestige of its informal, unpretentious, generally humble "newsletter" origins. The *Newsletter* was now a saddle-stitched (two staples on the outside spine) 16-page monthly booklet.[5] The front page had increased white space for the masthead, three columns instead of two (with the table of contents in a central boxed-and-shaded position), and all the editorial and subscription information contained in a boxed-and-shaded space on page two. In addition, the *Newsletter*'s title now appeared opposite the month and year in upper corners of all interior pages, an indication, possibly, of the extent to which articles were regularly being copied for use in presentations and tutor training sessions; essential bibliographic and reference information could now be easily included in all such copies.

In September 1993 (18.1), the most recent of the *Newsletter*'s physical evolutions took place—not as dramatic, perhaps, as some of the other transformations it had undergone, but striking nonetheless. The trademark pencil in the masthead was gone, replaced by a large, bold, all-cap "THE WRITING LAB" (with a script "W") and a smaller, all-cap, loosely tracked (i.e., stretched) "N E W S L E T T E R" underneath. Similar font changes took place in the print text, table of contents, and interior titles. The entire publication—interior pages as well as front page—went to a three-column format with a smaller, 9-point font (adjusted to 10-point in November 1994 [19.3]), presumably to allow the inclusion of more material within its 16-page space limitations.

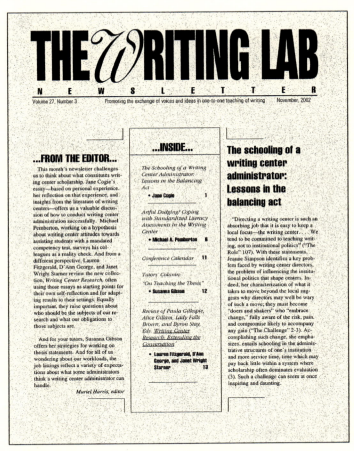

Figure 2. *Writing Lab Newsletter*, Volume 27, Number 3

APPENDIX 2
Subscription Fees and Subscriber Base of WLN (1977–2001)

1.1	(4/77)	Donations requested of "(perhaps a dollar?) to help cover duplicating and mailing costs, but this will certainly not be mandatory" (1). Mailing list numbers 49.
1.2	(5/77)	Donation checks should be made payable to Muriel Harris.
1.3	(6/77)	Donations of "a dollar or two" requested.
2.2	(10/77)	Donations of $2 requested.
3.5	(1/79)	Mailing list now "over 400."
4.1	(9/79)	Donations of $3 requested.
4.6	(2/80)	Answers questions about fees: there is "no subscription fee as such, your donation covers as long a time as your conscience permits." Mailing list is "over 650."
5.1	(6/81)	Donations of $5 requested, now specified as "for next year's newsletter." Checks may be made payable to Muriel Harris or the newsletter. Mailing list "grew from about 700 in September to over 950 in June" (1).
6.1	(9/81)	Mailing list now over 1000. Checks may be made payable to Muriel Harris or Purdue University.
6.3	(11/81)	Mailing list "almost 1200." Checks may be made payable to Purdue University or Muriel Harris.
6.1	(6/82)	Mailing list "over 1100." Checks should be made payable to Purdue University.
9.4	(12/84)	Harris issues a warning to those who haven't donated recently, saying the *Newsletter* will be deleting non-contributors from its rolls.
10.10	(6/86)	Donations of $7.50 requested.
11.4	(12/86)	*Newsletter* now has a "Non-Profit Organization" postage imprint.
11.5	(1/87)	*Newsletter* first describes itself as "A Publication of the NWCA."
12.2	(10/87)	Donations of $7.50 requested, $12.50 for Canada.
13.3	(11/88)	*Newsletter*'s ISSN (1040–3779) appears for the first time.
14.10	(6/90)	Donations of $10 requested, $15 for Canada.
16.6	(2/92)	Announcement of a price increase for "subscriptions" to $15 (US), $20 (Canada), $40 (overseas). "Donations" is still used in indicia.
18.5	(1/94)	"Donations" disappears from subscription information; "payments" is now used instead.

2

IN THE SPIRIT OF SERVICE
Making Writing Center Research a "Featured Character"

NANCY MALONEY GRIMM

For the last ten years, writing center scholars have been cheerily optimistic about the untapped research potential in writing centers. In 1993, for example, Michael Spooner referred to writing centers as "hothouses of knowledge making," acknowledging the tremendous amount of understanding about literacy that develops as one works in a writing center. Spooner, an academic book editor, was hoping some of "the breadth of expertise" would make its way into print (3). In the same year, Joyce Kinkead and Jeanette Harris concluded their edited collection, *Writing Centers in Context*, by commenting on a lack of writing center research, and particularly a lack of work on cultural and linguistic diversity. They encouraged research in this direction, speculating that the lack of development of writing center research might be because scholars had not yet addressed "the direction a writing center should take as a research center" (247). More recently (summer 2000), Kinkead and Harris observe that writing centers have still not reached their potential as sites of research, noting that most writing center directors have been too busy keeping programs "alive and healthy" (24).

I have heard many people who work in writing centers exclaim how much they learn in one day in a writing center. Indeed, many say that they learn more about how to be an effective teacher by working in a writing center than by taking courses in composition pedagogy. If there is so much learning happening in writing centers, what are the reasons for the untapped research potential, particularly research on the cultural and linguistic diversity that are the focus of so much writing center work? In this chapter, I'd like to explore that question as well as suggest ways to achieve the research potential of the writing center. An area of scholarship called the New Literacy Studies offers an exciting framework for thinking about research in writing centers, yet that potential cannot be achieved without an understanding of the issues that have blocked the development of writing centers as research centers.

One of the reasons for the blocked potential is suggested in Kinkead and Harris's reference to directors being too busy keeping programs alive to develop a research program. That programmatic busy-ness interferes with research time is echoed by other writing center directors. Harvey Kail (2000), for example, admits that he is intrigued by calls for research emphasizing what is learned in a writing center (he is referring to earlier calls made by North 1984 and Trimbur 1992). Nevertheless, he writes, "The problem for me in answering such calls is that it is late in my day when I get around to thinking of the writing center director as the writing center researcher—very late in the day" (27). Kail describes his priorities in ways with which many writing center directors will identify—"teaching, service, service, service, and then research—on our service" (28). Kail says that in order to make research "a featured character, not a walk-on part," we'd need to renegotiate the writing center statement of purpose.

Kail is right. Too often, writing center work is perceived as service, service, and more service. Although I have no problem thinking of the writing center serving students, I do have concerns when the same writing center is also perceived as serving faculty. In fact, I think one of the primary obstacles to making writing center research a "featured character" is located in this muddy vision of service to two different constituencies. Much of the muddiness is historical; many writing centers were established to remediate student writers and thereby lighten the burden of faculty. Linking the remediation project with the notion of faculty burden has created confusion about the primary constituency of a writing center. In the early years at the MTU Writing Center, we went to faculty to ask them to "send" their students to us, and we engaged in efforts to please faculty, to survey faculty, to assess faculty satisfaction, to gain faculty approval. Although writing centers have always prided themselves on the individualized work they do with students, there has always been a sense of looking over the shoulder to be sure the faculty approved.

As a result of this dual service mission, there has been a good bit of writing center scholarship directed at persuading faculty to value the work that happens in a writing center. In the early days, much of this work was essential—writing centers needed a supportive constituency. If the faculty saw no use for a writing center, budget cuts were inevitable.

Today, *some* scholarship still needs to be focused on educating faculty about what writing centers do. The faculty constituency is always changing and as it changes, fresh reminders about what happens in a writing center session are important. We must also continue to do research on our service. In the *NWCA Resource Manual* (1998) and elsewhere, Neal Lerner has thoughtfully demonstrated the range of questions we need to be asking about our practices, and I agree with his point that we must continue sharing the results of our local studies. I do not intend to undermine or replace these important kinds of research.

However, if writing centers focus exclusively on the kind of research that explains our services, there is little time left to develop research projects based on the unique level of access writing centers have to students, particularly students with diverse cultural and linguistic backgrounds. I believe that if writing centers developed a research direction that capitalized on this access, then faculty would have another reason for valuing what happens in a writing center. This would result in a healthier, more dialogic relationship with faculty, one that continued to ask for clarification of their expectations in student writing, but also brought to their attention the issues that students face when negotiating academic literacy. If the writing center mission were clearly focused on what we do with and for and because of students, then writing center research would bring this knowledge gained from interactions with students to the attention of faculty in local situations, such as faculty development workshops, as well as in more global contexts, such as publications intended for composition scholars. Spooner hinted at this shift back 1993 when he wrote, "It seems to me the writing center is uniquely situated not only to interpret the American academy to the transcultural student (or the non-Anglo American student), but also to interpret that student to the American academy" (3).

Unfortunately, when writing centers are represented as places driven by service, colleges and universities think about the writing center director as an administrator rather than a researcher or scholar. Recently, John Trimbur (2000) noted that although many writing centers are becoming multiliteracy centers, too often the role of writing center director is still perceived as entry level or non-tenure track staff. Such perceptions are serious obstacles to research. Trimbur recommends that a writing center director position be tenure track *and* potentially at an associate level. This would address the daunting expectation that a new Ph.D. can start a writing center and a publishing record at the same time. Importantly, Trimbur also calls attention to the developing multi-literacies function of a writing center, a reformulation that offers exciting possibilities for research as long as the institutional status of the writing center director is at an appropriate level. In addition, he points to universities where writing center directors have been hired at higher levels. Also, at this point in history, many writing centers now have tenured directors.

Like Trimbur, Lisa Ede and Andrea Lunsford (2000) are also enthusiastic about the potential for writing center research. They comment specifically on the team-based, collaborative research paradigm that writing centers offer, and the ways that writing centers, as multi-bordered, multi-positioned sites, could be catalysts for educational reform. By way of offering advice for developing the potential of writing centers to be catalysts for educational reform, they caution against having too local of a research vision. They credit writing center scholars like Muriel Harris, Lou Kelly, and Jeanne Simpson for having the stamina "to think and work globally as well as locally" (35). Many of the issues that arise from working with students, particularly students with diverse cultural and linguistic experiences, do have global dimensions, yet unless writing centers are perceived as places for addressing those issues, these dimensions will be unexplored.

To develop my ideas about how research can and should be a "featured character" of writing center work, I want to turn to some predictions made recently by Muriel Harris. In the millennial issue of *The Writing Center Journal*, Mickey authored a chapter entitled, in her characteristically optimistic fashion, "Preparing to Sit at the Head Table." Speculating on the future of writing centers, Mickey pictures writing center directors in influential academic positions. Always the realist, she cautions that we won't be sitting in those power chairs unless we pay attention to where the world is headed. According to Mickey, two issues particularly worth our attention are the role of technology and the changing demographics of our nation. Responding to the idea that commercial online tutoring may threaten campus writing centers, Mickey argues, "It's time to probe more deeply and to learn how to explain what we have to share with colleagues in other departments and schools on campus" (19). In this research call, Mickey is suggesting that we share what we have learned from students, but she is also saying we need "to learn" how to do this. Sharing what writing centers learn from students is clearly a kind of research that is not only an appropriate focus for the new millennium but also necessary for survival. If our students don't survive, neither will our institutions as we know them.

But saying so doesn't make it so. If making research a featured character of writing center work is something upon which so many scholars agree, there must be some other significant obstacle lurking underneath the surface. I think one of the primary obstacles to development of the rich research potential in a writing center is what literacy theorist Brian Street (1984) calls the autonomous model of literacy. Within the autonomous model, literacy is regarded as an individual skill. There isn't much to research if literacy is considered a value-neutral skill, and the individual writer is the sole locus of meaning making and skill building. When an individual fails to master the supposedly value-neutral skill of academic literacy, then the individual is to blame. Under this model, some students seem to work harder than others, or some students are smarter than others, or some students aren't focused, or some students don't know how to manage their time, or some students are simply unprepared and therefore don't belong at the university.

Many universities and many writing centers operate under an autonomous model of literacy, and many approaches to teaching composition are still strongly autonomous, focused on literacy as an individual attribute with little acknowledgement of the mainstream values and authority structures that are carried in academic literacy practices. The "hands off" indirect approach fostered in so many writing center training programs is also a part of the autonomous model. Many of the current expectations for writing center "research" are also informed by this model of literacy. The pressure to *prove* that writing center "intervention" makes a difference in student writing is part of the autonomous model. This expectation, usually voiced by higher administration, seems to be that one should be able to scoop up a piece of student text and determine that a few writing center sessions improved that text. Far too many variables, including the impossibility of deciding what constitutes "proof," affect the outcome, and far more is learned and understood and renegotiated in a writing center session than could ever be determined from looking at a student's text. Neal Lerner offers a thorough discussion of these issues in his chapter on assessment in this book. He, too, would like to see writing centers leave behind the twenty years of guilt about failure to prove their institutional value.

Let me be clear that I am not saying it is unreasonable to expect writing centers to provide evidence of what happens there. As a writing cen-

ter director, I gather quantitative data on an annual basis. What I am saying is that grade analysis, retention data, counts of student visits, and
surveys of student satisfaction do not shift writing centers from narrowly
defined service units to a more broadly defined research mission. As
Joan Hawthorne (2001) recently observed, "counting writing center visits doesn't really tells us whether or not our sessions are valuable to the
students who work with us." Hawthorne does suggest (and I agree) that
writing center research should be willing to ask hard questions. She
refers to the "confidence with which we can be wrong" as a possible
motive to pay closer attention to what happens in writing centers.

The ideological model of literacy, which Brian Street (1984) proposes as an alternative to the autonomous model, is one that demands a
willingness to question our good intentions. It doesn't suggest that we
blame ourselves for past misunderstandings, but rather that we change
our practices so that misunderstandings don't reproduce. An ideological model of literacy pays attention to literacies rather than *a* Literacy,
and it views these literacies as social practices rather than individual
skills. As a social practice, literacy is always attached to social values,
belief systems, and worldviews. With an ideological perspective on literacy, a writing center researcher pays attention to much more than words
on a page. Instead, the scope of attention is broadened to include not
only the text but also the conceptions, attitudes, and belief systems of
the individuals involved in the literate activity. An ideological model of
literacy requires a fundamental renegotiation of writing center purpose.
It asks us to serve students better by achieving a better understanding of
how literacy works as a social practice. It suggests a discovery approach
to research rather a prove-it approach. It insists on paying attention to
linguistic and cultural diversity. An ideological understanding of literacy
also changes our understandings of what counts as data and how one
interprets data. It encourages us to look at relationships, identities, cultural understandings, and more. It includes as data stories, interviews,
case studies, and ethnographic observations.

An ideological model of literacy is much more than a writing-across-
the-curriculum approach that attends to the different ways of making
meaning and using evidence and documentation in different disciplines. Although these issues remain important, an ideological
approach also destabilizes some traditional writing center dogmas. No
longer is the individual student alone the primary focus, but the individual's collective identity is also considered, along with the history of that

collective identity in relationship to the power structure of the university. Within the ideological model of literacy, color blindness is no longer an option. No longer is a tutorial represented as a peer relationship, but rather the asymmetries in the relationship of the two students working together are taken into account, particularly the differences in social situations and academic histories. If the tutor is white, urban, middle class, and the tutee is rural working class, then it is likely that the different values, assumptions, and experiences they associate with school literacy can undermine a tutorial relationship if they are not taken into account. This includes not only differences in dialect or language that appear on the surface of a text, but also ways that class and region affect the way one constructs an argument and the assumptions one makes about what counts as evidence.

Within an ideological model of literacy, no longer is the student represented as "needing help," but rather as coming to the writing center *to work* on understanding a potentially conflicted social context in which he or she is writing or reading or speaking or designing a particular kind of text for the first time. No longer is research done only to prove something to the institution, but also to change the thinking of the members of the institution. No longer does the pedagogy emphasize a hands off, indirect approach, but rather a direct and explicit unpacking of the understandings, beliefs, attitudes, and frameworks that underlie college literacy work. No longer is the writing center student represented as an undeveloped writer, but rather as someone who is an authentic beginner in a new discourse, new language, new social context, new culture, new power relationship and at the same time a fully developed individual in a community/culture/class unfamiliar to many in the university.

For example, within an ideological model, when a student from China "fails" to document sources, he is applying a cultural model that is embedded with Eastern values of group ownership. He may also be applying different conceptions of the role of writing in school. Under the pressure of deadlines and performance anxiety, he may also have been unable to sustain the dual identity needed to write as a Chinese citizen in an American university. Additionally, he is no doubt totally unaware of the tremendous sense of betrayal and despair that American teachers feel when they discover one of their students has plagiarized. In contrast, under the autonomous model, the Chinese student has simply cheated and is subject to disciplinary action for plagiarism. Within an ideological model, the conceptions, pressures, identities, and political relations are taken into consideration. These issues are considered within a context that acknowledges English as a world language. The fact that there are now more non-native speakers of English in the world than there are native speakers is entered into the conversations about how the university regulates language use (Kalantzis and Cope 2000, 144).

Some excellent models for literacy research can be found in recently published edited collections like *Local Literacies* 1998, *Multiliteracies* 2000, and *Situated Literacies* 2000, all of which incorporate Street's ideological model. The researchers in these collections think of themselves as representatives of the New Literacy Studies (NLS). I'd like to summarize just a few of the orientations found in the New Literacy Studies in terms of their potential for writing centers. Because the New Literacy Studies views literacy as a social practice rather than an individual attribute, it makes connections between empirical data and social theories. Some of the social theories that Barton, Hamilton, and Ivanic (2000) mention as significant to literacy research are "theories of globalization, media and visual design, social semiotics, bureaucracies and power relations, time, cultural identity, and scientific knowledge" (1). Their recent book, *Situated Literacies*, provides examples of research studies that begin with a detailed analysis of a particular literacy event. That event is then linked with theories that create a rich context for understanding. As a group, the NLS scholars share a commitment to a vision of literacy education which "recruit[s] rather than attempt[s] to ignore and erase, the different subjectivities—interests, intentions, commitments, and purposes—students bring to learning" (New London Group 2000, 18).

James Gee (2000) explains that the New Literacy Studies (NLS) is one of many movements that took part in the social turn away from emphasis on individual minds and behaviors and toward an understanding of how cognition and behavior are rooted in social and cultural understandings. As a NLS scholar himself, Gee argues that "reading and writing only make sense when studied in the context of social and cultural (and we can add historical, political, and economic) practices of which they are but a part" (Cope and Kalantzis 2000, 180). Gee encourages researchers to focus on *enactive and recognition work*, which he defines this way:

We attempt to get other people to recognize people and things as having certain meanings and values within certain configurations or relationships. Our
attempts are what I mean by 'enactive work'. Other people's active efforts to
accept or reject our attempts—to see or fail to see things 'our way'—are what
I mean by 'recognition work.' (191)

This project of enactment and recognition sounds like the focus of
writing center work to me. University professors expect students to
enact particular identities as writers and readers, and students either
accept or reject (or misunderstand) these attempts. I would argue that
the work of a writing center (or the research agenda of the writing center) is getting the rest of the university to see how literacy functions ide-
ologically and to understand the implications of that for students.

Let me offer an extended example to illustrate the implications of a
shift from thinking of literacy as an autonomous skill to thinking of it as
a social and ideological practice. On my campus, our writing center has
become the primary resource for students who speak English as a second language. Gradually, we are beginning to take a stronger role in ori-
enting faculty and administrators to the literacy understandings of these
students. Initially, this sharing of knowledge happened at a strictly local
level and was confined to providing information about the "services" we
provided to international students. But the more we paid attention to
what we were learning from working with international students, the
more quickly we made changes in the programming we offered. For
example, several years ago, we recognized the need of international
graduate teaching assistant students to practice oral English, and
applied for funding for a new program that provided opportunities to
practice oral fluency. Soon, the undergraduate writing coaches involved
in that program began talking with friends and members of student
organizations about how they were learning to listen to accented
English and coming to understand what it means to call English a world
language. In the process of learning to listen differently, their attitudes
toward international non-native English users, especially international
faculty members and GTAs, were changing. No longer did these undergraduates blame international teachers for having accents that inter-
fered with their education. Instead, they became advocates in campus
forums for a change in undergraduate attitude toward non-native teachers. These undergraduates even developed a special session for student
orientation that focused on learning to listen to accented English. In

other words, they were campaigning for different (and more positive) ways of "recognizing" international graduate students. Eventually, these same undergraduate students began writing papers about these new understandings for regional writing center conferences, and graduate writing coaches began to choose ESL issues as a research focus for their dissertations.

These changes developed when we spent less time focused on faculty perceptions of students' needs and more time focused on what we were learning from students about what they needed. Because we were also shifting our focus to an ideological model of literacy, it became easier to see the ways that local literacy issues linked up with larger social and cultural concerns. No longer were the ESL students simply having problems with documentation. Rather they were dealing with value conflicts between two different cultural ways with words. Our effectiveness with students improved as we developed a sense of how *deep* the issue of documentation goes. One frustrated dean recently compared learning to document sources to learning to drive on a different side of the road in another country. Although learning to drive on the other side of the road is awkward and initially disorienting, it doesn't involve value conflicts on the cultural or personal level. Rather than bristle at the dean's analogy, we can see it as a signal that more knowledge needs to be shared about how textual practices of documentation are embedded in cultural values.

Shifting from an autonomous to ideological understanding of literacy is a subtle but powerful factor in determining what one pays attention to, what one argues with, what one ignores, how one responds. Next year we plan to add more detail to our explanations of documentation in our work with ESL students, including some discussion of the emotional stake that American professors have in this literacy practice. We also plan conversations with the Dean of Students' Office, the place where the plagiarism cases are investigated. Research has become a 'featured character' of our writing center practice. Both graduate and undergraduate writing coaches expect to learn from their students, to connect that learning to social theory, and to share the connections they have made.

Because an ideological model of literacy pays attention to world views, to collective identities, to differences in cultural value systems, it shows us ways to improve our practice, and it points to places where research is needed. No longer is it easy to disregard the ESL student who has been accused (rightly or wrongly) of plagiarism. Rather, research into the situation is called for. What is the student's country of origin? What values does that country have regarding textual authority? What sort of identity has the student been expected to "enact" in the assignments leading up to this one? Is there a changed expectation in the assignment under question? Did the student "recognize" the change in identity expectations? What steps can be taken to clarify this enactment and recognition work on the part of faculty who gave the assignment, as well as the students responding to it? What rhetorical moves are available to a student who wants to enact a dual identity in a writing assignment? Is there a way to "recognize" the teacher's tacit expectations and still enact a different approach? Is there a way that writing center researchers can help faculty understand the layers of attitudes, values, world views attached to notions of text ownership, so that the social practices of documentation can be taught more effectively and recognized as far more than a technical skill? Is there (maybe) even room for asking if the American university might begin to think differently about documentation?

In addition to opening up a new research direction, the theoretical realignment offered by the New Literacy Studies actually strengthens the service that writing centers provide to students. One of the primary questions NLS researchers ask is "who benefits"? Rather than engage in research removed from students and everyday life, the NLS scholars are interested in studying how real people use literacy for real purposes in their everyday lives and how official literacies obscure power relations. Too often people think of research as something detached from students, and since many writing center people are attracted to writing center work because of the human contact and the satisfaction of working closely with others, academic research can sound unattractive. Because the NLS encourages research that makes learning conditions better for students, it may prove to be a more motivating approach to research for many writing center professionals. The desire to be of "service" has contributed to the service mission, and in its extreme form can lead to directors overextending themselves, but this same desire to serve can be linked more productively to a the strong sense of advocacy in the research conducted under the banner of New Literacy Studies.

The New Literacy Studies also provides encouragement for writing center researchers to involve students in research on extracurricular literacy practices, paying close attention to what students at the university do with literacy in their domains of choice. Because writing centers have direct access to students' lives, writing center researchers can learn more about how literacy is used in the rock climbing club, the bible study group, the fly fishing club, the coordination of winter carnival. Because we know so little about how students use literacy outside of school, I can't predict how these studies would inform what happens in the classroom or writing center, but I am certain such research would make things better for students by providing a clearer understanding of what's at stake for them in the classroom, of the ways their identities interact with academic expectations, and of the ways they use different kinds of text. Such an approach to research would feature students in active participant roles, whereby they create a legacy at the university and use literacy purposefully.

In addition to a strong sense of advocacy, another principle advocated in NLS research that may be appealing to writing center researchers is that which insists that all texts be treated equally. As Simon Pardoe (2000) explains, the research principle of *symmetry* disrupts the assumption that a dominant text is "coherent, homogeneous, purposeful, function or rational" while the novice text is "varied, inconsistent and lacking in coherent purpose" (162). When Pardoe applied the symmetry principle in his own research, he found that students' difficulties could often be traced back to the obscurity and ambivalence of the *official* accounts they were using as models. His study of students who were learning to write environmental impact assessment statements showed that while the professional documents were clear to the professor, a close study showed that there was lack of clarity about the relation of an environmental assessment to a development plan, that the relation of the assessor to the developer was obscure, that there was uncertainty about the data and methods used to predict future impact. Pardoe is not simply advocating for "charitable" readings of student texts, but rather for studying the links between a novice writer's text and the professional discourse. These links are both rhetorical and sociological. Studying them, as Pardoe argues, is a way to develop the sociological understanding that can inform our pedagogy. In my mind, the NLS research approach allows writing center researchers to frame understandings that derive from our practice, and to do so in a way that ultimately benefits students. Frequently, writing center workers learn to be better teachers in a writing center. We do this by learning to read official texts as students read them. This shift in perspective often reveals the gaps and lack of clarity in official texts.

Another emphasis in New Literacy Studies is the importance of understanding education as a process of transformation rather than assimilation. It sees learning not as a matter of development or leaving the old self behind, but rather as an expansion of repertoire. Importantly, it also emphasizes that the mainstream needs to be transformed in this process as well. To accomplish this, it tries to understand literacies in relation to their specific cultural location. Questions it asks seem appropriate to writing center practice: "Where is this text from? What are its multiple sources? What is it doing? Who is it doing it for? How does it do it? How do we get into it? What could it do for us?" (Kalantzis and Cope 2000, 148). According to Barton, Hamilton, and Ivanic 2000, we need to understand "what people do with texts and what these activities mean to them" and "how texts fit into the practices of people's lives, rather than the other way round" (9).

Another principle congruent with writing center work is that NLS researchers pay close attention to social context, often finding links between shifts in social context and changes in literacy practices. For example, NLS researcher Kathryn Jones (2000) presents her study of the literacy practices at a livestock auction in Wales, demonstrating the processes by which farmers become part of the abstract bureaucratic discourse. One of the key figures in the interactions is Stan, a retired Welsh farmer in his early seventies who enacts the face work commitment for the Ministry of Agriculture, Fisheries and Food bureaucracy. Helping the farmers as they fill out the new forms, Stan switches back and forth between Welsh and English, interacting with the farmers in ways that mitigate the controlling elements of the abstract discourse. By focusing on Stan's work, Jones shows readers how small town farmers are being inscribed into the global farming market, how a bilingual local event is taken over by monolingual forms, and how globalization is realized in a specific local literacy event. A small town social event becomes assimilated into the bureaucracy, and it loses its local character and neighborliness. Stan, as the key figure in this event, functions in ways similar to many writing center tutors in that they show students how to write at the university, how writing in college is different from high school, how to remove traces of neighborhoods and countries left behind, how to remove marks of lived experience in favor of abstract logic and reasoning.

Reading this account of the livestock auction evokes a sense of loss, but also a sense of wonder about how things could be different, how local differences and languages could be negotiated in the face of overwhelming economic forces. Because so much clearly depends on Stan, it is possible to read this thinking about how the "Stans" in writing centers might negotiate differently. It is also possible to see how Jones's analytical approach might be used in writing centers. For example, if such a research perspective were used in a writing center, a series of sessions with an ESL graduate student could be studied as literacy activities occurring in a specific university, at a specific time in curricular history, during a time of increased globalization, under a particular period of relations with that student's nation of origin. Within such a view, understandings of English as a world language, of economic trends, of political realities, of particular national identities, would be as significant as the particular text and discourse communities that this student operates within.

I want to make it abundantly clear that I am not proposing that anyone can just come into a writing center and begin this approach to research. In fact, the NLS would say that one cannot research in a context one doesn't understand. The projects I propose here, the ways of enacting and recognizing the multiple literacies in a writing center, are intended for writing center workers. Because this is research that addresses issues students face, it should involve writing center students in participant roles, be done by individuals familiar with the writing center purpose and theoretical mission, and respect the context of a particular writing center. To have a non-writing-center-affiliated faculty member or graduate student simply pop in to do a semester's research project would be a violation of all I am advocating here. I also make these suggestions assuming that the director is in a stable position and can set conditions about who can or can not undertake research in the writing center.

Some of this research might result in dissertations, books, or journal articles, and some of it may be suitable for web publication. Some of it may be appropriate for a writing center audience, but much of it should be appropriate for a larger audience of composition teachers and writing program and university administrators. If students are actively engaged in these projects, there is much they can learn about conducting research in real contexts, and much they can tell composition teachers. Some of the research questions that come to mind include the following: What stories might academically successful students of color have to tell entering students about adjusting to the Anglo mainstream university? What strategies have American students of color and international students developed for maintaining dual identities as writers? What approaches work best to explain American beliefs in documentation? How do students use literacy in their extracurricular activities, and how can we use this knowledge in ways that recruit (rather than ignore) their existing subjectivities? What options are there for making room in student texts for non-mainstream rhetorical choices? What do faculty need to know about schooling in China (India, Malaysia, etc.) that could support their reading of texts written by students of other cultures? What are the extracurricular strategies that third world students use in order to develop English literacies?

The research questions provoked by an NLS theoretical framework are congruent with the research direction proposed by Joan Mullin (2002). Mullin argues for ethnographic and longitudinal studies that move writing center scholars away from tired, overworked themes. She calls for research that is based on a more inclusive definition of "text," so that visual and oral texts become part of our focus, and she pushes for more consideration of the technological, international, global, and even spiritual questions that emerge from writing center work. She reminds us that we need to expect ourselves as well as our students "to dare to work at revision."

The research attitude I am proposing has in many ways been exemplified by Mickey Harris. Mickey's relentless efforts to educate varied audiences, her optimism, her insistence on connecting the local with the global, her habit of paying close, detailed attention to social issues, are all lessons appropriate to this undertaking. Mickey deserves credit for forging the initial productive and clarifying links with composition, a project that this sort of research would sustain and push even further. Although Mickey is often referred to in superhuman terms, she brings to her work and her interactions with others a sense of humor and humility, plus a strong connection with everyday realities. All of these qualities would support this research mission. Mickey says writing centers (particularly those most prepared to work with multilingual students) need to reeducate teachers and administrators about students who bring different languages to college. This is a "service" that requires the kind of research I am advocating here.

In conclusion, let me offer a few practical starting points for making research a 'featured character' of writing center work.

1. Revisit the writing center mission statement. Is it worded in a way that makes room for knowledge making and knowledge sharing? Does it take into account that this century's civic and workspaces will present the challenge of communicating a global context where understanding local diversity is essential?

2. Schedule time for research, reading, and reflection. Consider that time as inviolable as class time, or time for meetings with tutors and university administrators. Pick a time other than Friday afternoons, a time when the mind feels alert.

3. Put realistic restrictions on personal email and Internet access and other technological intrusions, which keep us responding to short-term urgencies rather than long-term priorities. If efforts to reserve time to think and to limit interruptions prove fruitless, perhaps it is time to begin campaigning for a support position for the writing center.

4. Find ways to layer research and service and teaching. Set up a personal reading program (include *Multiliteracies* on the list!) that also can be included in tutor training and that will generate ideas for scholarship in the writing center.

5. Form collaborative partnerships. Writing center directors at research institutions should look for partners at teaching colleges and community colleges. The many regional writing center associations can be places for creating research networks if conference coordinators dedicate time and resources for these liaisons. I don't mean simply setting up tables, but rather creating conference calls that encourage researchers to structure sessions that can lead to collaborative research on a particular issue.

6. Broaden the scope of writing center publication. Instead of another edited collection written for writing center professionals, plan a collection aimed at composition scholars or higher education administrators or (gasp!) the general public.

7. Find ways to allow personal passions and interests and histories to infiltrate academic interests. Whether that interest is labor history, visual design, self-help literature, contemporary spirituality, local politics, genealogy, or environmental advocacy, there are often ideas, perspectives, metaphors, and frameworks in those avocations that can enrich and motivate the exploration of writing center issues.

I believe that the dichotomies between research and service and teaching can be overcome. Research of the kind the NLS scholars endorse will improve the "services" of the writing center, and it will "teach" faculty and administrators and the general public about the new kinds of texts students can produce and the complicated identities they enact as composers. I hope that this fresh and theoretically informed approach to writing center research will encourage an exploratory fervor, one that replaces the victim-of-misunderstanding posture that emerges too often. The framework of the New Literacy Studies offers a way to renegotiate the writing center mission, to involve undergraduates in research, to improve retention by offering students legitimate roles as researchers, to contribute to the larger field of literacy studies, to enact principles of social justice, and to represent tutoring differently. It positions writing centers as change agents rather than protectors of the status quo, and it suggests a different way for writing centers to gain institutional legitimacy. It is research that changes people's minds in the same was that one's mind is changed by the diverse encounters in a writing center. In many ways, this approach has always been a part of the spirit of writing center work; it now deserves to be a 'featured character.'

3

WRITING CENTER ASSESSMENT
Searching for the "Proof" of Our Effectiveness

NEAL LERNER

Two words that haunt writing center professionals are "research" and "assessment." The first is too often held out as something others do to us, something we do not have time for, or something that is lacking in our field. The second is tied to our financial and institutional futures— if we cannot assess how well we are doing whatever it is we are supposed to be doing, we are surely doomed.

In this chapter, I reclaim these two words in several ways. First, I review the history of calls for our field to answer the assessment bell, calls that act as a sort of evaluative conscience, laying on 20 plus years of guilt about our inability or unwillingness to prove ourselves to our institutions and, ultimately, to ourselves. Next, I offer a critique of the few published studies of writing center effects, pointing out the logical and methodological complications of such work. Then, I turn to the larger assessment movement in higher education, particularly the work being done to study students' first year in college or university. I take from that research not only useful assessment tools that might be adapted to writing-center settings, but also important cautions about the nature of assessment work and its potential pitfalls. Finally, I offer some examples of real live assessment from the writing center I direct at my institution, not necessarily as exemplars for the field, but instead as indications that the work I call for can, indeed, be done. Overall, my intent here is to offer a clearer understanding of research to provide evidence of writing center "effects," its uses and limitations, and to put into a critical context the common call to investigate how well we are doing.

EVALUATE OR ELSE

For any of us engaged in writing center work, it always seems obvious that one-to-one teaching of writing is effective, and this belief has a long history. In 1939, E. C. Beck wrote in *English Journal* that "perhaps it is not too much to say that the conference method has established itself as the most successful method of teaching English composition" (594). Nevertheless, as writing centers moved from "method" to "site"—as Beth Boquet (1999) describes the evolution of the free-standing writing center—frequent calls for "accountability" followed, usually in response to threats from budget-conscious administrators or misguided faculty. However, the attempts to provide this accountability (or simply call for it) that have appeared in our literature often say more about our field's uneasiness with evaluation research than about the effectiveness of the work we do.

One source of uneasiness is with the use of statistics beyond the simple counting of numbers of students or appointments. In 1982, Janice Neuleib explained this uneasiness by noting that "many academics tend to wring their hands when faced with the prospect of a formal evaluation. English teachers especially have often not been trained in statistics, yet formal evaluation either explicitly or implicitly demands statistics" (227). For Neuleib, "formal" evaluation is necessary because "[good] tutoring and all that goes with it cannot be appreciated without verifiable evaluation techniques" (232).

While Neuleib's call is nearly 20 years old at the time of this writing, it is difficult to say that the field has answered her charge with a rich body of statistical research. The reasons for this absence are many, but most important, in my view, is composition's orientation toward qualitative or naturalistic studies of students' composing processes, as Cindy Johanek has pointed out (2000, 56). While I am aware that qualitative evidence can lend a rich and nuanced perspective to our evaluation studies (and have performed and will continue to perform such studies myself), I join Johanek in calling for additional research methods, namely quantitative or statistical ones, to understand more fully the work we do. Statistical evidence also lends itself to short forms, perfect for bullet items, PowerPoint presentations, and short attention spans—in other words, perfect for appeals to administrators and accrediting bodies. I would also argue that despite Neuleib's statement about our fear of numbers, our field is often under the sway of numerology, given the ways we have always counted who comes through our doors and why.

Nancy McCracken of Youngstown State identified the need to evaluate in 1979: "Many of us have had to expend so much effort convincing our funders of the need for a writing lab in the first place that I think that we have not adequately addressed the need for evaluation and the key issues involved" (1). To answer this charge, McCracken relied upon "error analysis of writing samples done at the start and at the end of the term" (1). This analysis (or counting, really) included "total number of words and paragraphs and rates of occurrence of focus-errors [errors identified by student and tutor from starting sample]" (1–2). While the pre-test, post-test design is encouraging, what is troubling here is a powerful focus on the text itself and the reduction of student writing into primarily mechanical features. It is difficult to imagine that the tutor[1] identified invention or revision strategies as a student's primary need and could evaluate progress on those tasks based on two writing samples; however, McCracken tells us that "demanding thorough diagnosis and evaluation has profoundly altered our staff's perceptions of their function and their effectiveness. It is enormously satisfying for the tutor to see clear evidence of progress where before it was only vaguely sensed" (2). Some students might surely have made "progress" of a sort, but McCracken does not provide accounts of how many students improved or how much improvement occurred in individual cases. Instead, we are left with one possible approach to proving the assumption that McCracken identifies and that many of us hold dear: "We have all had to discover ways to demonstrate what we know is the tremendous effectiveness of the writing lab experience for our students" (1).

A broad survey of the evaluative methods of this period was offered by Mary Lamb in 1981. Lamb surveyed 56 writing centers nationwide and found six "methods of evaluation": 1) basic statistics (i.e., usage data—nearly all centers reported this accounting); 2) questionnaires or surveys of students and faculty (used by half of the centers); 3) pre- and post-tests, usually of mechanical skills (only four centers collected writing samples in this method; the others used "objective" tests of English mechanics); 4) follow-up reports of students' grades who used the center (18% used this method); 5) external evaluations (14% of the centers surveyed used this method); 6) reports of staff publications and professional activities (7% used this method).

Since that time, I cannot imagine that the terrain has changed much. Ticking off the numbers of students who come through our doors and subdividing them according to categories that would make a census taker proud are about as easy as it gets and, for many of us, are adequate to the level of accountability to which we are held—at least the current level of accountability. But I am reminded of my first semester as a writing center director when I met with my division director and presented some nice tables on how many students we had worked with. "But of the hours you are open, during how many of those are your staff actually working with students?" Gulp! It seems my criteria for evaluation did not quite match up with my boss's criteria. That's not a good thing when it comes time for budget allocations (my staff salary budget was cut 40% by the end of that semester). I would also maintain that justifying our existences based upon how many students we work with will never get us very far. "Voluntary" writing centers (in other words, excluding those which students are required to attend or those centers that also run computer labs and count every time a student downloads an mpeg as a "contact") typically see no more than 10 to 15 percent of their student bodies, based on responses to that inquiry I and others have posted to the listserv WCenter over the last five years. That is not exactly a selling point. Thus, counting works fine when our supervisors give our annual reports about a close a reading as you might expect for columns of numbers subdivided by myriad categories. But when the inevitable budget crunch occurs, when the axe-wielding Provost is hired or a "back-to-basics" English chair rises from the ranks, those nifty tables and charts just won't cut it. In those cases we need to be ready with real evidence, convincing data, and a grasp of how to produce those figures.

Finally, the audience for our assessment efforts need not only be those who pull the purse strings. As Nancy Grimm points out in this volume, writing centers are uniquely positioned to investigate the ways that students—particularly non-mainstream students—encounter the cultures of higher education. With this research agenda, writing centers can move beyond simply defending their budgets and instead make significant contributions to these students, to our institutions, and to the knowledge in our field.

A REVIEW OF SOME EVALUATION STUDIES, OR HOW TO LIE WITH STATISTICS

The number of published statistical studies on writing center effects is quite few.[2] Two accounts that have appeared in *The Writing Lab Newsletter* are Stephen Newmann's "Demonstrating Effectiveness" (1999) and my own "Counting Beans and Making Beans Count" (1997). Both studies asked the same question: "Do students who use the writing center get higher first-year composition grades than students who do not?" Both studies used the same methods: compare students' grades who use the writing center with those who do not, but try and position students at similar starting points by using SAT Verbal scores. The assumption here is that two students with an SAT verbal of 450 would end up with about the same grade in first-year composition (FYC). However, if one of those students visits the writing center, that student's grade would be higher than the student with the same SAT score who did not visit. Thus, the hope is that the "intervention" of the writing center pays off in tangible results, namely higher course grades.

Both Newmann and I did report such results. Newmann writes that "the lower SATs [of students who were tutored] and smaller percentage of As [for students who were not tutored] suggested that the Writing Program helped less able students who were willing to work harder to perform as well as their peers" (9). My claim was that "students at the lowest end of the SAT verbal benefited the most [from writing center visits]; on a one-hundred point scale, the mean grade of this group was five points higher than students within the same SAT verbal range who did not come to the Writing Center" (3).

Two studies, similar methods, similar triumphant results; unfortunately, both are about as statistically and logically sound as the flat tax. Three assumptions underlie both studies: (1) that students with lower SAT scores are at a disadvantage in first-year composition courses; in other words, that there is a strong relationship between SAT Verbal scores and final grades in FYC; (2) that a student's final grade in FYC is an indication of her or his writing ability; and (3) that students will receive the same grade in FYC regardless of the instructor. The first assumption is fairly easy to disprove. For my institution, for the combined first-year classes from 1996 to 1999 or 488 students, the correlation between students' SAT Verbal scores and FYC average[3] was equal to .12. In non-mathematical terms, this result says that the relationship between the two scores was extremely weak (a correlation of zero indicates no relationship; correlations of -1.00 or 1.00 indicate the strongest relationship possible). In fact, the correlation between SAT Math and FYC grades was higher (.20) than the one for SAT Verbal! Thus, for my institution at least, trying to predict FYC grades based upon students' SAT Verbal scores just does not work.

The second assumption—that there is a strong relationship between a student's FYC grade and his or her writing ability—is one that should be troubling to anyone who has taught the course. Sure, some students benefit tremendously and flourish in terms of their writing. Others come to us with considerable skill and leave at about the same level.

Many are somewhere in between. In other words, tying writing center effects to FYC grades is troubling territory when we really do not know for sure if the grade is a fair assessment of the goals that the writing center holds for its student visitors.

The third assumption—that grading is consistent across FYC sections—is also troubling. When I conducted the study I refer to above, my division director and I realized that one instructor gave almost all of her students very high grades (and very few had visited the writing center!). I do not bring this up to condemn that colleague—perhaps she was working on a contract system or some other method that allowed almost all of her students to meet her criteria for high grades—but my point is that FYC grades in most places (or at least in my institution) are not particularly consistent across sections/instructors.

So, are the difficulties inherent in these sorts of studies[4] the primary reason why we generally avoid conducting them in the first place? Perhaps. However, we do not have to look far in order to understand how to make powerful statistical arguments. In the last two years, I have become increasingly involved in research on and the development of academic activities for students' first-year, and in particular, first-year seminar courses. That body of literature is a valuable resource for ideas and justifications for research on writing center effects.

IF THEY CAN DO IT, SO CAN WE—LEARNING FROM STUDIES OF FIRST-YEAR SEMINAR

What is perhaps most interesting about the literature on first-year seminar and other programmatic attempts to provide support for first-year students is how the descriptions often echo writing center themes. For example, Betsy Barefoot, the Co-Director of the Policy Center on the First Year of College, has described a dilemma familiar to many of us:

> A pervasive and central problem is that many of the programs and activities that constitute the 'first-year experience' are in a continuous battle for status within the academy . . . never becoming a central, sustainable part of the institution's fabric. First-year programs often have a single champion rather than broad-based institutional support and frequently operate with a minimal budget or no budget. (quoted in Cuseo 2000, 2)

In response to this need to "institutionalize" first-year programs, many researchers have engaged in an impressive array of studies; however, what distinguishes much of this work from writing center assessment are the efforts to tie evaluative research to the goals the institution holds for its students, whether those are simply retention or are part of larger general education goals. Barefoot (2000), again, offers the following three observations about administering and evaluating first-year seminar courses. I, however, have substituted "writing centers" for "first-year seminars" to demonstrate the applicability to our field:

> [Writing centers] are not a magic bullet that will change student behavior. [They] can serve as one piece of a comprehensive [educational] program—a linchpin of sorts to give coherence to the curriculum and co-curriculum.
>
> [Writing center] effects can be multiplied through connections with other structures and programs such as learning communities, advising, orientation, and residence life.
>
> Assessment of [writing center] outcomes is important. If [writing centers] are to survive the vicissitudes of changing administrations and fluctuating resources, there must exist some evidence that the [writing center] is doing for students and for the institution what it was designed to do. (3–4)

Thus, we need to think broadly about research on writing center effects, not just about how many students came through our doors or if those students were satisfied, but about how do our writing centers contribute to the teaching and learning goals that our institutions hold dear? How do we begin to investigate such matters?

A FRAMEWORK FOR RESEARCH ON WRITING CENTER EFFECTS

M. Lee Upcraft and John Schuh (2000) lay out a comprehensive eight-part framework for assessing students' first-year experience, one that I will adapt to writing center work. Assessment should include the following: 1) keep track of who participates, 2) assess student needs, 3) assess student satisfaction, 4) assess campus environments, 5) assess outcomes, 6) find comparable institution assessment, 7) use nationally accepted standards to assess, and 8) assess cost-effectiveness. For many of these points, I will also show some of the assessment attempts I have been making in my own writing center.

1. *Keep Track of Who Participates.* As Mary Lamb pointed out in 1981, counting who comes through our doors is something that nearly every writing center does and reports on, and is often the extent of our evaluative attempts. In the five years that the MCPHS Writing Center has been open, I have faithfully submitted those usage reports to my dean.

Certainly, demonstrating usage can provide persuasive evidence that we are meeting our goals. For example, if a writing center was targeted to certain student populations (e.g., first-year students or non-native English speakers) reporting on how many of *those* students were served can be a much more impressive and meaningful number than percent of total student body (which, as I pointed out earlier, is quite low in most cases). For instance, the MCPHS Writing Center was primarily intended to meet the needs of students in first-year composition, and we usually find that between 50 to 70 percent of the first-year class comes through our doors—a much more impressive number than percentage of the whole student body. We also have consistently found that 60 to 75 percent of the writers we see self-identify as non-native English speakers, a persuasive number to show administrators who are concerned about providing academic support for this growing population at my college. Thus, we need to keep counting, but our counting needs to have a specific focus and should not be the extent of our evaluative efforts.

2. *Assess Student Needs.* Upcraft and Schuh (2000) ask, "What kinds of services and programs do first year students really need, based on student and staff perceptions, institutional expectations, and research on student needs? Put another way, how do we know if what we offer 'fits' our first-year students?" (1). This is a powerful question when considered in light of our field's often-stated desire to be "student-centered." How much do we know about the needs of writers who come to our centers, and, perhaps more importantly, the needs of writers who *do not* visit us? How does writing center work fit into current theories of student learning and development (see, for example, Haswell 1991; Baxter Magolda 1999)? I cannot say that I have fully engaged in researching these powerful questions; however, this past academic year I did survey FYC students and had particular questions for students who did not visit the Writing Center. What I found was that the primary reason for students not visiting was that the hours were inconvenient (40% of the responses), followed closely by "Did not need to receive feedback from a tutor" (32%) and "Primarily worked with classroom teacher" (24%). However, 86% of the students who did not visit agreed with the statement that "The Writing Center is for any student engaged in any writing task," and 82% indicated that they would make use of an online Writing Center if one were available. These findings indicate that in terms of students' needs, we can do a better job of scheduling available hours or of creating on-line services, but that we are not limited by students'

remedial definition of our work. Thus, feedback from students who did not use our services this past academic year gives valuable input on the assessment of current efforts and indications for future ones.

3. *Assess Student Satisfaction.* This area of evaluation is one that many writing center directors pursue, and we often find that students are highly satisfied with our services, particularly if we survey them right after a session is completed. However, it is difficult to sort out if writers are just trying to be supportive of their peers who work in the writing center or if they were genuinely satisfied. James Bell's (2000) approach to this dilemma was to survey writing center users at three different points after their session: immediately afterward, two weeks later, and two months later. He found that satisfaction remained high over time: "Two months after a 45-minute conference all impact might be expected to have dissipated, but three-quarters of the clients agreed or strongly agreed that they could still apply what they had learned, and two-thirds agreed or strongly agreed that it would continue to help them in the future" (22). Bell's assessment protocol is a practical and powerful example for our field to follow.

One other important constituency often left unassessed is faculty. What are faculty perceptions of the writing center? At the end of the 2000-01 academic year, I distributed a survey to faculty[5] and found results that were encouraging: On a five-point Likert scale (five = strongly agree and 1 = strongly disagree), the highest mean rating, 4.9, was for "I feel comfortable referring my students to the MCPHS Writing Center." The two next highest responses were for "Students who utilize the Writing Center make discernible improvements in their writing" (4.5) and "I view the Writing Center as a valuable resource even for competent writers" (4.5). Faculty also indicated they were aligned with our intent to help all student writers by showing fairly strong disagreement (2.5) with the statement "The main function of an effective writing center is to serve primarily the weakest student writers." The survey also provided a public relations opportunity to let faculty know that the Writing Center is concerned about meeting their needs, including our availability to help faculty with their writing in progress, a survey item that was met with surprise by quite a few responders.

In addition to our own surveying, a great opportunity for writing centers is to connect with larger institutional efforts at surveying student satisfaction. Offices of Institutional Research, Student Affairs, or other campus entities are increasingly using instruments such as the College

Student Experiences Questionnaire (Pace and Kuh 1998) to investigate student satisfaction with a wide variety of their educational experiences. While specific questions about writing centers will likely not appear on the national standardized surveys, they will contain questions about academic support services, or they often have the ability to be customized. Thus, important allies for any writing center director are those survey creators and administrators on your campus. Assessment of writing center satisfaction should be seen as part of a larger institutional effort.

4. *Assess Campus Environments.* In the context of first-year programs, Upcraft and Schuh (2000) note, "It is critical to take a look at first-year students' collective perceptions of the campus environments within which they conduct their day-to-day lives. For example, what is the campus climate for first-year women? What is the academic environment, both inside and outside the classroom?" (2). As applied to writing centers, these can be powerful questions, particularly as we look not merely at "effects," but at the environment of the writing center itself. What is the students' perception of the writing center? How is space used by students and staff? What determines the flow of traffic? What is the writing center climate for different student groups: women, men, non-traditional students, non-native English speakers? It is often claimed that writing centers are "safe havens" of sorts,[6] but how systematic have been our attempts to understand this environment from the perspective of writers, tutors or faculty?[7]

5. *Assess Outcomes.* While many institutions increasingly describe their work with students in terms of "outcomes," writing centers have been slow to take up this challenge, partially because of fears that outcomes talk might reduce the complexity of the work we do to "measurable" gains outside of the goals we hold for our centers. However, consider Upcraft and Schuh's (2000) broad categorization of outcomes as applied to first-year programs: "Of those students who participate in [our] services . . . , is there any effect on their learning, development, academic success, transition to college, retention, or other intended desired outcomes, particularly when compared with non-participants?" (2). In other words, it is important to think broadly of writing center outcomes, not in terms of the narrowest measures—students' command of mechanical skills—but in terms of such things as students' development as writers and success as college students, as well as the ways the writing center contributes to the professional development and future success of its tutors.

Researching these sorts of outcomes is quite challenging, of course, but also quite necessary to establish writing centers as essential academic components. A natural effect of such work might also be to have us broaden our individual missions vis-à-vis our institutions. After all, the goals we hold for our writing centers—whether articulated formally in mission statements or less formally in our promotional materials and annual reports—provide the first focus for our assessment efforts. But those goals themselves can often be broadened to include not just our effect on student writers, but our effect on the entire institution. Such is the strategic work of making writing centers central to the conversation about writing at our institutions, to paraphrase Stephen North's charge (1984, 440).

In terms of the outcomes measures I have pursued, I cannot say I have quite measured up to the challenge I offer. Nevertheless, I have collected and analyzed a broad range of writing center data and have plans for continued analysis.[8] For example, in order to investigate the achievement differences between first-year students who used the writing center and those who did not, I combined four years worth of data on first-year students, as shown in the table below:

TABLE 1

First-Year Students, 1996-99

	Mean SAT Verbal	Mean H.S. GPA	Mean FYC GPA	Mean First-Year GPA
WC Users (307)	487	3.23	3.07	2.73
WC Non-Users (181)	499	3.11	2.78	2.42

All of the above differences between writing center users and non-users are statistically significant,[9] with the exception of SAT Verbal scores. In other words, the two groups did not start at different levels according to SAT Verbal scores, but those who did visit the Writing Center at least once during the academic year had First-Year Composition grades and end-of-first-year GPAs that were higher than students who did not visit the writing center.

Alert readers are by now remembering the condemnation of my own and other studies several pages earlier. However, I need to frame the results above in a somewhat different way. SAT Verbal scores *are* a measure of *some* ability; it is just a statistical reality that they have little relationship to FYC grades. However, by showing that SAT Verbal scores were not significantly different for writing center users and non-users, I am showing that these two groups were starting from a similar footing, according to this measure (and let me add that it is a measure that administrators will recognize immediately). My previous cautions about relying on FYC grades and about studies that do not take into account teacher effects are well worth considering here. However, my argument for positive writing center effects is bolstered by "big" numbers. By looking at data across multiple years, multiple students, and multiple teachers, but applying the single variable of writing center usage, I am making a pretty convincing argument that this single factor—visiting the writing center—has a pretty powerful relationship not just to students FYC grades but to their overall first-year GPA, despite the broad variation in those other factors over the four years for which I am accounting. In terms of the single outcome of students' grades, visiting the writing center makes a difference.[10]

One other way of considering the contribution of writing center visits is through the statistical technique of multiple regression, which calculates the contribution of several factors on some outcome. In my case, I used multiple regression to find out how well the factors of students' SAT Verbal score, SAT Math score, high school GPA, and number of writing center visits can predict first-year GPA. Writing center visits were a statistically significant variable in the entire equation,[11] lending more support to the idea that the writing center makes a difference.

One common critique of such findings is that students who visit the writing center get better grades because they are more motivated. To explore this hypothesis, I used the results of the Learning and Study Strategies Inventory (LASSI, H&H Publishing), a self-reporting instrument of "readiness" to learn, which we had first-year students complete during summer orientation for the 1999-2000 academic year. Two of the LASSI measures address "attitude" and "motivation," so I compared the scores of students who visited the writing center that academic year with those who did not. What I found was that neither of those factors—as well as the eight other LASSI measures—showed statistically significant differences between the two groups. In other words, according to that instrument and for that academic year, writing center users were not more motivated than non-users.

My use of the LASSI (unfortunately, for only a single academic year because we have not administered it since then) is an example of how we can connect our writing center assessment efforts to larger institutional attempts to collect data. Many institutions, including my own, administer the CIRP survey (The Higher Education Research Institute) to incoming freshman every fall. The CIRP provides a great deal of demographic data, as well as an indication of students' high school study habits and attitudes.[12] Tremendous possibilities exist to use these data to compare students who use the writing center with those who do not, as well as to compare these groups according to results of satisfaction surveys, such as those I mentioned earlier.

One more obvious area for writing center outcomes research is the specific contribution writing centers make to students' development as writers. In 1981, Mary Lamb expressed surprise that only four of the 56 centers she surveyed collected "pre- and post-test samples of writing" (77). I doubt that situation has changed much since, usually because centers are not set up to collect such data, and a whole host of complexities would surround such a procedure (e.g., sorting out non-writing-center influences on students' development, creating the logistics to collect consistent samples, coordinating the grading/evaluation of the samples). I can report that I did make an attempt at such a study, using the diagnostic essay that a group of first-year students wrote during freshman orientation, comparing that essay to a similar writing task—a required Writing Proficiency Exam that students wrote within a year after completing FYC—and then calculating whether writing center visits would make a difference in students' "improvement" over the two tasks. While I did find that the grades on the later writing sample were significantly higher than the first (grading was done by two independent raters), writing center visits were not a significant factor. Several complications confound these findings, however. Students knew that the diagnostic essay did not "count," so perhaps that writing effort was less than characteristic. Graders also knew which essay was the diagnostic and which was the proficiency exam, thus biasing their judgment that the latter task could be of superior quality. Finally, while I did control for teacher effects with this sample—all students were from my sections of FYC—only one out of 46 students did not visit the writing center; thus, I could not separate students into two clear groups. Perhaps almost all benefited from their writing center experience! Nevertheless, the research design I used holds promise for future efforts at examining the effects of writing center visits on students' actual writing, whether on a single task or on multiple tasks.

One approach to understanding the effects of writing center sessions would be to examine the influence of conference dialogue on student writing or to ask, "Are there components of the tutor-writer conversation that get incorporated into a student's subsequent draft?" This question has been explored in the context of elementary and high school students' writing conferences with their teachers (see Vukelich and Leverson 1987; Sperling 1991), but not on the college level or in writing center settings. It would be one way to understand not just writing center effects, but the process of learning that we believe goes on in writing center sessions.

An additional area of writing-center effects are the benefits that tutors—whether peer or professional—draw from their work. Molly Wingate (2001) has reported on the ways that her undergraduate tutoring staff at Colorado College benefit from their writing center work, including higher grade-point averages and more satisfaction and higher rates of annual giving as alumnae as compared to the rest of the student body (9–10). Indeed, the acknowledgment of the writing center as an ideal place for the training of composition teachers is long standing (see, for instance, Almasy and England 1979; Clark 1988; Zelenak et al. 1993). Thus, our understanding of writing center "outcomes" can be broadened far beyond students' command of English mechanics or grades in first-year composition, and can instead be expressed in ways that administrators, colleagues, and students will understand and value.

6. *Find Comparable Institution Assessment.* While we often recognize the particulars of the local context within which our writing centers are situated, we also often seek comparisons with similar institutions. In times of particular need—budget cuts or salary justifications—the requests appear on WCenter with a strong sense of urgency. Research on writing center effects should similarly be considered within the scope of other institutions, whether that is the results of our efforts or our methods. Our field is a relatively young one in this sense—national "benchmarks" do not necessarily exist, accreditation efforts have primarily stalled, and the central collection and dissemination of writing center data is logistically challenging. One hopeful sign in this direction is the creation of a Writing Centers Research Project at the University of Louisville (see http://www.louisville.edu/a-s/writingcenter/wcenters/wcrp.html). This "think tank," archive, and research center is a new venture and one that will certainly raise the possibility for the kinds of cross-institutional comparisons that Upcraft and Schuh (2000) call for in terms of first-year programs.

7. *Use Nationally Accepted Standards to Assess.* Similar to the item above, our field has not necessarily created national standards that might be used to gauge our effects. The International Writing Centers Association has created a useful self-study document (see http://faculty.winthrop.edu/kosterj/NWCA/nwcadraft.htm), and efforts have recently linked writing center assessment experts to the Writing Programs Administrator consultant-evaluator program. However, the political terrain of calls for "standards" can be quite rocky; in the history of our field such calls are usually associated with back-to-basics movements, attacks on non-standard literacy practices, and a pedagogical focus on mechanics. One useful framework in this debate is Alexander Astin's (1993) notion of "talent development" as the preferred goal of our institutions. In Astin's words, "The fundamental premise underlying the talent development concept is that true excellence lies in the institution's ability to affect its students and faculty favorably, to enhance their intellectual and scholarly development, to make a positive difference in their lives" (6–7). Astin contrasts this view of "excellence" with long-held notions of institutional assessment based upon the amount of resources held (including high-quality students and faculty, library holdings, campus facilities) and the reputation accorded the institution, usually according to the amount of resources. Thus, in the national-ranking view that predominates, institutions that add little more than networking possibilities for their graduates continue to be held in much higher regard than institutions that move students much farther along the developmental continuum, and assessment efforts are focused on the former and ignore the latter.

The applicability of Astin's ideas of "talent development" fit well with the goals of our writing centers, where our efforts are focused on the development of students' writing processes and on our tutors' professional development. If we are to develop standards for writing center excellence, such a view should predominate, particularly given the paucity of resources many writing centers are facing. Perhaps even our long-standing attempts to escape the label of "remediation" can be reconsidered when we realize that working with the most underprepared writers allows for the greatest amount of development, a charge that few other campus entities embrace as fully as writing centers do.

8. *Assess Cost Effectiveness.* This final component is one that makes most of us take pause. In the context of first-year programs, Upcraft and Schuh (2000) ask: "Are the benefits students and the institution derive

from the programs and services targeted to first-year students worth the cost and how do we know?" While we are reluctant to ask that question in terms of writing centers, and are quick to acknowledge the difficulties in calculating costs and benefits, budget-conscious administrators always have—and always will—ask such a question. However, by engaging in the assessment procedures outlined in this framework, we will be in a much stronger position to argue for the benefits of our work and to show the relative costs. These need not merely be in reductive terms, i.e., dollars and centers. Instead, we need to think broadly about our contributions to institutions, considering our writing centers' contributions to campus life and climate, to general education outcomes, to our institutions'commitment to academic excellence. Given the paucity of most of our budgets, the work we do comes at a relative bargain—now it is incumbent upon us to demonstrate that bargain with sustained research and assessment.

AND IN THE END

My intention in this chapter has been to demonstrate that research on writing center effects does not require an additional graduate degree or a small army of assessment "experts." Collaborating with colleagues across our institutions can serve the dual purpose of capitalizing on local expertise and sending the message that the writing center is serious about assessment. For institutions with graduate programs, writing center assessment can provide an important venue for graduate students to put into practice the methods they are learning in the classroom (see, for example, Olson, Moyer, and Falda 2001).

In 1979, Nancy McCracken wrote, "No matter the size of the writing lab, for several different purposes and at several different points in its development, the director has to justify the lab's existence" (1). That need has not gone away in the intervening 22 years, but hopefully now we can avoid the defensiveness of "justification" and instead begin to assess our work in ways that we feel are meaningful and useful.

4

SEPARATION, INITIATION, AND RETURN
Tutor Training Manuals and Writing Center Lore

Harvey Kail

> *It has often been said that one of the characteristics of the modern world is the disappearance of any meaningful rites of initiation.*
>
> Mircea Eliade

Much of the daily business in writing centers takes its shape from the ongoing necessity of recruiting new tutors and training them for the complex conversations between writer and reader that constitute the main event of writing center life. The entire training process—from interviewing potential recruits to designing and teaching the training course to celebrating the graduation of yet another group of peer writing tutors—prominently shapes the way tutors and tutor trainers alike come to the literacy work that they do together in writing centers. It is reasonable to assume, then, as I do here, that tutor training manuals are among the most important texts for authorizing writing center lore, our collective knowledge of ourselves.

Training manuals obviously make available to researchers a particularly concentrated source of information about tutor training practices, and because tutor training is at the center of so much of writing center life, these texts also provide a relatively complete picture of the educational theories and loyalties that have shaped the development of writing centers since the early 1970s. The research value of tutor training manuals might be even more broadly conceived than that. A tutor training manual might also be viewed as a kind of master narrative, an educational creation myth, if you will—a tale of the writing center tribe. What I propose to do here is to interpret tutor training texts as if they were narratives rather than manuals, read them for their story rather than focusing exclusively on their exposition and advice.

My research proceeds by excavating from the expository materials of the training manual genre the initiation tales that tutor training texts can be interpreted as implicitly telling. This excavation process, which I hope both to demonstrate and to justify, proceeds on the assumption that there are, in fact, meaningful initiation rituals in modern life, and that training writing center tutors might just possibly be one of them. Such a reading takes us not only into the theory and practice of writing centers, it may take us as well into their originating impulses and ambitions.

In his classic study of cultural celebrations and initiations, *The Rites of Passage* (1909), anthropologist Arnold van Gennep identified three major phases of the initiation story: "separation, transition, and incorporation." In his *The Hero With a Thousand Faces* (1956), Joseph Campbell brought van Gennep's classic work into a more contemporary, psychoanalytic context. I have used Campbell's better-known narrative schema of *separation, initiation, and return* as a template for this study and a tool in my analysis of tutor training manuals. It is my thesis that an initiation story, a *bildungsroman* of sorts, can be read among the metaphors and minutiae of tutor training texts, an initiation story that can tell us, like all good stories do, a bit more about who we are and what we care most about.

In Campbell's composite narrative of the rites of passage, the action proceeds as follows:

> The hero sets forth from his or her commonday hut or castle, is then lured, carried away or else voluntarily proceeds to the threshold of adventure. There the hero encounters a shadow presence that guards the passage. If the threshold is successfully crossed, the hero journeys through a world of unfamiliar yet strangely intimate forces, some of which threaten or test the hero, some of which give magical aid. When the hero arrives at the nadir of the quest, he undergoes a supreme ordeal and gains a prize or reward. The final work is that of return. At the return threshold the hero emerges from the nether world of the quest bringing a boon that restores the world. (30)

Based on the crucial events in the initiation sequence of "separation, initiation, and return," my research systematically asks the same set of questions of a number of tutor training texts.

- Who or what calls the prospective tutor to the "adventure" of the training course in the first place?

- What happens at the threshold crossing? What sort of break is suggested in educational business as usual?
- What trials and tests must be undergone? What kind of aid is received?
- What is the prize or reward to be gained at the "nadir" of the quest?
- What difficulties, if any, must be endured as the tutor "returns"?
- What does the tutor bring with her to "renew the world"?

Call to Adventure? Nadir of the Quest? Renew the World? Such quasi-anthropological terminology and the cultural assumptions that underpin it might all seem a bit preposterous when applied to tutor training manuals. In our quotidian writing center world, where the institutional deadlines of the academic calendar have long since supplanted the tribal rituals of the initiation ceremony, and where magic no longer has cultural currency and myth has become a subject rather than an experience, we are hardly likely to think of tutor training manuals in the same context as the founding tales and texts of human consciousness. It surely is a stretch to think of tutor training as residing within the same mythy ether and narrative impact as Odysseus's journey home to Ithaca or Coyote's ascent from the underworld or even Luke Skywalker's quest for atonement with his father. Writing center tutors are not culture heroes, after all, not "world redeemers." Tutors are simply ordinary folk, usually young, doing relatively mundane work, occasionally tedious but hardly dangerous, in ordinary not magical ways.

At the same time, I am persuaded that tutor training can and frequently does involve a powerful and transforming rite of educational passage, one that vividly plays out the trajectory of separation, initiation, and return. Peer tutors emphatically do separate from the mass of other students on campus, endure a rigorous initiation into writing and leaning, and then return with this dawning knowledge and developing self to tutor their peers. A transformation may be at hand in their lives. I am not alone in this belief in the transforming power of an initiation into writing center work. Tutor training manuals all claim that the experience of becoming a writing tutor is something very special in the world of higher education, and that being selected to go through a tutor training program and then becoming a writing center tutor uniquely empowers individuals. As Paula Gillespie and Neal Lerner point out in the *Allyn and Bacon Guide to Peer Tutoring* (2000), to cite only one example, the experience of writing center tutoring may "change your life, if you allow it to" (9).

I would like to demonstrate my research into tutor training manuals by examining in detail the initiation stories that might be excavated from three early and particularly influential tutor training manuals: Muriel Harris' *Teaching One-to-one: The Writing Conference* (1986), Kenneth A. Bruffee's *A Short Course in Writing* (1972), and Irene Lurkis Clark's *Teaching in a Writing Center Setting* (1985). For those interested in writing center lore, these three texts open up a rich vein of scholarship and theory, a mother lode from which many other tutor training manuals have mined much of their own ore. Be forewarned, however. Reading tutor training manuals *as if* they were coming of age stories told in the heroic mode of the questing hero of saga and myth will no doubt distort as well as reveal what they attempt to explicate. My attitude on this issue is that one sees some things inevitably at the expense of others. On with the stories!

MURIEL HARRIS, *TEACHING ONE-TO-ONE: THE WRITING CONFERENCE*

Muriel Harris's *Teaching One-to-One: The Writing Conference* is surely one of the most influential of the writing center tutor training manuals. It brings copious yet sensibly pruned composition scholarship to bear on its discussion of the writing and the tutoring process. It grounds itself firmly in empirical research data while, at the same time, it situates tutoring within a wide matrix of information and research styles, thus providing writing tutors with access to valuable interdisciplinary information and strategies. It makes judicious use of mock tutor dialogue, a now conventional but particularly tricky feature of tutor training manuals. It is even-handed and generous in its tone, offers sound and practical advice on preparing to tutor, and takes itself seriously without a hint of patronizing either the veterans or the rookies it hopes to convert to the one-to-one conferencing method. It is a classic.

If we read *One-to-One: The Writing Conference* as a covert initiation story, however, the same materials take on a somewhat different and more charged perspective. A very interesting tale of separation, initiation, and return emerges. It might go something like this:

> Students and teachers have become separated from each other by the authority and the mystery of the teacher's knowledge. This difficult and seemingly unavoidable separation must somehow be bridged and a reconciliation effected. In order to prepare the student writer for true independence of thought, one must help demystify the writing process.

Demystifying the writing process, however, necessarily involves the teacher and student in an act of reconciliation, for it was within the very conventions of the traditional classroom relationship that the mystery of learning to write took shape in the first place! Through the rehabilitation of the relationship between teacher and student, the writers may be set free to think and write on their own. The one-to-one writing conference is the ground upon which this reconciliation can best be won.

The Call to Adventure

Teaching One-to-One calls prospective tutors to the adventure of tutor training from two distinct yet allied academic communities: experienced classroom teachers, on the one hand, and novice tutors, on the other. Both are likely to be imprisoned behind a wall of suspicion, ignorance, or lack of confidence. The experienced classroom teacher may have even become bewitched, as it were, by the falsehoods of classroom pedagogy. He may be unaware of the problems inherent in his world of abstract discussions about essay organization or textbook generalities about the writing process, or, even more importantly, he may unwittingly be involved in the unproductive relationships that characterize much composition teaching in traditional classrooms, where we "abandon [students] when they are most likely to need help" (8). Stuck in the assumptions and miasma of classroom life, the experienced classroom teacher may even have strenuous objections to the idea of the one-to-one conference: "How can it be done with thirty students per class?" or "What a tiresome way to proceed" or "It simply takes too much time" (4). Why, he asks, take a chance on something different? Why not simply stay put?

Novice writing lab tutors, on the other hand, are similarly if ironically trapped by their *lack* of teaching experience. Although their absence of classroom experience frees them from the false assumptions and prejudices about the one-to-one conference method that holds back the experienced teacher from the adventure of one-to-one conferencing, it simultaneously leaves the novice tutor with a corresponding lack of confidence and "unwarranted fears" (2) about their ability to help others to write well. Why put oneself in the embarrassing position of being expected to help a complete stranger with his writing when one is burdened by self-doubt? It is much safer for novice tutors to stay home in their "commonday hut or castle" than to venture out.

"These people," according to Muriel Harris, "must be lured into some elbow to elbow contact with students" (1). They must be persuaded to leave the ease and pleasures of the status quo of the classroom for the genuine rigors of the quest. The "call to adventure" in *Teaching One-to-One* is sounded in a variety of ways, all designed to break down the misconceptions about conferencing that keep the hero stuck at home. In a self-described tone of "evangelistic fervor," Harris offers the reluctant heroes bias-busting arguments that favor one-to-one pedagogy. She quotes testimonials from well-known composition researchers such as Charles Cooper and Janet Emig, who have themselves already successfully answered the call of the writing conference adventure. Furthermore, and perhaps most persuasively, she cites numerous empirical research studies that demonstrate how the one-to-one method makes advantageous use of the writing process model. Study after study, Harris argues, show not only an improvement in writing but also an actual savings of time as a result of the conferencing method. Reasonably speaking, then, there is nothing to stop the potential tutor-in-training from advancing forthwith to the "threshold of adventure."

Except, of course, the hero's own inertia. Having no reason *not* to engage in doing something is not quite the same thing as having a very good reason really to want to go, to answer the call, to trade in one way of doing something for another. *Teaching One-to-One* promises the prospective tutor more than just effective arguments against his arguments to stay home. It suggests not only efficiency and productivity in the teaching of writing through conferencing, but additionally and most importantly, it also promises that a new relationship with students can be forged in the process. Instead of the "fear" and alienation that most students feel toward their composition teachers (21), a relationship based on trust and mutual respect can be forged. The "invisible walls between teacher and student" can be "dissolved," and in their place may come a recognition of the "human connections and . . . the individuality of the person with whom we are sitting" (41). At this point, the reluctant but now sufficiently intrigued heroes begin packing their bags. The crossing of a threshold is at hand.

The Threshold of Adventure

To achieve this desired new relationship, the classroom teacher must cross the Threshold of Adventure, going through a kind of transformation. Instead of appearing to the student writer as the authoritarian source of mysterious rules and ruthless red ink, the hero/teacher must emerge on the other side transformed into a coach, a mentor, a kind of magic helper. "Personal attention is magic," Muriel Harris argues, citing a colleague. "It gets writers going again when they've hit some rough spots, and it makes them want to write again"(9).

Crossing the Threshold of Adventure itself, however, is risky business. Not only are one-to-one conferences "exhausting" and the level of concentration demanded "high," but the give and take of one-to-one teaching is so intense that it can even "fry one's brain" (27)! Even more ominously, both experienced classroom teachers and novice tutors risk inviting chaos into the teaching-learning process by converting to the one-to-one method. Unlike the structured and predictable classroom environment, with its conventionally determined rituals and familiar order, its comfortable distances and hierarchical certitudes, the writing conference may "sometimes. . .amble down several paths before finding a direction; at other times, it's difficult to define what was accomplished in all that talk." To make matters more complex, there are no typical or predictable tutorials: "Exact similarity isn't possible because writers are not alike. Even the same writer at different times, with different assignments, has different concerns."

Breaking with the traditional expectations of classrooms in exchange for the perplexing and unpredictable intimacy of the conference format calls for a radical change in the teacher's orientation to learning and teaching. In spite of the dangers that lurk at the Threshold of Adventure, Harris urges the heroes to "plunge in" anyway (1), to take heart and embark on a night sea journey of discovery! This journey on the "Road of Trials," as Campbell calls it, will involve the questing hero in a succession of tests that may tempt him to fall back into or reassume the teacher role that is so deeply engrained in our sense of what it is to be a teacher. For instance, one may be tempted to share with writers the solution one has in mind for the problem the writer is trying to solve. Indeed, one's very training in composition may ironically serve to undermine the power of one-to-one conferencing and to stop the quest dead in its tracks. Teachers "primed and ready to discuss composing strategies, cohesion, audience awareness, or whatever else teachers value" (33) are likely to fall into the trap of making student writers dependent on the teacher's expertise rather than directing the writer toward the most important goal of the educational process, the writer's independence. "The dangers of robbing students of the initiative are great," Harris points out, and resisting the temptation to lecture at the student or ask obvious, leading questions—to simply transfer classroom consciousness to the conference setting—requires experience and discipline.

To gain understanding and practice, Harris provides tutors with intricate strategies and procedures to help them help others along the road of trials. Tutors learn to listen and to question, to diagnose, and, as appropriate, to show and even to tell. They are also introduced to interdisciplinary resources that they can call upon for "magical" aid, becoming acquainted with exotic domains of knowledge, such as cognitive psychology, therapy and counseling, even cultural anthropology. None of these strategies or approaches, however, resembles the usual textbook explanations that state rules or give examples or guidelines to follow. Instead, they are embedded in the context of the one-to-one conference, where teacher and student are always "working together on the student's own writing" (132). These conversations are not "mysterious" but "normal," not abstract but specific, not general but rooted in the goal of "helping this student seated next to me to become a better writer" (133)

The Nadir of the Quest

As the hero gains practical knowledge, working in the immediacy of the one-to-one setting, the myths of teaching writing that have formerly trapped experienced teachers and novice tutors alike in a world of generalities, abstractions, and unreal relationships will begin to be exposed for the falsehoods that they are. Instead of the usual mystification and missed connections, the heroes of this tutor training manual will experience a vision of how they can arrive at real contact with students. My research suggests that it is this contact or union between teacher and student writer that gives Muriel Harris's *One-to-One: The Writing Conference* its underlying sense of vital purpose.

It is as if the relationship between teachers and learners has been corrupted by schooling itself, and needs repair and reunification. The institutions of higher education, with their emphases on products rather than people, evaluation rather than instruction, competition rather than collaboration, through long practice have formalized and structured the separation between student and teacher into the curriculum itself, rendering their human relationship adversarial rather than mutually supportive. In Muriel Harris's writing lab creation myth, the

teacher/coach and student/writer break through these forms of alienation and atomization and embark together, writer and writing guide,
on a mutual "journey of discovery."

The journey follows the intricate movements of the writing process
itself, which, though it may bend and twist, and sometimes appear to
flow backwards, always leads to a generative sea. One must, with the
help of composition scholarship tempered by personal experience,
learn to trust the writing and revision process. The tutor can learn what
tricks and turns the writing process might take in its tortuous route
toward meaning, and can warn the student writer of impending crevices
and swamps, keep the student writer moving when he is discouraged,
help the student retrace his steps when he has lost the way.

Should all go well in the course of their intimate travels together, stu-
dent/writer and teacher/coach may find that the writing process
becomes increasingly transparent, losing some of its mystery for the student and becoming, instead, the subject of an intense and highly specific conversation. Communication barriers may begin to come down.
The authority of knowledge that has manifested itself in the form of
grades and written teacher comments may be replaced with helpful
advice and friendly talk. Writers and readers will begin to recognize
each other in a more intimate and individual way. The institutionalized
unreality of classroom consciousness will give way to the intimacy of two
individuals traveling on the road to meaning together, with mutual
respect and even affection. Along the way, a sacred, educational union
may be achieved.

The Return

The intense and intricate dialogue that characterizes the relationship
of the tutor and the writer during the Journey of Discovery becomes not
only a source of immediate and individualized information for the
writer but also, ideally, a part of his own, individual, writerly consciousness. Because the tutor has not merely talked about the writing process
to the student writer, but participated in that process with him, the dialogue between tutor and writer may prove sufficiently intense and productive that it will be internalized in some measure into the novice
writer's own understanding and memory. The more the student writes,
the more the encouraging but firm voice of the magic helper/coach
will be sounded from within the writer, himself. Citing Deanna
Gutschow, Harris argues that when students "master this inner dialectic,

they can . . . look inward rather than outward for critical evaluation" (22). In effect, the voice of the tutor will become intertwined with and a vital part of the student's writing process itself.

It is here that the reconciliation between writing teacher and writing student is confirmed. As a result of the intellectual intimacy of one-to-one tutoring, the writing tutor's passage across the "return threshold" is achieved through another act of transformation. The tutor is carried, as it were, across the return threshold within the very protocols of the student's own writerly memory, an integrated and integral part of how the writer writes. Thus, teacher and student are fully reconciled. When the hero-writer emerges into the world of meaning-making, she will bring with her the internal voices of a demystified writing process, and thus the boon of independent thought.

KENNETH A. BRUFFEE'S *A SHORT COURSE IN WRITING: COMPOSITION, COLLABORATIVE LEARNING, AND CONSTRUCTIVE READING*

Kenneth Bruffee's groundbreaking work on collaborative learning and peer tutoring is widely acknowledged in writing center scholarship, yet his tutor training text, *A Short Course in Writing*, first published in 1972 with the subtitle *Practical Rhetoric for Composition Courses, Writing Workshops, and Tutor Training Programs*, is surprisingly rarely cited. Perhaps it has been too well disguised as a composition textbook to be recognized as a tutor training manual. Still, there is arguably no more influential story for writing centers than the one Kenneth Bruffee tells in it.[2] *A Short Course in Writing* presents a purposeful, systematic, and detailed pedagogy for training writing center peer tutors that has been and continues to be at the forefront of social constructionist theory and practice in composition studies and in writing center lore.

Reading *A Short Course in Writing* through the lens of *A Hero With A Thousand Faces* presents an immediate problem and an immediate reward. The problem is that *A Short Course in Writing* tells a story without a hero. Central to Kenneth Bruffee's project in this training manual is the premise that collaborative learning deconstructs the very image of the writer as hero. In *Elegaic Romance: Cultural Change and the Loss of the Hero in Modern Fiction* (1983a), Bruffee argues that the novels of such writers as Joseph Conrad, Ford Maddox Ford, F. Scott Fitzgerald, and Robert Penn Warren illustrate that the hero of the quest romance novels of the nineteenth century did not survive into the twentieth. "There is no modern hero," Bruffee announces. In the hero's place emerges an "exemplary modern figure,"a literary type "who exposes and copes with the delusion of hero worship and outgrows it" (15).

The immediate reward to a narrative reading of *A Short Course in Writing* is that it is hard to imagine a more ironically appropriate lens through which to examine this training manual than the progression of "separation, initiation, and return." As it turns out, even narratives without heroes have a story to tell. The collaborative learning story told in *A Short Course in Writing* might go something like this:

> The "exemplary figure" and a group of like-minded friends arrive at the threshold of adventure together. In order to cross it, they must depart from one community, of which they are an integral part, and join another, which may not necessarily be overly glad to see them. This difficult process of saying good-bye and saying hello may be facilitated by the formation of a transitional community of knowledgeable peers. Formed for the purpose, this temporary community must carry the exemplary figures, who may come from diverse and even antagonistic backgrounds, across the threshold of adventure together, seeking to learn the language, mores, assumptions, and goals of the new community they wish ultimately to join. To succeed, they must learn to learn with and from each other, to strive toward mutual aid rather than to struggle in mutual competition. At the nadir of their quest they achieve at-one-ment with the new community. Their final task is to avoid the allure of the status quo of change, the danger of becoming enthralled by their own transitional experience. If the exemplary figures are successful in breaking free of the temporary loyalties and obligations they have established as part of their journey together, they will be welcomed at the return threshold, where they will begin yet another conversation in the never-ending conversation of mankind.

The Call to Adventure

The Call to Adventure in *A Short Course in Writing* is sounded from a community outside the writer's own. Let us call it the community of literate adults. Its members are a stern and imposing lot, but they are not without charm. More importantly, they have real power and authority that, for educational reasons, they wish to redistribute. They call to the exemplary figure, barely discernible from his or her peers, all of them deeply embedded in their social context, to join them in a world of sophisticated literacy in which the important work of the academy, government, business, and the professions gets done.

What happens next is crucial. If the exemplary figure and peers want to identify themselves sufficiently with the virtues and benefits of sophisticated literacy, or if they feel sufficiently compelled to do so, they will have to make a break from the security offered by not being literate in the discourse of the academy. They will to some degree have to give up the attraction of the old neighborhood, the satisfactions and security of the known, along with the safety of their familiar, home grown vernaculars. These ties with the status quo are powerful, so much so that even exemplary figures are not likely to make the break alone. If, however, a skillful and dedicated representative of the community of literate adults—call this agent a tutor trainer—intervenes in the process by helping students form themselves into institutionalized, accredited, academic gangs, they might make the break into literate discourse together.

The Threshold of Adventure

The crossing of the threshold of adventure in Bruffee's collaborative learning story is a very stressful time, since it necessarily involves a conflict of social loyalties and individual identities, a period of "brother-battle" in Joseph Campbell's terms. The transitional subgroup of potential tutors, with its collective aim of joining a new community, raises considerable conflict among its individual members. Issues of authority, loyalty, and identity are likely to be felt, if not remarked upon, by all. At the threshold crossing, tutors-in-training are likely to be looking in two directions at the same time: back to the familiar and the comfortable, forward to the strange but the promising. For the transitional subgroup, there may be no easy way back and no easy way forward. The familiar life horizons are being outgrown; the crossing of a threshold is at hand.

The crossing of the threshold of adventure is made possible when the members of the subgroup become so absorbed in their mutual work that, tenuously at first but with increasing confidence, they transfer their allegiances from their former communities to their newly formed transitional subgroup. In effect, the exemplary figures learn to say good-bye to one community by learning to say hello to another. The threshold crossing remains a dangerous time in the collaborative learning story, however, long after the work has advanced. The attraction of the old ways might prove so enduring and the stress of the new ways so discomforting that the transitional subgroup might well dissolve at some point, its members fleeing back across the threshold, back home.

This complex process of intellectual and social acculturation is shaped by the writing and peer response tasks that are at the heart of the peer tutor training process in *A Short Course in Writing*. Writing an original argument paper and then writing a detailed critique about someone else's argument paper while he or she writes a detailed critique of your essay systematically engages the exemplary figures in the roles of writers, readers, and critics. Through the extended intimacy of this elaborate exchange ritual, the exemplary figures begin to exercise and develop their critical judgment among themselves, learning through mutual risk to grant genuine authority to each other. As a result, they begin to recognize themselves as serious and effective writers and thinkers. The nadir of the quest is close by.

The Crunch

At some point along the road of adventure in *A Short Course in Writing*, the exemplary figure may come up against "the crunch." The crunch is a form of rebellion directed against the strict authority of the formal writing assignments that constitutes the writer's training in *A Short Course*—the infamous three-paragraph essays on which Bruffee steadfastly insists. Students are likely to become "irritable and impatient" with these forms of argument—proposition and two reasons, strawman and one reason, concession, etc.—feeling that this kind of controlled writing is destructive of their creativity if not their very identity. This is the writing course "crunch," Bruffee says, and "no writing course should be without one" (130). It provides the moment at which student writers and peer tutors-in-training face the same question: "Am I going to govern my words and my ideas, or am I going to go on letting my words and ideas govern me?"(131). The crunch is a period of change in the writers' sense of their relationship with writing and with discourse conventions. Because of the "deep and complex relationship" between language and identity, "people cannot change the way they formulate and express idea without undergoing some change in themselves" (130).

The Nadir of the Quest

Thus, to learn is to change—learning is change—and "change hurts," Bruffee points out (131). Throughout this uncomfortable period of saying good-bye and trying to say hello, the tutor trainer can help the struggling exemplary figures by providing them with as much sympathy and encouragement as possible. At the same time, the trainer must firmly hold to the *Short Course* forms and tasks. The crunch, like some psychological ogre that threatens us at the gates of knowledge, must be confronted and defeated. "To grow as writers," Bruffee maintains, "[tutors] must endure the crunch and come out successfully on the other side with new confidence in their writing ability and new confidence in the worth of their own ideas" (132).

With the sequenced writing and critiquing tasks to guide its members, and if the crunch is successfully endured, the transitional subgroup arrives at the nadir of its quest: at-one-ment with the community of literate adults. The quest culminates when the exemplary figures have "learned the language, mores, and behavior that is the norm in. . .the new community. . .and by accepting the assumptions and goals that are the working premise of the new assenting community" (*Collaborative Leaning and the Conversation of Mankind*, 642).

The Return

Even as the student writers/tutors attach themselves to their new community of knowledgeable peers, their passage across the return threshold is not certain. Nostalgia—"the allure of the status-quo of change"—may set in among the members of the transitional subgroup. They may become stuck in a sentimental attachment to their transitional subgroup culture. It is up to the representatives of the community of literate adults to make sure their new members feel that the hazardous journey was worthwhile and that they are now, indeed, writers among writers, teachers and learners recognized among other teachers and learners. This acceptance is confirmed by the new members' acknowledged ability to engage in "normal [writing center] discourse," the proficient use of their new community's prevailing symbol system. Their reward is their ability to participate in and thus to renew the never-ending "conversation of mankind."

IRENE LURKIS CLARK, *WRITING IN THE CENTER: TEACHING IN A WRITING CENTER SETTING*

Irene Clark's *Teaching in a Writing Center Setting*, originally published in 1985 and now in its third edition (1998), brings a new dimension to the dynamic relationships involved in writing and tutoring writing: a vital sense of place. If the theme of Muriel Harris's *One-to-One* is reconciliation between teacher and student in the name of the writer's independence, and if the theme of Bruffee's *A Short Course in Writing* is the redefinition of those relationships in the name of interdependence, the theme of Irene Clark's *Teaching in a Writing Center Setting* is the shaping importance of the setting of the quest, the writing center itself. The setting of this story is the story. In a very palpable sense, the writing center is the major theme, if not the actual hero, of this tutor training tale. It might go something like this:

> The prospective tutor is irresistibly attracted to the adventure of tutoring by the educational energy on the other side of the threshold. Something dynamic is going on over there in writing centers. They are somehow flourishing in the academic desert! What are they all about? To make his way toward this energy source, the tutor-in-training must renounce the dark forces of product and embrace the uncertainties of process, both in writing and in tutoring writing. Once he crosses the threshold of adventure, the tutor-in-training will first enter into a state of anxiety and trepidation. He will go through self-analysis and role playing.
>
> The psychotherapist Carl Rogers will appear to help ease his way. He will read scripts of tutor dialogue and be introduced to an extensive range of composition scholarship as it becomes transparent and experientially achieved in the happy marriage between theory and practice that constitutes the writing center setting. If all goes well, he will arrive at the nadir of the quest, the very heart of the writing center, where he will hear the tale of the goddess of learning, Mrs. Prestopino. Activated now by both self-knowledge and tutor lore, the tutor will soon be free to intervene in other students' writing process at all stages. At the return threshold, his final challenge is to follow the arduous path between legitimate and illegitimate collaboration. The hero crosses the return threshold holding aloft his boon: the keys to the writing center.

The Call to Adventure

The threshold of adventure in *Teaching in a Writing Center Setting* marks the boundary line between the old ways and the new ways in composition studies. Crossing the threshold is accomplished by listening to the story of the Great Paradigm Shift and the Rise of the Writing Center. Back in the old days, years and years ago (in a university not unlike this one), colleges and universities were pretty much the province of the elite. Students liked to write because they passionately liked to read. In fact, college students were identifiable as college students precisely because they already knew how to write when they arrived on campus. That's the way it used to be. Then things began to change. People who didn't love to read and write (at least in English) started going to college. They were smart enough, no doubt, but perhaps not experienced enough or lucky enough at writing. This made the students nervous, and it made their colleges and universities nervous, too. The students didn't know what to do, and the professors didn't know what to do. So, relying on tradition, the professors talked at the students about writing, and then marked up the students' papers when the students were done writing them and "handed them in." Sometimes, it must be acknowledged, the professors wrote nasty things to the students, perhaps not realizing what they were doing—such was their despair. The situation really was untenable for students and faculty alike. The crossing of a threshold was at hand.

Astonishingly, the writing center, heretofore thought of as the remedial fix-it shop of college writing programs, emerges to occupy some of composition studies' prime educational real estate, located on the other side of the Threshold of Adventure. It is just down this hall, then up the stairs, turn left and look for the blue sign: Writing Center. It is in the library. It is in the English building. It is in the student center. It is in the study skills center. (It is actually in a box at Ohio University). Wherever it is to be found, the writing center is the place where contemporary composition theory and practice are most efficiently and usefully joined within the powerful, writing-process paradigm: One helps others to write for college not by giving lectures on writing or by assigning how-to books or by marking up products in order to grade them. One helps others to write by engaging them in acts of "writing, talking about writing, getting feedback on one's writing, and then rewriting and rewriting, preferably in a comfortable, nonthreatening setting" (vii). What could·have been better for the composing process than writing centers? What could have been better for writing centers than a research based, step-by-step elaboration of the composing process?

The special source of the writing center's surprising institutional vitality, however, is its flexible and nonthreatening setting, where grades have been banished, where instruction adapts to individual necessity, and where students can obtain help with their writing at any stage in the composing process. The writing center becomes in *Teaching in a Writing Center Setting* not merely a room where students happen to be tutored, but a far more encompassing yet particularized setting in the academy, a unique locale with its own institutional history and its own legitimate brand of scholarship. Flourishing on the margins of academe while simultaneously redefining its geography, the writing center, a utopia of composition theory and practice, calls the hero to adventure.

The Threshold of Adventure

After being introduced at the threshold crossing to the history of writing centers and to various approaches to composition theory that inhabit therein, the tutor is invited first to turn *inwards*, to anticipate what lies ahead on the journey toward that initial tutorial. By first interrogating his own writing process, by reflecting on his own positions concerning evaluating writing, and by remembering what it was like to be a student—the tutor/hero can safely cross the threshold of adventure, balancing the anxiety such a crossing provokes by discovering what he already knows about writing.

Buoyed by this information, the tutor is then instructed to turn *outwards* toward the needs of the student writer. What is helpful for her? What will put him at ease? How can the authority of the tutor be subtly negotiated so as to empower the student writer rather than the tutor? Finally, the tutor must look to the silent third partner in the tutoring relationship, the teacher taskmaster, who secretly inhabits the writing center cleverly disguised as "the assignment." How can writing assignments be best understood? How can a response to them be invented? What tools are available? What does the teacher really want?

Through analysis and writing exercises, examples and strategies, student-tutor dialogue and interpretations thereof, the tutor-in-training moves through the complexities of the adventure toward the simple but profound tale at the nadir of the quest, the story of Irene Lurkis Clark's graduation dress.

The Nadir of the Quest

Just at the point where novice tutors are starting to grapple with some of their most daunting training tasks, such as diagnosing student writing and helping writers to manage revision, they come face-to-face with a piece of writing center lore as iconographic as any we are likely to find in tutor training manuals. At the nadir of the writing center creation tale told in *Teaching in a Writing Center Setting*, the tutor comes face-to-face with one of the resident goddesses of writing center lore, Mrs. Prestopino.

All the young women in the eighth grade were required to take a sewing class in order to make their own graduation dresses. So every Tuesday and Thursday afternoons, a bunch of very silly and generally incompetent young girls would sit in Mrs. Prestopino's sewing room, diligently working on our creations. Of course, some of us were better seamstresses than were others, and so, the rate at which we worked and the kinds of problems we had varied considerably among us.

Mrs. Prestopino was able to cope with the differences in her students, though, because she was a wise woman with some extremely sound pedagogical principles. Rather than requiring every girl to work on the same task at the same rate, she sensibly allowed full scope for the individual differences. Serenely, Mrs. Prestopino would sit at her big sewing table at the front of the room, seemingly undisturbed by girlish chattering or the whir of the sewing machines. When any girl had a problem or needed instruction in the next stage of dressmaking, Mrs. Prestopino would then summon the girl to her table and give her the necessary help (93).

Mrs. Prestopino's wise pedagogical principles—praise something in each student attempt, give practical tasks that focus initially on global problems, keep tasks simple—provide an object lesson at the nadir of the quest. More importantly, her story also suggests an entire ethos for the writing center setting: the safe if somewhat disorderly environment created by Mrs. Prestopino's serene presence at the big table amid the undisturbed chatter of the students; the almost immediate access to genuine expertise that will be freely and wisely given; the talent for recognizing just what each student needs when she needs it; the indefatigable commitment to find something praiseworthy in every attempt; the arrangement of the pedagogical whole on the basis of the differences of the individual parts, not the other way around; and the unquestioned significance of the task that each girl has had set out for her by the authority of the institution—something appropriate to wear to her own graduation. Here surely is one of the master narratives of writing center lore.

Having heard this founding tale, and buoyed by what inspiration it may provide, the writing tutor must hurry on her way. There is much still to be learned in the highly developed world of contemporary writing centers: dealing with learning disabilities, working with computers, working with non-native and dialect speakers, tutoring students who are working on research projects or writing a literary essay, among others. The breadth and depth of expertise expected of the writing center tutor is considerable, and the extensive wardrobe that the writing tutor must be prepared to model comes with all the accessories.

The Return

Having worked his way by now through a range of subdisciplines and practices, and an expansive bibliography of writing center scholarship, the tutor-in-training arrives at the return threshold. After so much travail and so near to the end of his quest, it may seem cruel, but here at the return threshold the very success of his journey is threatened by a nasty paradox: the more the novice tutor knows about writing center tutoring, the more difficult, not easier, it becomes to act within its limits. Even a lot of knowledge might be dangerous. The real world of writing centers, the one that is in actual operation on the other side of the return threshold, may well be flourishing, yet it must manage its flowering in the edgy ambiance and ethical brambles that mark academic culture. The very non-interventionist policies and strategies that had at one time promised to keep the writing center safely insulated from its vocal critics in the academy, those who would accuse the writing center of aiding and abetting student plagiarism, for instance, now threaten to congeal into an unfortunate orthodoxy that could well marginalize the center's very mission to improve student writing. The serene and ordered ethos offered by Mrs. Prestopino's sewing circle does not, as it turns out, entirely take into account the complex and troubling issues that full participation in university intellectual life are likely to raise. In order to cross the return threshold of adventure, and become a full-fledged member of the writing center fellowship, the tutor-hero must learn to walk "the fine line between legitimate and illegitimate collaboration," between not intervening too much in others' writing and not intervening enough. The return threshold crossing is marked by a narrow and perilous route that snakes its way across the dismal swamp of authority and authorship in the academy. To successfully cross the return threshold is to move from acting out of habit or defensive bureaucratic policy to the sort of flexible and informed judgment required in the real world setting of colleges and universities.

If he can negotiate this last test, the tutor-in-training crosses the return threshold of adventure, holding aloft the prize, the boon, the magic talisman: the keys to the writing center.

I hope that my reading of these three tutor training manuals as if they were quest romances or creation myths has not gratuitously caricatured their pedagogical purposes, on the one hand, or overinflated their cultural significance, on the other. The temptations of these two extremes were constant companions throughout my research. At the same time, I would argue that my reading does persuasively interpret tutor training manuals as powerful stories of initiation. I would argue further that these "tales of the tribe," such as they are, collectively and individually inscribe a number of the most enduring themes of writing center lore:

- By reuniting the learner with the teacher, the writer with the reader, one-to-one conferencing can humanize both participants and demystify the writing process.
- By systematically introducing students to each other as credible writers, thinkers, talkers, and listeners, peer tutoring can change students' lives and reinvigorate campus literacy.
- By creating a knowledgeable and flexible academic culture around one-to-one conferencing and collaborative learning, writing cen ters can thrive.

What about those of us who are tutor trainers and writing center directors? What might these manuals-as-myths tell us about ourselves? For one thing, they suggest a more satisfying explanation of why we are so very, very busy. After all, we are the ones who recruit the tutors from their banal schedule of classes, calling out to them to step beyond business as usual and to come to a special place called "Peer Tutoring" or "English Internship" or simply "ENG 395." We are the ones who construct and reconstruct the intricate, sequential writing tasks and the elaborate tutorial rehearsals that constitute the "road of trials" of tutor training itself—even videotaping the proceedings for later study. We are the ones who provide as much "magical aid" as scholarship and experience make available to us, perhaps more aid than even hero-tutors can take advantage of, so afoot are we with our mission. We serve, too, as the "shadowy figures" that guard the thresholds of adventure, making sure the rites of passage are fully observed. Once in a while we even have to say "No, you can't have the keys to the writing center." (We are not particularly good at that.) When we witness the heroes struggling across the return threshold, we are there, too, on the other side, offering congratulations and welcome to the new initiates, along with a slice of pizza with outlandish toppings or a hot bowl of chili made with our own hands in our own kitchens. "Would you be interested in going to the National Conference on Writing and Peer Tutoring?" we ask between bites. "We're having an organizational meeting next week to put together a proposal, and you are invited."

Not only does the cycle of tutor training shape much of a writing center director's professional and even personal life, but my research into tutor training manuals also suggests that we deeply identify ourselves with the themes of these tutor training initiation stories. Narratives of alienation and reunion, social and cultural transformation, marginalization and eventual validation—the tutor training stories as I have excavated them from tutor training manuals remind me very much of the history of our own collective "heroic" struggle to establish writing centers in universities and colleges. Our creation myth might go something like this:

> Having answered the call to adventure sounded from the pages of the "MLA Job Information List" or "The Writing Center Journal" or from the bulletin board at the local employment office advertising a CETA job at Kishwaukee Community College, we embark on an arduous quest to achieve the elusive prize, the boon, the reward at the nadir of our writing center journey: at-one-ment with the academy. The Threshold of Adventure is hidden in a former classroom across the hall from the book-store annex, at the literal and figurative margins of campus life. The sign on the door says "Writing Lab." We open it, cross over the threshold, and find ourselves transformed and at the cutting edge of undergraduate education. We soon adapt to the paradox of our educational centrality and our tenuous status. We take ourselves seriously. Somewhere up ahead, if we can figure out where ahead really is, we hope to find a "tenure home" for the writing center. Magical aid is in short supply at the dawn of writing center time, but at least there are some federal dollars and local grants-in-aid to be had, some one-time monies to ease us across the threshold, to get us going. Along the way, we receive invaluable guidance from talented and generous colleagues, who know what we are in for and try to help. Mostly we make things up as we go along the road of trials, where no one else seems to understand or care a fig for what the idea of a writing center is; they just want a plumber to fix the literacy leak. A few of us miraculously get tenure-track positions, or at least long-term professional appointments associated with writing centers. We are at the nadir of the quest: at-one-ment with the academy. Some of us get tenure; many of us get screwed. Those who survive the tenure trial take a big, sabbatical breath and then set out on the long and necessarily repetitive passage to the return threshold, which is marked clearly by a sign we ourselves have

written. The sign reads "Wanted: Writing Center Director, Tenure-Track, Big Bucks! Enter Here." Up ahead of us, hazy in the distance but clearly discernible, we can see others with whom we have journeyed crossing over the Return Threshold. They disappear from sight almost immediately, but the writing centers themselves, the true heroes of this story, soldier on toward the ever-receding horizon. They are thriving in the future that is taking place just on the other side of the Return Threshold, a future where writing centers have become as permanent a part of the academy as writing itself.

5

POWER AND AUTHORITY IN PEER TUTORING

PETER CARINO

"Power" and "authority" are not nice words, especially to writing centers, who have always advertised themselves as nurturing environments, friendly places with coffee pots and comfy couches for the weary. These words are further muted by calling students who work in writing centers peer tutors, peer writing consultants or some such formation that includes the word *peer*. The use of undergraduate peer tutors has powerfully shaped writing center practice for more than twenty years, and the idea of peership has served in center scholarship to represent writing centers as the nonhierarchical and nonthreatening collaborative environments most aspire to be. As early as 1980, Thom Hawkins, in "Intimacy and Audience: The Relationship Between Revision and the Social Dimension of Peer Tutoring," lauded writing center work as "a reciprocal relationship between equals, a sharing in the work of the system (for example, writing papers) between two friends who trust one another" (66). Kenneth Bruffee's model of collaborative learning (1983b), which Hawkins cites and many centers adopted, did much to shape initial constructions of the tutor as peer. Though in the middle 1980s, John Trimbur's "Peer Tutoring: A Contradiction in Terms" called into question the notion of "peerness," pointing to the unequal positions tutor and tutee often hold in terms of rhetorical knowledge and academic success, Trimbur recommended training tutors in nondirective questioning methods to preserve the peer relationship as much a possible and to encourage collaborative learning rather than hierarchical teaching. As Carrie Leverenz wrote of peer tutors, "it could be said that they are experts in not appearing to be experts" (2001, 54).

Two essays in the *Writing Lab Newsletter* demonstrate tutors' difficulty in always remaining peers. As tutor Jason Palmeri (2000) put it after discussing a session in which a tutee lost confidence in him because he could not show her how to integrate source material as expected in her discipline, "I came to realize that authority is a central part of peer tutoring" (10). Palmeri goes on to lament that once this student lost confidence in his authority, she had far less interest in their sessions. Julie Bokser (2000), a new director, concludes an essay by questioning the purpose of suppressing directive behaviors learned on the job by older tutors who have worked in corporate settings where people are more comfortable in hierarchical arrangements. Bokser issues a call "to resituate discussions about collaboration and peerness within the locus of discussions about power and authority" (9). These complaints, coming from a tutor and new director rather than the community's "name" theoreticians or practitioners, suggest a grassroots problem that tutors face daily and that has remained problematic in center scholarship—the question of tutorial power and authority. This question has had a long and unresolved history in the writing center community, and likely will remain one of the more difficult questions as the community continues to develop. In this paper, I will attempt to sort out why writing centers have been uncomfortable with wielding power and claiming authority, how they have masked these terms in the egalitarian rhetoric of "peerness," how centers might gain by refiguring authority as a usable descriptor in discussing tutorial work, and how tutors might be trained differently to recognize and use their power and authority without becoming authoritarian.

POWER, AUTHORITY, AND THE WRITING CENTER'S DISCONTENTS

Historical work on writing centers, such as that of Beth Boquet, Irene Clark and Dave Healy, as well as some of my own, has demonstrated that centers have long been uncomfortable with power and authority. First, as instructional sites that require funding and resources but neither generate FTE credit hours nor award grades, centers have always been (and in many cases still are) vulnerable to budget cuts and seen as expensive peripherals for remediating students considered unprepared. Furthermore, as instructional sites but not classrooms, student service units yet instructional (in contrast, say, to the health center or financial aid office), centers have been difficult to classify in the taxonomy of university entities, despite their aspirations to disciplinary status. They are neither fish nor fowl. While their ambiguity makes them hard to define, it also makes them easy to marginalize. The initial positioning of centers figures heavily in their attitudes towards the unfortunate yet unavoidable power relations that govern the large majority of American universities. Having felt the pressure of being on the bottom of hierarchical relationships in the university, centers have been loathe to take an authoritative position in their work, preferring a peer tutoring model that promotes a nonhierarchical relationship between tutor and student.

Before proceeding further, however, I would like to say that like others who work in writing centers, I am certainly no fan of hierarchical relationships. None of us likes to feel less empowered than another in interpersonal relations, and students who enter writing centers should be made to feel as comfortable as possible, if for no other reason than basic human decency. However, to pretend that there is not a hierarchical relationship between tutor and student is a fallacy, and to engineer peer tutoring techniques that divest the tutor of power and authority is at times foolish and can even be unethical. Yet to some degree, that is what writing centers have done. Much tutor training routinely includes community-endorsed noninterventionist dictums, if not dogma, that instruct tutors to never hold the pen, never write on a student's paper, never edit a student sentence or supply language in the form of phrases or vocabulary. Irene Clark and Dave Healy, in "Are Writing Centers Ethical?" (1996), catalogue a number of examples of articles propagating these dictums, most notably Jeff Brooks's "Minimalist Tutoring: Making the Student Do All the Work," a piece originally published in the *Writing Lab Newsletter* (1991) and reprinted in *The St. Martin's Sourcebook for Writing Tutors* (1995). Brooks's essay encapsulates nondirective pedagogy in its title, and such instruction is then justified by egalitarian notions of peership that maintain that doing otherwise would be to appropriate the student's text, to take ownership of it. In other words, except for a few notable exceptions, writing center discourse, in both published scholarship and conference talk, often represents direct instruction as a form of plunder rather than help, while adherence to nondirective principles remain the pedagogy *du jour.*

In the past few years, some center scholars have questioned notions of peership and nondirective pedagogy on ethical and political grounds, though they remain in the minority. The beginnings of this line of questioning were adumbrated in 1990 in Irene Clark's "Maintaining Chaos in the Writing Center: A Critical Perspective on Writing Center Dogma." There Clark attempted to dislodge such dicta that the tutor never hold the pen or that the best answers to students' questions are more questions from the tutor. Though Clark's essay appeared in the Tenth Anniversary Issue of the *Writing Center Journal,* it was essentially a lone and unjustifiably ignored voice in a community espousing nondirective pedagogy, though perhaps not being able to implement it consistently given the diverse needs of students and the complexity of tutorials. This latter point is borne out in a 1994 essay by Alice Gillam, Susan Callaway, and Katherine Hennessy Winkoff. Tellingly entitled "The Role of Authority and The Authority of Roles in Peer Writing Tutorials," Gillam et al. organize their essay with an opening review of writing center theory, demonstrating the hegemony of nondirective methods based on the tricky notion of peerness. They then move to a section on practice, showing how tutors in their center— often torn between needing to follow the party line and needing to exercise authority—struggle with role conflict, and how students are often confused by the tutors' behavior. However, published in *The Journal of Teaching Writing,* rather than in a venue more regularly read by center directors and scholars, this essay, despite its high quality, had little or no influence on the community and is not even listed in the Murphy, Law, Sherwood bibliography of 1996.

In 1995, however, the community could no longer ignore challenges to nondirective pedagogy with the publication of Linda Shamoon and Deborah Burns's "A Critique of Pure Tutoring" in the *Writing Center Journal.* Aside from their wickedly subtle pun on "peer tutoring" in the title, they unapologetically attacked writing centers' seemingly unflagging allegiance to a nondirective peer model, characterizing its tenets as a "bible" in the most inflexible sense of the term. They then demonstrated how master-apprentice relationships in music and art constitute a kind of directive tutorial and are an accepted and fruitful practice, arguing that tutorials in these disciplines "are hierarchical: there is an open admission that some individuals have more knowledge and skills than others, and that the knowledge and skills are being 'handed down'" (141). Needless to say, this essay caused much gnashing of teeth and rending of garments on WCenter, the community's online discussion group. A year later, Irene Clark, this time as a co-author with David Healy, attributed the community's long commitment to nondirective peer tutoring not to a saintly sense of egalitarianism, but to writing centers' attempts to mollify faculty who suspect tutoring is a form of plagiarism. Accusing centers of having adopted a "pedagogy of self-defense" (34), Clark and Healy dare centers to stop pretending that tutors do not do some work for students, arguing that directors must educate faculty about postmodern ideas of authorship whereby no single author is fully responsible for any text, and that what goes on in tutorials is no different than what goes on in the production of most professional writing. From a more political stance, Nancy Grimm, in *Good Intentions: Writing Center Work for Post-Modern Times* (1999), has questioned the ethics of nondirective methods, contending that in adopting them centers unwittingly "protect the status quo and withhold insider knowledge, inadvertently keeping students from nonmainstream culture on the sidelines, making them guess about what the mainstream culture expects" (31).

Examined closely, all of this is tough talk. If centers, as Clark and Healy (1995) maintain, embraced nondirective collaborative pedagogy largely as a defense mechanism, then the dominant practices of writing centers in the last twenty-odd years have been little more than a rationalization of the frightened. If Grimm (1999) is right, then centers are not just cowards but dupes, political pawns in some larger power structure they serve unawares. And if Shamoon and Burns (1995) can be believed, centers are immature—unable to face the fact that "some individuals have more knowledge and skills than others," something small children quickly learn. Cowardly? Gullible? Childish? Even if I am engaging in a bit of rhetorical hyperbole in representing the implications of these scholars' postions, these are strong words. They do not describe the writing center directors I know, and I think Healy, Clark, Burns, Shamoon, and Grimm would agree. Nevertheless, their exposure of the problematics of a nondirective collaborative peer model of tutoring helps to account for the anxieties tutors such as Palmeri (2000) and Bokser (2000) articulate.

Unpacking each of these critiques uncovers the issues of power and authority beneath them, issues imbricated in the institutional position of the writing center but carrying over into the pedagogy of peer tutoring. Many accounts of writing centers in the 1970s, as Clark and Healy (1995) demonstrate, show writing centers acceding to a mission of providing grammatical instruction and drill, the fix-it-shop model. These centers were given the authority to deliver this type of instruction perceived by the public and university adminstrations as necessary to acculturate underprepared students admitted to the academy under open admissions programs. Simultaneously, other centers, influenced by the emerging process pedagogy in composition, began to take authority for more than grammar, tutoring students in rhetorical matters as well and thus engaging in a power struggle with the classroom for the authority to teach students to write, an authority usually reserved for the classroom. This binary arrangement—center for grammar, classroom for rhetoric—never reached detente, as is evident in the anticlassroom rhetoric marking much writing center scholarship of subsequent decades (see Hemmeter 1990), and as remains clear in the fix-it-shop image of centers that still persists for some faculty, administrators, and many students. Rather than a division of authority or acceptance of a compromise position—e.g., both classroom and center teach writing, but just differently—a power struggle ensued that continues today. In terms of institutional positioning, the classroom held and continues to hold the stronger position, given that it generates credit hours and awards grades, the very blood of the university.

While the classroom holds the high ground, the hegemonic position afforded by institutional recognition, writing centers have functioned more like a minority party, recognized as a voice but lacking institutional power, operating pedagogically somewhat clandestinely, while simultaneously attempting to work through the system through extended services—WAC linkages being the most obvious—to increase their authority and power base within the institution. These struggles continue, and while some centers have won strong positions on their campuses, others remain struggling, and laments about marginalization, though sometimes seeming counter productive to more successful centers, still inflect the community's discourse. Still other centers, though empowered on their campuses, consciously take a subversive stance, seeing as their duty exposing students to what they perceive as the oppressive power structures of the university and society itself (Grimm 1999; Davis 1995).

Although centers vary in institutional power and authority, as well as taking different stances toward their positions, they have almost uniformly maintained their identity as nonhierarchical, friendly places where students can feel welcome. Though many teachers would argue that the same applies to their classrooms, centers have the added luxury of being positioned where they do not have to give grades. This is both an advantage and disadvantage. As mentioned, their failure to generate credit hours may make centers seem a frill to university administrators. Furthermore, students so acculturated to tangible rewards—they speak of "getting something out of a class," "getting good grades"—may wonder what they "get out of" going to the center, what they "get for" spending an hour of their busy week talking with someone about their writing. For many, the answer is "better grades," an answer that writing centers have often seen as grubbing and vulgar, preferring rather to follow Stephen North's claim that the center's job is "to produce better writers, not better papers" (1984, 438). While this mission has satisfied writing center directors, it is unlikely too many students would accept it, though they may unwittingly become better writers through their work in the center (and thus earn better grades). Thus students sometimes come to the center expecting work to be done for them in exchange for the time they sacrifice, an attitude which further pushes centers toward a nondirective peer pedagogy.

Not having to assign grades, however, also becomes a reason to contrast the center advantageously against the classroom. Students can, it is claimed, feel relaxed and unintimidated as they might not in a teacher's office or in class. They find creature comforts such as the three Cs of writing centers—coffee, cookies, and couches—and they interact with others supposedly like themselves—students. This is the image of the writing center as "safe house" or student sanctuary, a place beyond the competition, evaluation, and grade-grubbing that supposedly marks the classroom. Centers have taken pride in this image in presenting themselves as student advocates, while turning to it for succor when feeling the sting of marginalization (if we lack clout, at least we are nice). But when taken too far, the safe house metaphor has also contributed to an identity that is not only unrealistic, but that also has adversely affected peer tutoring. The "safe house" metaphor rests on maintaining a non-hierarchical environment at all costs, which, though imperative in the atmosphere of the center, in a tutorial can undermine the tutor and lead to dogmatic applications of nondirective peer tutoring principles. It is these principles that Shamoon and Burns (1995) castigate in their call for more directive tutoring in which the tutor takes more authority, wields more power, and is only a peer in perhaps belonging to the same age group and sharing the status of student.

While I agree with Shamoon and Burns, as well as Grimm (1999) and Clark and Healy (1996), that peer tutoring has been represented by the community and translated into practice, often uncritically, as a largely nondirective egalitarian enterprise, I believe that peer tutoring should not be dismissed, but refigured in terms of the way authority and power play themselves out depending on the players in any given tutorial, a refiguration I will now attempt.

WHAT DO WE MEAN BY PEERS?

Peer tutoring has been a powerful pedagogy for writing center teaching and student learning. However, when the word *peer* has been interpreted in the extreme, it has been distorted to support the kind of nondirective tutoring that understandably rankles some center scholars and practitioners. At the same time, the enshrinement of nondirective tutoring is understandable in the context of writing center history. On the one hand, as Clark and Healy (1996) argue, this pedagogy helped deflect charges of plagiarism, but on the other, I would argue that center workers were as concerned about plagiarism as teachers were, and developed nondirective pedagogy not only to deflect criticism, but also because they believed it worked. Based on questioning methods, whether designated Socratic or Rogerian, nondirective tutoring can cue students to recall knowledge they have and construct new knowledge that they do not. Anyone who has worked in writing centers knows that when nondirective tutoring clicks, it is wonderful, and its effectiveness accounts for some of the zealotry of those who endorse it but then impose it upon situations where other strategies are necessary.

An ideal peer tutorial in the nondirective mode proceeds something like this. A third-year chemistry major comes into the center with a draft of a lab report and meets with a tutor, let's say a second-year literature major and skilled writer. The two are peers in that both are students, and both are committed to being good writers:

Tutor: You seem to have your thesis at the end and the first part talks about your steps in the experiment. Is that the way you want it?

Student: Yes, we are supposed to use an inductive pattern and draw a conclusion.

Tutor: Ok, that's good. Now, on the third page you talk about mixing the chemicals and then heating them, but you don't explain why. Do you see what I mean? Could you add a transition to get the reader from one to the other?

Student: Yes, I could say how I mixed the chemicals until they got syrupy, that's how they should be, before I put them on the Bunsen burner, something like "Once the chemicals thickened to a reddish

> syrupy consistency, they were placed on the Bunsen burner." And
> then add some stuff about the temperature. . .

Tutor: Yes, that would really help.

This snippet illustrates nondirective peer tutoring at its best. The tutor
asks questions; the student answers in ways that lead to improving the writing. The student takes responsibility for the content, which the tutor, a literature major, cannot be expected to know, justifying the placement of her
thesis based on knowledge of the rhetorical structure of the lab report, and
even takes a step toward becoming a better writer in supplying a concrete
example of the tutor's reference to an abstract rhetorical term—*transition.*

This tutorial not only exemplifies the effectiveness of nondirective tutoring, but Bruffian collaborative learning as well, with the tutor learning that
a thesis in a lab report (though usually called something else) is more desir-
able as a conclusion based on induction, something he can file for future
reference, just as the student can the definition of transition. Both student
and tutor share authority and engage in collaborative operations to
improve the text. It is important to remember that in adopting a nonhierarchical pedagogy of peer collaboration, centers were heavily influenced by
Kenneth Bruffee's work on collaborative learning (1993), which originated
when he was directing the writing center at Brooklyn College. Coupling the
mutual benefits to tutor and student with the theoretical underpinning of
Bruffian collaborative learning, this tutorial is exactly the way writing centers would like to represent their work—effective in practice and under-
pinned by theory. In fact, this tutorial works so well that it becomes a myth
for self-justification. Unfortunately, the myth is seductive, and directors
want to believe such tutorials happen far more often than they do, use
them to represent center work, and try to train tutors to approximate, if not
attain, them consistently, all the time knowing at heart that such tutorials
are rare, many are messier, and most are far messier.

Furthermore, to pretend this tutorial is exemplary is not only to
ignore its rarity but to misread Bruffee somewhat. While certainly he
placed much faith in students' ability to learn from one another, his
sense of collaboration included the assumption that the tutor had some
authority. Discussing training tutors at Brooklyn under Bruffee's super-
vision, Marcia Silver (1978) argues "probably the single most important
condition for teaching writing is the willingness on the part of the student writer to accept criticism and grow as a result of it" (435). This is
tough love, not the egalitarian, nonhierarchical presentation of tutor

and student as "two friends" cited in Hawkins (1980) at the outset of this essay. The tutor is expected to criticize, and the student is expected have a skin tough enough to put the criticism to good use. However, blind adherence to a nonhierarchical ethic of peer tutoring treats the student as if he or she is a high-strung child, and can also lead to inefficiency if the tutor refuses to take authority when necessary.

Witness this tutorial in which the tutor will not deviate from nondirective principles. This time the tutor is a journalism major minoring in theater; the student, an undeclared freshman writing a review of a campus production for an introduction to theater class:

Tutor: After reading through your paper, I am wondering why you spent the first page writing about you and your friends on the way to the theater.

Student: I don't know. That's what happened. We met in town, then drove to campus, and had a hard time finding a parking space, like I said.

Tutor: Do you think that is important for the reader to know?

Student: Well, I thought I would put it in to get started and I thought it was neat the way we got lucky and got a space just when we thought we'd be late. I wanted to start with something interesting, and I thought the play was really serious, heavy.

Tutor: It is interesting, but how do you see it relating to the play?

Student: I don't know. Should I take it out?

Tutor: That's up to you. What do you think?

Here the tutor continues nondirective questioning to a fault in the name of preserving the peer relationship. It is obvious that the student lacks knowledge of the conventions of a play review, but instead of taking authority for teaching him, the tutor coyly "wonders" about the way the student opens the paper. No one can implicate this tutorial for plagiarism, and the tutor certainly maintains a nonhierarchical peer relationship with the student, but it is doubtful that anything other than adherence to principle has been achieved. If the student does cut the superfluous introduction, it is likely the cut will be more the influence of the tutor's doubts about it than from a writerly decision by the student.

Compare a second version of the same tutorial, in which the tutor draws upon his knowledge in journalism and theater, takes some authority for the text, and exercises some power in directing the student

Tutor: After reading your paper, I see you have a long part about getting to the theater. Have you ever written a play review before?

Student: No. I put that in because I thought it was interesting the way we got the parking space at the last minute. I wanted to start with something interesting before doing all the stuff on the play, which I thought was really serious, heavy.

Tutor: Yes, it is good to start with something interesting, but did your teacher explain anything about how to write the review?

Student: No, we just have that little sheet I gave you saying we had to write the review, how many pages, and when the play is on.

Tutor: Well, in a play review, you might have a short introduction, but you should start as close to the play as possible because your purpose is to help the reader decide if they want to see the play or not. You need to cut the part about getting to the theater and start with the sentence where you say "*Oleanna* is a play that will make people think." That is a short direct sentence, and it previews what follows.

Clearly, the tutor here takes more authority, is more responsible for the shape the paper will take. In addition, the tutor uses her authority—familiarity with the conventions of play reviews and the rhetorical need to consider audience—to provide instruction that will be useful to the student in completing the paper as well as others in the future. Strict adherents to nondirective methods might argue that the tutor is appropriating the student's paper in directly telling him to cut the long introduction, or wielding too much power over a student who seems to have little himself in terms of this assignment. Although beneath the surface of the first exchanges there may be a slight bit of contentiousness on the tutor's part and defensiveness on the student's, the tutor does not belittle or exclude the student, but uses her authority to transmit knowledge and power to direct the student for the purpose of helping him complete the task. Undoubtedly there is not the sharing of authority seen in the tutorial on the chemistry lab report, where the student is much more knowledgeable, but nevertheless there is a sharing of the work as the student, though lacking authority, remains attentive and explains his motivations to the tutor.

Tutorials, then, I would argue, depend on authority and power, authority about the nature of the writing and the power to proceed from or resist what that authority says. Either tutor and student must share authority, producing a pleasant but rare collaborative peer situation as in the tutorial on the lab report, or one or the other must have it, and in writing centers the one with it is more often the tutor, as is the case in the second tutorial on the play review. Writing centers should not be ashamed of this fact. Of course, there are caveats. In some tutorials, authority may be lacking on both parts, because every tutor cannot be expert in all types of writing. Or power can be misdirected. For example, the student writing the theater review has the power to resist the tutor and not cut the irrelevant introduction. Or the tutor may wield power without authority, misleading the student, as is evident in the following excerpt, again with a literature major tutoring a chemistry student, this one less able, on a lab report:

Tutor: You seem to have your thesis at the end and the paper talks about your steps in the experiment. Is that the way you want it?

Student: I don't know. Why? This is chemistry. I thought thesis sentences were for English papers.

Tutor: No, most papers have a thesis and usually it comes at the beginning.

Student: You mean the part where I say the chemicals turned into a clear gel when heated to a certain temperature.

Tutor: Yes, can you put that in the first paragraph so the reader knows what you found?

Student: Ok, I get it now.

This tutorial goes immediately astray because the tutor lacks authority, in that he misdirects the student based on his own experience of placing the thesis sentence first, something generally not done in lab reports. The student, though somewhat suspicious, does not wield power to resist, because the institution of the writing center and the position of authority it awards the tutor cows him into acting on the tutor's misleading advice. The only benefit of the nondirective technique here is that it somewhat preserves the environment of the center as "safe house", because the tutor's question gently raises the possibility of moving the thesis rather than directly telling the student about the (mis)perceived thesis problem. Yet in the end, the "safe house" is not safe at all because the non-directive method is worthless without some authoritative knowledge on the structure of lab reports. Nor would directive tutoring work in this case, because without the knowledge of the conventions of the lab report, the tutor would be unable to help—to direct—the student about the placement of the thesis.

In this case, the tutor, lacking knowledge, lacks power and authority beyond that conferred by being the tutor—a situation analogous to that which Palmeri (2000) describes when he cannot show the student how to cite sources in her discipline. Granted, the tutorials above are invented, but I would argue that similar tutorials happen regularly. Invented or not, they illustrate the wide variety of tutorials that occur in writing centers every day, a variety conditioned by the degree of power and authority brought into the tutorial by tutor, student, and assignment. All of these tutorials demonstrate that no matter what techniques are used, both parties (ideally) or one (more commonly) must have some knowledge at hand, must occupy the position of power and authority in a hierarchical relationship. In the first tutorial on the lab report, the student fortuitously had the knowledge and only needed it to be drawn out by the tutor's cues; thus the tutorial worked exceedingly well. In the second, neither knew the conventions of the lab report, and the tutorial went awry because knowledge was not available. In the tutorials on the play review, the first tutor had the knowledge but chose to withhold it in the name of egalitarianism, thus abusing power and authority, while the second exercised them responsibly to instruct the student. I realize here that I am seeming to treat knowledge as an entity, a thing, rather than something constructed, as is readily accepted in postmodern thought, but in many tutorials the knowledge, for student and tutor, *is* something to be retrieved or transmitted. Though the conventions of the lab report and the play review are constructions in that they are agreed upon by writers and readers of such pieces, for the tutor and student the conventions are fixed and transmittable knowledge, because neither has the authority or power to change them without negative consequences in the situation offered by the assignment and tutorial.

IMPLICATIONS FOR TUTOR TRAINING

Writing center professionals like to point out that every tutorial is different, and the samples discussed illustrate that claim. What they do not like to point out is that very often one tutorial is better than another despite efforts to train tutors. In the twenty-fifth anniversary issue of *The Writing Center Journal*, longtime writing center scholars and practitioners Lil Brannon and Stephen North claim that "if we are honest, we know the quality of the work is uneven" (2000, 11). This is a rare admission, given the protective and defensive stance writing center scholars usually take regarding peer tutors. The party line runs something like this. Tutors are effective because they are peers trained to be nondirective. In this sense, their authority comes from not having any. If they know more than the students, they use nondirective questioning to ensure that they don't end up doing students' work for them. If they know less than the students, they again rely on nondirective questioning to draw out the student's knowledge of the subject. Nondirective tutoring thus becomes the antidote for having too much authority, or too little.

Certainly tutors should continue to be trained to maintain a comfortable environment for students, treating them with kindness, understanding, and respect. Though raising the spectres of power and authority in this essay, my purpose is not to turn the writing center into just another impersonal office on campus. Students must face enough of those already, and, as much as possible, writing centers should maintain the atmosphere of the safe house. At the same time, tutors need to learn that the center is not the local coffee house, and tutorials just a chat about a paper or assignment. In short, a nonhierarchical environment does not depend on blind commitment to nondirective tutoring methods. Instead, tutors should be taught to recognize where the power and authority lie in any given tutorial, when and to what degree they have them, when and to what degree the student has them, and when and to what degree they are absent in any given tutorial.

When they can do so, they can proceed using techniques—nondirective or directive—based on their position in the tutorial. As in the tutorial on the play review, the tutor should know to take the lead and be more directive when tutoring an inexperienced freshman in an introductory theater course. To shackle such a tutor by training him or her only in nondirective methods, in the name of maintaining a nonhierarchical peer relationship, is to shortchange the student lucky enough to be paired with him or her, a point Bokser implies when she chafes against the training in nondirective methods that would have her suppress assertive behaviors that would help the student. At the same time non-directive methods should be maintained for situations in which the tutor does not have authority, and needs to draw it from the student. When such is the case, a question such as "Do you want your thesis last?" becomes a real question, and not a ploy to push the student to move it where the tutor thinks it belongs. Similarly, when tutors lack authority in one area—organizational conventions for a particular type of discourse, for instance—they should feel free to move the tutorial in a direction in which they feel more authoritative. The tutor who tells the chemistry student to move the thesis to the beginning would have been better off to direct the student to ask the instructor about the organization and then perhaps move to matters of style and even grammar, raising questions about wordy constructions, vague pronoun references and the like. Unfortunately, writing center orthodoxy would train him or her to reserve those areas for last, or to shun a tutorial that works primarily at the sentence level as the demeaning stuff of the fix-it shop, rather than value it as a service to the student based on the authority available in the tutorial.

In an unpublished study of students' and tutors' perceptions of directiveness, Irene Clark found that tutors view their tutorials as less directive than students do in terms of contributing ideas, making corrections, and the degree and influence of conversation. She attributes this result partly to the tutor training "that had emphasized the importance of allowing students as much opportunity as possible to develop their own ideas, urging consultants to guide and suggest rather than lead" (n.d., 16). While such training is necessary, to a degree, it contributed to tutor views or tutorials that countered those of the students, even if one considers that students may have, conversely, overestimated the contributions of the tutor. It is troublesome that tutors feel the need to see themselves as less directive than they likely are, for given the challenges and complexity of tutoring, tutors should not be made to feel inadequate when they cannot live up to an orthodoxy of nondirective pedagogy, whatever reasons, pedagogical or political, may underlie it.

While presenting a fully developed method of tutor training is beyond the scope of this paper, I would like to offer a few possibilites. The watchword in tutor training should not be nondirective peership, but flexibility. Tutors should learn to shift between directive and nondirective methods as needed, and develop some sense of a sliding scale.

- More student knowledge, less tutor knowledge = more nondirective methods.
- Less student knowledge, more tutor knowledge = more directive methods.

As it stands, this scale is admittedly reductive. It would also have to account for what educationists call "the affective domain," that is, the various personality traits of tutors and students. Timid students, despite a lot of knowledge, might require both nondirective and directive methods, nondirective questioning to draw forth what they know, directive prodding to make them take responsibility for the text. Likewise, less knowledgeable but gregarious students might benefit from nondirective questions to question a hasty but wrongheaded enthusiasm, or directive warnings when they are stubbornly blundering into moves that could result in a disastrous response to the assignment.

Clark's study further lends credence to a more flexible approach. In addition to suggesting that training influenced tutors to perceive their sessions as more nondirective than they might have been, Clark found that students who rated themselves as "good" writers viewed tutorials as less directive, while students who rated themselves as "adequate" or "poor" writers saw the sessions as more directive. I would maintain that there is a good chance that these perceptions were accurate, that more able students needed less direction than the less able. It's common sense. However, whether out of political timidity or an excessive commitment to egalitarian principles, writing centers have not wanted to admit it—until recently.

Clark's NWCA study, coupled with the earlier sporadic efforts cited above and more recent voices, indicates that centers are beginning to be more courageous in describing their work. In a recent case study of a complex tutorial between a male Ph.D. student tutor and a female student in first-year composition, Jane Cogie (2001) demonstrates how, from session to session and moment to moment, tutorial methods shift from directive to nondirective and, as a result, so does the authority of the participants. When Ken, the tutor, in a directive move, tells Janelle, the student, that she seems to be critiquing a "stereotype," the term turns up in her revision as an organizing principle and point of focus, greatly expanded. Similarly, when he *tells* her that interviews are a valid method of research, she is able to expand the paper significantly. Ken's moves here are directive, yet Janelle's use of his directives makes them her own. We have here not plagiarism, but teaching and learning. Cogie concludes:

> The point here is that given the dual need for guidance and authority in most students, any strategy involves risk. Fostering student authority is not a matter of following a single approach and avoiding another. The authority of students may grow from moves as diverse as asking them tough questions, providing summaries or terms to help them conceptualize points and build

confidence, and helping them negotiate assignment demands, gain the necessary situated knowledge, or try out aspects of the writing process. (47)

Fortunately, I think the kind of tutoring I am calling for and Cogie describes has been going on for a long time in many centers, without being widely acknowledged. While centers have always valued and elicited students' input, they have also had the good sense to place student needs before orthodoxy. I turn for evidence here to Mickey Harris's recent professional memoir, delivered as the Exemplar's address at the CCCC 2000 and subsequently published in CCC (2001). On the one hand, in discussing the early days of her center at Purdue, Harris describes a very safe house, happily recounting tales of tutors dragging in old sofas, decorating the lab, and raising funds to buy piz-zas. She relates ways in which she trained tutors not to dominate tutori-als. On the other hand, she speaks of finding "crevices where the conversation permits [her] to adopt a mentor role" (436), and her sum-mary of what went on in her lab shows a sensible mixture of nondirec-tive and directive methods that drew upon the students' authority without stifling the tutors'.

> When students had no idea how to begin an assignment—or even what it was
> asking for—we addressed that with questions and suggestions for strategies,
> and we learned how to help writers acquire the strategic knowledge they
> needed to achieve goals such as how to add more content or organize what
> they had written. . . . We supplied information they didn't have (answering
> such questions as "So what goes in an introduction?" "What is my instructor
> telling me to do here?" "How do I cite this in MLA format?" "What goes in a
> personal statement for this application?") and tried to re-explain whatever
> parts of our explanations they didn't get. (432)

Here it is evident that Harris's staff is exercising their power and authority ("suggestions," "supplied information," "answering ques-tions"). At the same time, Harris states how "some deep personal dis-comfort with rules and power structures led [her] to revel in creating and strengthening the guidelines for a non-hierarchic place like our Writing Lab" (435). This is not to say Harris is not practicing what she preaches, or that she contradicts herself, but rather to show how she maintained the safe house atmosphere without divesting her staff of the power and authority needed to serve students.

I suspect many other centers were doing the same, but just not talking about it. This may have been partly, as Clark and Healy (1996) charge, out of fears of being seen as contributing to some faculty's notions of plagiarism, or out of an overly simplified notion of peership and a misreading of collaborative learning theory as always egalitarian learning. Whatever the reason, nondirective, nonhierarchical methods not only have held sway, but also given rise to the dogmatic dicta that disturb commentators such as Shamoon and Burns (1995). This would be relatively harmless, a group of writing center directors keeping "our little secret," as Beth Boquet (1999) has called it, that sometimes tutors do more than ask questions, sometimes they do write on students' papers, sometimes they do question the quality of assignments they see—in other words, sometimes they wield power and exercise authority. The problem, rather, is that when tutors are trained as if this does not happen, or hear the same espoused and nodded at approvingly at writing center conferences, they feel guilty or deficient for failing to live up to the doctrine—Bokser (2000) and Palmeri (2000) are cases in point and very likely not alone.

All this is not to say centers should become authoritative, dictating to students what they should do or not do, but if they are to confront and negotiate the inevitable presence of power and authority, like their tutors, they will need to take responsibility for what they know and do not know. They will need to educate faculty in the ways in which directive tutoring is not plagiarism, but help. They will also need to take authority for what some faculty expect of them—help in grammatical and stylistic matters—without worrying that they will be stereotyped as fix-it shops or grammar garages. Finally, they will need to continue to educate faculty about what they don't know, and encourage faculty to clarify their expectations and provide students with instruction in the way of disciplinary convention, even if only in the form of copies of successful papers from past students furnished to the center. Power and authority are not nice words, but they don't have to be bad ones, either, when the actions they represent are addressed honestly and responsibly. Writing centers can ill afford to pretend power and authority do not exist, given the important responsibility they have for helping students achieve their own authority as writers in a power laden environment such as the university.

6

BREATHING LESSONS
or Collaboration is . . . [1]

MICHELE EODICE

My purpose here is to invite an *apperception,* what William James says in *Talks to Teachers* "means nothing more than the act of taking a thing into the mind" (1958 [1899]). It sounds simple, but with all the different minds reading this, I understand the challenge I have in making my think piece yours. Despite the fact that we share some prior knowledge of writing center work, what each of us brings to this reading "no sooner enters our consciousness than it is drafted off in some determinate direction or other, making connections with the other materials already there." In the 1890s, James wrote:

> A little while ago, at Buffalo, I was the guest of a lady who had recently taken her seven-year old son for the first time to Niagara Falls. The child silently glared at the phenomenon until his mother, supposing him struck speechless by its sublimity, said, "Well, my boy, what do you think of it?" to which, "Is that the kind of spray I spray my nose with?" was the boy's only reply. That was his mode of apperceiving the spectacle. (1958 [1899], 112)

You will, of course, build a first perception (of the following proposition, say) based on your previous conceptions and experiences (with collaboration, for example), although it is my hope that you will recognize a "natural wonder" when you see one.

Collaboration is a word I wish was not a word at all. I wish then that collaboration was understood as ineffable in all we do, not because I don't wish it ever to be challenged or acknowledged, but because I believe, as Michael Blitz does, that collaboration is like the "air we breathe."[2] Like many travelers who sometimes wish for fresher, healthier air in a cabin full of strangers, or like a poor swimmer gulping and gasping, I often have my moments of distress: wishing for breathable air, for a writing partner, for voices of collusion; longing for the better angel of my nature.

Yet whether the air is fresh and sweet or rank and polluted, I find I do most of my *writing* work with others. And yes, whether the air is fresh and sweet or rank and polluted, I find I do most of my *work* work with others. In analyzing these trace elements in the air—the alchemy of collaboration—I find its daily work of "transforming something common into something special"[3] so rooted into my habits and deeds that I no longer question its life in mine.

But air is not *nothing,* not neutral, and we know that academics are often dismissed if critique is missing. So I take up a tactic that other academics have used: I avoid my interior work and focus instead on what is wrong with everyone else. For example, I find fascinating those who insist that this alchemy of collaboration is an "inexplicable or mysterious transmuting"[4] which is too scary to engage in, or, when it is in fact a practice for some, there is no effort to make it visible and valued. One result: institutional resistance to collaboration gives students permission to ignore, dismiss, or cheapen learning and writing with others. Thus, I foolishly set out in my pedantic, missionary way to convert other academics to my practice of *uber* collaboration and to help them experience the joys I find inherent in writing with others.[5]

Along the way I have learned something about conversion experiences: first, I am driven to get you to write with others and to get students to embrace a collaborative view of writing themselves, yet I watch all kinds of text-production marching on, oblivious to my mission. Where I believed I must bring collaboration, I find it working fine; I realize that writing centers themselves practice one of the most powerful forms of collaborative learning (and yes, collaborative writing) embodied in the peer-consulting model. However, when asked, many writing center directors will say that their peer relations, their relationships with their institutions, their identity politics, are anything but collaborative, and they may even say that what happens in consulting sessions is not *really* collaborative writing. Paradoxically, then, a set of tropes continually employed to describe our relationships and positions in our institutions foreclose on possibilities of uncovering (and thus *teaching*) what undergirds both our tangible daily practice and our abstract desire: collaboration.

Collaboration (in, over, during?) text production—the writer-to-writer talk, the mix of handwriting coloring a document, the shared excitement about a simple (re)construction, the alternate achievement of clarity or chaos in the feedback, the way time passes differently, the un-aloneness of work—all of these embody our centers. The material practices and the ethos generated in writing centers emanate and travel—whether to online environments or virtual peer tutoring, or to satellite locales in residence halls or community centers, or to your home office or favorite coffee shop. Although we seem to recognize these activities when they fall within our own brick and mortar or electronic environments, we often fail to carry them beyond—to the offices, committees, programs, and faculty who could learn from us.

TROPES

In a 1990 article, Virginia Perdue and Deborah James found the following state of things unfortunate:

> [B]ecause the teaching that occurs in writing centers is often informal, collaborative, and egalitarian, it is invisible. And this invisibility makes writing centers vulnerable to uncertain budgets, staffing, and locations, but most importantly, vulnerable to the misunderstanding that marginalizes writing centers . . . within our home institutions. (quoted in Harris 1992, 272)

Although written over a dozen years ago, this claim still gets some heads nodding. We have read plenty of listserv posts and articles about how to make ourselves visible: we need direct and clear reporting lines, we should learn to count beans and disseminate our data, and on and on. In addition to these sensible practices, what we could be doing to insure visibility is what we do best, and what we do in a powerful collection of moments all the hours we are open: collaborate. Writing centers have been called exemplars of the "best" kinds of communication (informal, collaborative, egalitarian), pedagogy (informal, collaborative, egalitarian), and caring (informal, collaborative, egalitarian) that the academy can offer. In "best" practices models, learners, teachers, and administrators read about and adopt methods that others have discovered to work. Who in your institution is adopting your practices? What can we do to help them do this?

By consistently reviving the tropes of marginality, disappointment,[6] and disciplinarity-above-all-else, we have abetted our institutions, allowing them to draw our perimeters. It is perhaps what Elizabeth Boquet calls the "promise of containment" (2002, 66)—securing a program fund, a director, or a space in exchange for "squirreling away certain student populations" (67)—that makes us complicit, paralyzing our efforts to get out more. The hold this margin/containment trope has on us has become embedded in our lore to such a degree as to become *doxa*—we pass along these beliefs and their resulting practices to the detriment of future generations of writing center leaders. As James Sosnoski reminds us:

> Intellectuals like to think they are less subject to orthodoxy than they actually are. As "native" practitioners they may laugh at the naïve views "foreign" administrators have of their customs, but they obey the curfews. (1994, 99)

Why do we romanticize our status by hanging on to the idea that our land is more important than anything else (the Scarlet O'Haras)? Why are we always riled up for a feud, or reveling in our loner status, thinking ourselves such radical and subversive outposts? Alternative, supplemental, radical, marginal—our identity preempts contact outside our walls. A kind of reciprocity with institutions could help to convert the identity of a marginalized site, although this would no doubt force us to give up the cachet of self-defining as the subversive-radical-moveable feast-carnival-safe house-literacy club. Frankly, I am afraid some of these terms have become parodies of their original meaning. If we could flip the *working on the margins* thing to a *working the margins* thing (since, after all, margins are required, useful, in any textual work[7],we might see that every department, every member of our academic communities, is struggling with a range of issues—from budget to pedagogy—and that while our farm may be on the outskirts of town, our campuses need what we grow there. How then do we now go back on our original and implicit "promise" to contain and remain apart in order to unlearn the tropes? I think the following story corroborates that these tropes have come to define us for ourselves in particular ways, and they have also influenced the way others construct us.

> *A faculty member in English stopped by, his first time since we opened five years ago, and his office is right downstairs. He said, "I know that you don't usually work with really good writers, but I have a problem. I have a student who is writing good papers but she wants more. She gets A's, but she keeps bugging me for more; she wants me to tell her how she could improve the papers even more, just for herself, not for a grade. I don't know if you have anybody here who has dealt with that and maybe could talk to her?"*
>
> *Instead of feeling defeated by his assumptions, his clear misunderstanding of what we do and in fact what teachers can do with student writing, I looked on this communication as an opening, an opportunity.*

I thought he wanted some guidance, to hear about some (new) ways he could conference with his student, but it was suddenly clear that he expected only to hand off both the student and her papers to us. I suggested that he and the student and I and a writing consultant get together to talk; I was already anticipating what all of us could learn, what I could take back to our consultant practicum meetings; hell, I was even thinking of videotaping the session.

However, he wished not to be further involved in learning how he or we might do this work with a "good" writer. What ended up happening was that a few of our consultants took the papers and wrote responses to the writer in a kind of blind exercise (I didn't tell them the back-story). We all took a look and then discussed the feedback, how it works when good writers don't want to be done with their writing. We asked ourselves, what can school-sponsored writing do beyond its deadline, beyond its terminal grade? Finally, we hooked up with the student and had a great visit.

We often collect these stories to justify a further retreat to our margins; by doing so we rub salt in our wounds and nurture our cynicism. My attempt to collaborate with this faculty member enacts, rather, a kind of collaboration with refusal. As my friend and assistant director, Emily Donnelli, says, "collaboration is not collaboration only when it is with those who deserve it or with those who are sufficiently enlightened." I really hate the fact that Angela Petit's (2001) assertion below can still be true:

As long as significant numbers of students and faculty believe that writing centers are places where only 'bad' writers go, these centers will affirm the distinction that the academy wishes to draw between its own study of privileged texts and the types of writing students produce. (52)

My impulse to turn this encounter into more than placating a faculty member helped to maintain the construction of our writing center as a place for collaboration, not as a place for "affirming the distinction that the academy wishes to draw." From this experience, and others like it, I wish to offer a way of seeing that what we do with collaboration every day in our writing centers can empower us to dismantle its borders and perform a kind of collaboration that will benefit both us and our institutions. In order to do this, I invite you, as reader, to collaborate with my proposition as well.

RIGHT UNDER OUR NOSES

It is a joy to be hidden but a disaster not to be found.

D.W. WINNICOTT

Let's start closest to home and move outward. John Trimbur urges us "to see tutoring not simply as a dyadic relationship between tutors and tutees but as part of the wider social and cultural networks that shape students' emergence into literacy" (1992, 174). The best thing we can do (indeed the thing we do best) is to help students see how several dimensions of their lives are collaborating in a text; after all, the act of visiting a writing center isn't the only thing that constructs a student as a writer. As Stephen Ferruci reminds us, "students do not operate in the context of a single department or discipline" (2001, 7); they are, in fact, getting around much more than we are. Trimbur seems confident that we can take some credit for this foundational kind of collaboration: "I can't think of a place as ideally situated to carry on the kinds of extended conversation necessary for students to make sense of their . . . experiences as readers and writers" (178). Richard Behm (1989), like Alice Gillam, Kenneth Bruffee, Andrea Lunsford, and others, captures the spirit of our work:

> [T]he tutor and the learner are truly collaborators, peers involved in a give and take, a communal struggle to make meaning . . . a very basic act of sharing, one that often extends well-beyond completing a particular academic exercise. In fact, I am convinced that peer tutoring and other kinds of collaborative learning gather power in proportion to the degree of cooperative involvement in the endeavor. (6)

One step, then, can be recognizing and studying the collaboration—and I would say the collaborative writing as well as the collaborative learning about writing—that takes place in our centers. Muriel Harris asks us to "examine the difference . . . to disentangle" and distinguish the types of collaboration that we see and practice (1992a, 369), but I want to see the sameness, too, by collapsing the categories she defines as collaborative writing and collaborative learning about writing into an encompassing collaboration. What we do with student writers is much more like the collaborative writing we practice when we academics, writers, or teachers seek feedback, participate in peer review, or work with editors; it is much more a form of intrusive caring about texts; it is much more an exchange than a one-way service.

Without the bumpy seams between forms of collaboration, we can see spread out before us the many viable research questions embedded in our everyday work. Can we extrapolate from what we do daily with students and engage genuinely in corresponding practices? Below I provide some examples of research questions stemming from my daily work. Look at what gets generated when we simply let our "insider" inquiry get turned outward:

> *I admit I engage in—and inculcate my writing consultants to do—what Sally Crisp calls "assertive collaboration." What always surprises them then is when I reveal that one of my primary goals in working collaboratively with writers is to help foster self-directed learning. Now I am interested in how the consultants themselves view collaboration: How blurry are their lines? What collaboration experiences have they had that they link to the development of their own self-directed learning? Have they worked through how these are related? Have I?*
>
> *What happens when this talk and facilitation and pen passing is over for the moment? What do students count as "help"? What matters to them enough to call a session successful, fun, or a waste of time? How likely are student visitors to characterize their work here as collaborative?*
>
> *Moving, for example, to the term "consultant"—which implies collaboration—rather than tutor—which stems directly from a transmission model of learning—might help us redirect our understanding that for the consulting model to work, the consultant must lean in, must be invested in learning from and with the client, must be prepared to exploit the moment.*[8]

So then, realizing the richness of research questions springing from our home soil, might we move what is central to our centers out of the center? This next step can be inspired by our daily practice (or perhaps nonpractice) and asks us to look at what we do as writers ourselves. In a book called *Weaving Knowledge Together: Writing Centers and Collaboration*, Carol Haviland admonishes us:

> [I]f we believe the writing center is a community for all writers, we have to use it for our own writing; we have to occupy the writer position as well as the tutor, teacher, and director positions. It is not enough to claim that any of these can be a learning position; it is important to act on our claims. (Enriquez, Haviland, Olson, and Pizurie 1998, 120)

After getting into "the writer position" ourselves, we can bring our many conceptions of collaboration into dialogue with one another, and begin to hear how our identity and thus our relationships are negotiated in the academy. Nancy Grimm, in *Rearticulating the Work of the Writing Center* (1996), recognizes that even though over 90% of colleges have writing centers, "we might expect a stronger presence of writing center voices in composition forums" (523). In many cases our individual effort to influence our closest cousins has fallen short; yet we should not miss the opportunity to go beyond moving (only) our English department colleagues. The core activities of academics—team research, committee work, peer review, grant writing, visiting the library, watercooler exchanges, conference presentations, listserv participation, advising students, grading papers, and teaching scheduled classes—all fall within the scope of collaboration. I look for ways in; for example, like Carol Haviland, I want to talk back to the pervasive attitude that faculty *collaborate* but student writers *cheat* (Enriquez, Haviland, Olson, and Pizurie 1998, 119). Ironically, it seems collaboration is the *only* practice to which academics do not want to acculturate their students. While both plagiarism and collaboration are addressed by writing centers for the faculty community, collaboration is most often framed as a qualifier in relation to an official writing center position on plagiarism. If this is the only way we can conceive of intervening on this issue, we have not collaborated; we have merely fallen back on our promise to contain. I take Grimm's call to "share more . . . to move out of silence and into dialogue" (1996, 539) not just to carry student voices and experiences outside our doors, but to carry ourselves and our gifts to our distant relations. Haviland and Denise Stephenson (2002) are certain, as they echo Ede and Lunsford (2000), that "at their best, writing centers can use their intensely collaborative work to make traditional university borders more permeable than can other more firmly fixed programs" (381). Collaboration trumps the old tropes.

LEAN IN

> *We must clink that glass and talk to our colleagues.*
>
> MURIEL HARRIS

Many of us would count our administrative reporting as the most necessary and tangible form of communication beyond our centers. With Richard Miller (1998) and Jo Koster (in this volume), I recognize the asset they believe will lend the helping hand in conveying our local and global goals for higher education reform: our proficient rhetorical skills. Summoning these skills to our advantage makes sense, of course, but don't we know that and do that pretty well already? Might we be a little too attracted to and obsessed with this form of communication (this is not collaboration, yet)? Are we overlooking an additional solution right in front of us, because we fear that this effort might compromise (our) identity in untenable ways?

Lean in.[9] It's okay to be what Richard Miller (1998) calls an "intellectual-bureaucrat." We are already adept at hosting this blend—both inter- and cross-disciplinary, both service and scholarship, both teacher and administrator—but do our institutions recognize our skill at hybridization? Have we communicated this well with our colleagues? Have we even accepted this hyphenated identity ourselves? In his discussion of the identity crisis of the writing center director and our positions relative to our institution's organizational structures, Stephen Ferruci states that "by establishing the context of the relationship in oppositional terms, us against them, [we] undermine the director's authority as an administrator, since the director needs to be 'near the center' of the institution to enact change" (2001, 5). His critique of Tilly Warnock and John Warnock's suggestion that "it is probably a mistake for centers to seek integration into the established institution" (5) is useful support for my position: we should not "maintain a critical distance from the institution"—we should, in fact, become integral as models for its leadership through collaboration.

It is in our interest for growth in our work to work at our "growing edge." If we start by accepting this hybrid role we already embody—understanding that the intellectual in us can "collaborate" with the (welcome or conscripted) bureaucrat in us—we then possess the capacity to expand beyond our borders. We already possess the traits of the intellectual-bureaucrat; any reflection on our work, our interests and talents, and our future goals should tell us this. What Miller outlines is what we see when we look in the mirror:

> [O]ne who takes on the hybrid persona of the intellectual-bureaucrat would . . . possess remarkable tolerance for ambiguity, an appreciation for structured contradictions, a perspicacity that draws into its purview the multiple forces determining individual events and actions, an understanding of the essentially performative character of public life, and a recognition of the inherently political character of all matters emerging from the power/knowledge nexus. (1998, 213)

I carry this persona into my campus interactions, but this necessitates abandoning the traditional connotation of bureaucrat in order to allow a balance of intellectual contributions. Two affirmations from sociology motivate me: 1) my work requires others and 2) gosh darn it, people like me (and I am learning to like them too). If we can insert ourselves more into campus life, because this "consistent social intercourse" is a *requirement* "if human characteristics are to be preserved," then a significant personal and professional development can obtain: "the selves we are are to a great extent a product of our social contacts" (Sprott 1970, 28). In short, we are the relationships we have.

Yet for many of us, it is difficult to trust the process, to trust the academy's record of rewarding collaboration. I want to believe with social psychologist George C. Homans that the following is true:

> Interaction leads to mutual liking . . . [and] if the interactions between the members of a group are frequent in the external system, sentiments of liking will grow up between them, and these sentiments will in lead in turn to further interactions over and above the interaction of the external system. (quoted in Sprott 1970, 53)

GOOD CITIZENS

It happens that currently here at my institution a different generation of administrators (and I use generation not in relation to a person's age, but in relation to their paradigm, say) with "good intentions" considers me a "good soldier" (for weathering budget cuts, for leading difficult committees, etc.). I reject that title, but I am unashamed to embrace the title of "good citizen." It is not difficult for me to accept this role, as I see it linked directly to the process of engaging in "good work."[10]

With Miller (1998), I agree that composition itself has barely been able to carve out a disciplinary space beyond mainly talking to itself, and that it is indeed "a mistake to abandon the ethic of service that defines the field in the hope that doing so will bring about a broader respect for [our] intellectual work" (103). When I say we should reformulate and embrace service, I am not trying to invalidate the experiences of the adjunct, the untenured, those challenged by a disenfranchising relationship with the academy when I ask us to reexamine our conceptions of service. I am not suggesting a sacrifice in time, reputation, or values. Consider how fortunate we are even in being given the luxury of reading this book. Have our several advanced degrees helped us grow our *acquisitiveness* or our *inquisitiveness*? Are we ashamed to work for others, in service to others, in a helping profession? James Sledd (2000), in a curmudgeonly reflection, believed service ought to be a goal of our work, one that might even allow the WPA or WCA to "become that rarity, an honorable and effective manager" (30). Many of us relay our disappointment at administrative work and its status; we begin to internalize a kind of managerial mind-set that allows us to reduce our work to tasks. What if we were to trade *management* for *leadership*? Annette Kolodny (1998) asks us to see future academic leadership as "an inclusive collaborative activity" so that all players can "work together as true partners, sharing information, and negotiating priories" (30). In the name of improving learning experiences for students—whether they have walked into our writing centers or not—we should gather up our service energy, our rhetorical gifts, our diverse scholarship and "get out of this place."[11]

A COLLABORATORY

Where then should we go? Collaboratory models of interaction are found primarily in the sciences, where networks of cooperation and inquiry increase the potential for results and dissemination while strengthening the epistemic or knowledge-building culture of an institution (see, e.g., Lunsford and Bruce 2001).

Collaboratory models of interaction at our institutions—arrived at physically, like the one we built here in our library; or constructed as work groups, like the ones I helped form for our campus; or erected virtually in Blogs, Wikis, Blackboard and OWLs—can support both short-term projects and long-term commitments, and develop into sites of intense research and scholarship as well.

Whether we have a formal, visible collaboratory at my school or not, I have learned as if in one. In just this last year alone, I have learned from my colleagues in business about boundarylessness, in biology about memes,[12] in social welfare about the strengths perspective, and from the librarians I learned about all kinds of good stuff. For writing centers, whose history is full of scrambles for turf, for a stable budget line, for a physical space of their own, purposely seeking a boundaryless state sounds risky. Yet this move could take Boquet's (2002) call for "high risk, high yield" tutorial practices to a new level: administration without a net. Replace *tutor* with *director* in the following prompts Boquet has created: "[H]ow might I encourage this tutor to operate on the edge of his or her expertise? Where's the place where, together, we will really feel like we're jammin' and how did we get there?" (81). Taking this micro-to-macro view helps us see the parallels between our tutors' work in here with our possibilities out there.

A collaboratory requires a level of comfort with boundarylessness. Todd Jick and others from business management education predict that

> when vertical, horizontal, external, and geographic boundaries are traversable, the organization of the future begins to take shape. When these found boundaries remain rigid and impenetrable they create the slowness to respond and the lack of flexibility and innovation . . . that signals failure.[13] (quoted in *Electronic News*, 1996)

When readying to take such a risk, it helps to start with an existing strength and build outward, to see micro versions of interplay that can contribute to our health and growth in the bigger picture. Through my work with faculty and students in our School of Social Welfare, I have learned about an abiding theory in practicing "social" work, one that has, in fact, come to be identified internationally with my university's program: the strengths perspective. According to the program's web page:

> [T]he strengths perspective arises from the profession of social work's commitment to social justice, the dignity of every human being, and building on people's strengths and capacities rather than focusing exclusively on their deficits, disabilities, or problems. As an orientation to practice, emphasis is placed on uncovering, reaffirming, and enhancing the abilities, interests, knowledge, resources, aspirations and hopes of individuals and communities. This approach assumes that the articulation and extension of strengths and resources increases the likelihood that people will reach the goals and realize the possibilities they have set for themselves.[14]

Most of our centers already work from this strengths perspective. For example, we do not endorse a deficit model of education; in writing centers, we start where students are. For this next generation of collaboration to work, all parties, including the students themselves, must "assume that students bring ideas and experiences to learning situations that advance and enrich the understanding of others" (Muir & Blake 2002, 3). By taking this strengths perspective to heart, we might begin to recognize and activate our fundamental resource: we are really good at understanding and practicing collaboration.

A story:

> *Andrea Lunsford (1995) wrote that "collaborative environments and tasks must demand collaboration" and I have taken this statement very seriously. A few years ago*

I worked with our student senate here on a proposal to fund a writing center site in the main undergraduate library. The result is a space that is designed to offer a writing center service most evenings of the year, but during the rest of the time the space is called the Collaborative Learning Environment, a location in the library that is set up specifically to encourage group work, talk, and collaboration. So, this collaboration with the library staff and the student senate resulted in a collaborative learning environment for everyone—sans territorial possessiveness, sans demarcation of spaces for students and those for scholars. These kinds of achievements cannot be claimed by departments or programs working alone or working only from a motive to preserve or contain or justify their existence.

This result is potentially an exemplar of how we think learning is constituted and valued in our institutions; at a Research I (Doctoral Extensive) university such as mine, the "story" of this achievement is only as good as the scholarship that can be produced from it. The way then to move collaborative action at an administrative level is to pursue opportunities within our programs to engage in collaborative research. James Sosnoski (1994) calls this a move toward *concurrence.* From student writing groups to university-wide committees, to joint inquiry, *concurrence*

construes our work as collaborative rather than competitive . . . [it] is a non-hierarchical form of organization. Concurrence converges upon the mutual recognition of a painful problem . . . [and] by concurring, [groups] do not seek conformity; they seek the coincidences among their differences. A common ideal or *telos* does not hold the group together. Intellectual compassion and care hold the group together. (218)

Some of my best friends are librarians,[15] and some are other writing center directors, two groups that Liz Rohan (2002) labels "hostesses of literacy" in an article that uncovers similarities in both of our service models. In her critique, Rohan recognizes that the kind of "theorizing" that Elizabeth Boquet (2002) calls for, or the "knowledge-making" that Sharon Crowley calls for, should work as a ballast against a purely service model of our work. Think of yourself—good citizen—arriving in the collaboratory to now generate theory about the many dimensions of your work, your service, your leadership, your teaching. An organic outcome of our interactions with tutors, student writers, faculty, and all members of our college communities should be this continual discovery of useful theory. For me, the kinds of actions we take with others beyond our walls can be brought together within the collaboratory; joint inquiry, co-authoring, collaborative grant oversight, team teaching—all and more can foster and exemplify this theorizing and knowledge-making—sending a clear message that our work goes well beyond residual notions of *service* (that we *serve* our English departments, for example) to incorporate the potential of an intellectual-bureaucrat's brand of service. Rohan suggests, drawing on the work of Boquet, that we convert the rich archive of lore and narrative about our daily work to acts of unmasking, storytelling, and theory-building:

> Boquet suggests that 'theorizing,' rather than purely managing or masking the stories and the conflicts that they may represent and foster, may help raise the status of the work performed in stereotypically domestic spaces, and make visible this parlor of the academy. . . .
>
> The future of education might lie therefore in knowledge-making achieved through dialogue . . . in which knowledge is conceived through dialogic exchange, or as Boquet suggests, through story telling. (69–73)

This storytelling requires both teller and listener.

A PROMISING FUTURE

When Kinkead and Harris predicted in "What's Next for Writing Centers" (2000) that the twenty-first century writing center will be more "reliant on technology and need more second-language acquisition specialists," they spoke of the needs *inside*, what I propose moves us *outside*, beyond even their observation that

> [W]e are poised to assume a more prominent role in the institutions and communities in which [we] exist. Increasingly, writing centers are no longer seen as supplementary but as programs that are central to the mission of the school and essential to its being competitive in terms of attracting and retaining students. (23)

In addition, the terms *de-centered, satellite,* and *virtual* are often featured in predictions of our future—yet these terms are typically described as valuable always in conjunction with emerging technology, not as assets on their own or representative of a holistic programmatic goal to become more "central to the mission of the school." Contraptions are only that—contraptions are not collaboration (and this coming from someone who loves contraptions).

Likewise, I run the risk of implying that I agree entirely with Terrence Riley's (1994) argument that an "unpromising future" is in store for us if we "lean in" too far, whether that means committing to technology or disciplinarity or marginality as our method of survival. I believe that we can—and should—uncover our shared intelligence and expertise about collaboration *in order to* "lean in," and then to "lean in" with a bucketful of it. With Riley, I fear that we are mapping out a disciplinary territory in order to assimilate to the mainstream of higher education (which supposedly means we have "arrived"), and then we have to account for all we have lost (and all we will lose if we withhold our collaboration) in the process.

> In an attempt to secure something of value, we will end up recreating most of the debilitating hierarchies that we wished to escape. The peer relationship, collaboration, spontaneity, freedom, equality, courage; the excitement of interaction, the energy of student culture—replaced by constructions of expert and amateur, of protocol, instruction and tradition. (31)

The possible "lost" can be resuscitated. It is my assertion that identifying collaboration as the common denominator of our work—a universal conveyance (without assuming a cookie-cutter methodology that is played out the same way in all institutions)—allows us to overcome or supersede the very real effects of what Riley predicts we will encounter if our primary motivation is to build yet another academic empire. I, for one, would be willing to let go the tether of discipline for the subject. Valuing the subject (of writing, teaching writing, coaching writing, whatever) over the discipline, "in which staking out a certain argumentative orthodoxy seems to be more important than engaging with a sense of cultural dynamism" (Hills 2002, xiii), means working toward a sustainable rather than a contingent relation with education in the broadest sense. Which is exactly what we think writing itself has the capacity to do, right?

I used to be very irritated by the following assumption about the desired result of our efforts—a statement we have heard from many a naïve newbie: "We want to work ourselves out of job." We reacted: it is just plain wrong-headed thinking, we said, that we wouldn't really want to be available anytime for any writer; that "good" writers don't need us; that if we put enough student writers up on the lift, diagnosed their writing problems, and sent them on their way, eventually there would be no new student writers to serve. All this to say that now I wonder if writing were imbued so deeply and naturally as a habit of mind and a habit of connection, and internalized so effectively as a habit of learning on our campuses, that we would no longer need a "Center."[16] We would carry on deliberate, productive conversations about writing, in writing, for writing with our technology support staff, our librarians, our student services folks, our center for teaching facilitators, our first-year-experience program designers, our faculty from anthropology to zoology.

This then is my small message to my affinity group: professional and social networks are already formed and formidable within the writing center community; these are powerful and productive and ferry our goodies back and forth to each other, but to go beyond this we need to become a "smart mob"[17]—a homegrown initiative that utilizes our workaday knowledge to reach others in ways that can impact policy, influence administrative and institutional leaders, and help us grow leaders from among our writing center fellows. We can and should *demand* collaboration and continue to work toward boundarylessness, even with the knowledge that these actions will never be fully accomplished, completed.

CODA

I think you know I would never presume to teach you to breathe, to do something you do so naturally already, something you do fairly well, something you do to continue along, much without thinking; but I might slap you on the back if you were gasping for air.

Or . . .

Look around, feel the spray, see the natural wonder.

7

(RE)SHAPING THE PROFESSION
Graduate Courses in Writing Center Theory, Practice, and Administration

Rebecca Jackson
Carrie Leverenz
Joe Law

The development of graduate courses devoted to writing center studies (theory, practice, and administration) is a relatively recent phenomenon, one we attribute to several key factors: (1) the reality of various kinds of administrative work—writing program, writing center, WAC—for PhDs in rhetoric and composition; (2) specific local exigencies; (3) the growing professionalization of writing program and writing center studies, in particular the emergence of a new generation of rhetoric faculty specifically trained in these areas, and the steady growth of scholarly literature devoted to writing program and writing center issues (Hesse 1999); and (4) a consequent increase in interest among rhetoric graduate students in writing program and writing center careers—in the practice of administration as intellectual and scholarly work. Our principal concern here is with the ways in which graduate courses in writing center work shape and are shaped by the professionalization of writing centers, and the visions and interests of the next generation of writing center specialists. We begin with what might be called the "professionalization debates" in writing center studies—looking closely at arguments both for and against the actuality and/or desirability of writing center professionalization. We then turn our attention to graduate courses in writing center theory, practice, and administration, exploring the ways in which they enact and reshape the professionalization debate. We end with brief case studies of our own graduate-level writing center courses and implications of such courses for the future of writing center work.

PROFESSIONALIZING WRITING CENTER WORK

Graduate-level writing center courses might be seen as marking a significant stage in the professionalization of writing centers, part of the identifiable pattern that can be traced in the evolution of most academic disciplines. The essays collected in Mary Rosner, Beth Boehm, and Debra Journet's *History, Reflection, and Narrative: The Professionalization of Composition,* 1963–1983 (1999) take a variety of approaches to tracing that professionalization, often mixing anecdote with analysis to show the emergence and recognition of composition as an academic discipline. In their different ways, these essays suggest a similar overall pattern, which might be summarized fairly simply: (1) practitioners recognize that what they do differs fundamentally from the work done by the larger group with which they are associated; (2) practitioners form alliances that eventually are formalized, often in the form of local, regional, or national organizations; (3) practitioners develop a body of scholarship, often developing conferences, establishing new journals, or creating other means of disseminating that scholarship; (4) as this new field of study becomes sufficiently visible, it is gradually acknowledged (or at least tolerated) as a legitimate field of inquiry; and (5) it eventually takes its place with other disciplines taught in the academy. The fourth and fifth phases of this process are especially important, since together they enable a discipline to reproduce itself within the context of a larger institution and under the sanction of that institution. Although such a simple description strips away most of the complexity of professionalization, its very crudity may be useful in raising some fundamental questions, particularly the implications of that concluding phase.

This very general pattern does seem to describe the gradual professionalization of writing center work. Although writing center scholars have problematized our various narratives of origin (e.g., Carino 1995; Carino 1996; Boquet 1999), the concerns they address are symptomatic of a discipline's awareness of itself as a distinct entity. Equally important are the venues in which these essays have appeared—whereas Carino's two essays tracing the history of writing centers appeared in *The Writing Center Journal,* a publication likely to be read only by specialists, Boquet's more recent essay was published in a special issue of *College Composition and Communication* celebrating the fiftieth anniversary of CCCC. The fact that Boquet's essay was selected for this special issue signals a wider recognition of the importance of writing centers (and the study of writing center work).

Further evidence of this kind of recognition may be inferred from the inclusion of Muriel Harris's recent *College English* article, "Talking in the Middle: Why Writers Need Writing Tutors" (1995) in the fourth edition of *The Writing Teacher's Sourcebook* (Corbett et al. 2000), marking the first time writing centers have been represented in this frequently consulted resource. The presence of writing centers as a separate category in other resources, such as *The Bedford Bibliography for Teachers of Writing* (Bizzell et al. 2000), and the number of sessions devoted to writing centers at national conferences (thirty-one such sessions were identified in the topic index in the CCCC program book in 2000) provide further evidence of the increased scholarly interest in writing centers. Perhaps the most certain sign of academic acceptance is the number of dissertations involving writing centers in recent years. A quick look at *Dissertation Abstracts* between 1990 and 1999 shows twenty-six doctoral dissertations (and two master's theses) directly focused on writing center work; in addition, writing centers are important enough to figure in the abstracts of twenty-three more theses and dissertations.

Together, these developments have led to a sense of professionalization, even a sense of disciplinarity, that is now being perpetuated in graduate courses dealing with writing center theory and administration. The way in which a graduate course on writing centers may further that professionalization is evident in the stated goals of one such course:

> By semester's end, you should be able to
> - discuss the evolution of writing centers and writing center practices over the last 30 years
> - discuss the various theoretical orientations that form/have formed the foundation of writing center practice
> - engage in ongoing scholarly conversations about the relationship between writing center theory and writing center practice
> - start a writing center
> - administer a writing center (and all that this involves)
> - design and conduct writing center research studies of your own.
>
> (Jackson)

This ambitious set of goals, taken from Becky's class, would certainly prepare future writing center administrators to enter the field with a clear sense that it is a field, that it has a history (a complex, contested history, in fact), that all practice is informed by distinct theoretical or philosophical stances, that research can and should be conducted in a writing center. In short, we would assume that the student who actualizes these goals will be and will be perceived by others as a professional. Furthermore, the very existence of such a course suggests that writing center professionalization has reached the final stage of being institutionalized as a discipline, or as part of a discipline, within the academy.

INSTITUTIONALIZED SUBVERSION: THE PARADOX OF PROFESSIONALIZATION

The reality, however, is much more complicated. Like the larger discipline of Composition Studies, writing center directors and teachers began to form a community not only because of a shared commitment to a certain kind of intellectual work with student writers, but also because of a need to share resources and strategies for addressing what many still consider a marginalized status within institutions of higher education. While it is true that any new group of scholars seeking to establish themselves as a discipline or field is likely to face institutional resistance, writing centers face more than resistance to a new form of knowledge; they face the common prejudice within universities against valuing work deemed as service. That prejudice remains common despite the work of those, most notably Ernest L. Boyer (1990), who call for recognizing—and valuing—the "scholarship of service" as well as the "scholarship of discovery."

Differences between the institutional(ized) values of academic professionals and the values writing centers wish to embrace as part of their professional identity constitute one reason writing center workers themselves continue to debate the benefits of being professionalized. For many academic professionals, the work of the profession is most often described in terms of the production of research, the credentialing of majors, and the reproduction of professionals through graduate programs. As many writing center scholars have argued, the work that writing centers do is not driven by the mandate to pass on an officially sanctioned body of knowledge, but instead grows out of the specific needs of students and other constituencies in very local contexts. For example, while some writing center professionals have expertise in writing across the curriculum or English as a second language, others are experts in professional writing or writing assessment. If writing center professionals do share a common pursuit that differs from what others in the academy are doing (as the first step in becoming professional-ized), it is the pursuit of individualized instruction in writing. As Harvey Kail (2000) puts it in an issue of *The Writing Center Journal* devoted to the future of writing centers, "What distinguishes writing centers in acad-eme is their willingness and ability to engage student writers sentence by sentence, phrase by phrase, word by word, comma by comma, one to one, face to face. No one else in the academy can or wants to do this work, but everyone wants it done—now" (25). This focus on addressing individual students' needs rather than inculcating them into a definable discipline is one reason writing center work is not seen as professional by other academic professionals.

While many writing center professionals do produce research, that research is closely tied to practice. Indeed, a recently published bibliog-raphy of the last twenty years of *The Writing Center Journal* reveals a pre-ponderance of articles dealing with tutor training and the art of the individual conference. This practical emphasis supports Kail's (2000) contention that writing center directors are primarily occupied with teaching and administration. As Kail puts it, "[R]esearch is something we have added on after the original writing center creation myth was well established in our minds and embedded in our job descriptions. . . . As Writing Center Director my priorities are teaching, service, service, service, and then research—on our service" (28). In the same issue of *WCJ*, Lisa Ede and Andrea Lunsford argue that writing centers are well situated to contest common academic assumptions about research: "Rather than a model based on highly competitive individual research, writing centers foster team-based and collaborative research. . . . [S]uch research aims less toward individual advancement and more toward pro-grammatic and institutional improvement. . . . In such research, theory and practice exist in a reciprocal and dialogic relationship" (35). Ede and Lunsford emphasize the degree to which the values associated with writing center work—including writing-center-based research—differ from those of the traditional academy: "[I]n writing center work, the extrinsic reward structures of the university—represented by grades and class standing for students and promotion criteria tied almost com-pletely to individual 'original' research for faculty—is replaced by intrin-sic rewards measured in improved performance and satisfaction for students and faculty alike" (35). They note, however, that working against institutional norms can be risky, for research tied too closely to practice is often devalued. Thus, for writing center professionals, step three in the professionalization process—the development of a body of scholarship—is a complicated one, for while writing center workers have produced research of value to each other, the value of this scholarship to the larger institution remains in question.

In spite of widespread evidence that writing centers already are professionalized through research, journals, books, tenured faculty appointments, and the creation of writing-center-focused graduate courses, established writing center professionals continue to deliberate about what this evidence means. As Lil Brannon and Stephen North (2000) argue in their recent essay "The Uses of the Margin," although writing centers are much more common than when they both were assigned the task of starting writing centers in the late 1970s, "So far as we can see, not much has changed in this 20-year-old description of our work" (9). Brannon and North point out that writing centers continue to be underfunded; the staff is still typically dominated by student workers that change from term to term; and writing centers continue to be ignored or disrespected by the institutions that house them, even when student demand for writing center teaching is high. Such were the conditions in the mid-1980s that led Stephen North (1984) to publish his now canonical essay "The Idea of a Writing Center" in an attempt to make a case for the importance of writing center work to his non-Compositionist colleagues.

What is particularly interesting about the professionalization of writing centers is that while no professional wants to be despised or misunderstood, some writing center professionals do argue for caution in pursuing a fully professionalized status if that status requires that we give up what Brannon and North (2000) call an "(en)viable" place on the margins of the institution, free from the constraints of semester calendars, course objectives, and the inevitable grades associated with the "real" business of higher education (8). Of course, in exchange for this seeming freedom, writing centers have the additional burden of justifying what they do. While some writing center professionals struggle to justify the value of their research, others struggle with the institutional demand to produce traditional research that takes them away from their writing centers. Such struggles have led to disagreements within the writing center community about the benefit of having tenure-track status (the ultimate mark of professionalization), especially in institutions where research is the significant factor in awarding tenure. Having tenure-track status may be a sign that writing center directors are professionalized, but if such status require them to give their research agendas greater priority than the administration of their writing centers, they may be striking a devil's bargain. Directors with non-tenure-track appointments may have less status as professionals, but may be freer to devote their energies to administration and the kind of research valuable to writing centers without the fear of losing their jobs for focusing too much on administration or teaching or doing research not deemed scholarly enough.

Another example of the ambivalent professional status of writing centers is the conflict that can arise between the literacy values of writing center professionals and the literacy values of the institution that houses the writing center. Although academic freedom is an important value that colleges and universities are ethically obligated to protect and that academic professionals have a right to expect, writing centers (and other branches of Composition) often find themselves being asked to support literacy values that they would rather resist. As professionals, writing center workers should have the freedom to teach writing as they see fit, and yet, writing centers are often called on to support basic writing programs with questionable placement procedures, to tutor students who must sit for state-mandated competency tests that privilege status quo literacies, to limit collaborative practices seen as academic dishonesty by other professors. Nancy Grimm (1999) has argued persuasively that this conflict in literacy values arises when the institution's modernist concept of literacy (that individual, unified subjects should speak a single discourse) bumps up against the postmodernist reality of fragmented subjects enacted through multiple literacies, something especially apparent in writing centers. As Grimm sees it, "Just as postmodernity pushes against the limits of modernist beliefs, so does writing center work expose the limits of existing literacy practices in higher education. But because writing centers are funded for modernist reasons (to improve the clarity, order, and correctness of student writing), writing center workers too often must avoid questioning taken-for-granted university assumptions in order to fulfill their designated function" (2). Granted, being a professional who is able to marshal the authority of a body of scholarship puts one in a better position to act to change these expectations than would someone arguing from local conditions only. Still, being a writing center professional does not mean the kind of academic freedom in one's teaching and research experienced by professors teaching upper division courses in the major or graduate seminars to their devotees.

One of the values that writing center professionals are initiated into, then, is the practice of questioning what it means to be professionals within the larger field of higher education. While such initiation once typically occurred on the job, increasingly, graduate-level writing center courses serve as sites where questions related to professionalization can be addressed explicitly and systematically. Focused on complex problem solving, on strategic ways of approaching the constellation of issues writing center directors inevitably face, these courses emerge as sites of acculturation and critique, preparing students to participate in, complicate, even resist and reshape the conversations and context within which their work is situated.

We began our exploration of graduate-level writing center courses with documents from our own courses, then turned to Brown, Jackson, and Enos's (2000) "Survey of Doctoral Programs in Rhetoric" to locate similar courses in programs across the country. Profiles from the survey indicated that at least 12 doctoral programs in rhetoric offered either a course in writing center administration exclusively (5), or a course in writing program administration (8) with a writing center component (see Table 1).

TABLE 1

Doctoral Programs with Graduate Courses in Writing Centers
or Writing Program Administration

Institution	*Course Focus*
Ball State University	Writing Programs
Florida State University	Writing Centers
Iowa State University	Writing Programs
New Mexico State University	Writing Centers
Purdue University	Writing Programs
Syracuse University	Writing Programs
Texas A&M University	Writing Centers
Texas Tech University	Writing Programs
University of Illinois-Urbana Champaign	Writing Programs
University of New Hampshire	Writing Centers (and WAC)
University of Kansas	Writing Programs
University of Southern Mississippi	Writing Programs
Washington State University	Writing Centers

Our next step was to request recent syllabi from instructors at each institution who had developed and/or taught the writing center or writing program administration course listed in their program profile. In all, we gathered ten syllabi, including those from our own courses. Again, courses and accompanying syllabi fall into two primary categories: courses in writing center theory, practice, and administration (6); and courses in writing program administration (6) with a writing center component (see Table 2).

TABLE 2
Syllabi Received

Institution	Course Title	Instructor
Ball State	"Professional and Administrative Issues"	Carole Clark Papper
Florida State	"Teaching for Multiple Literacies"	Carrie Leverenz
Iowa State	"Writing Program Administration"	Carol David
New Mexico State	"Writing Centers: Theory, Practice, and Administration"	Rebecca Jackson
Purdue	"Writing Program Administration"	Shirley K. Rose
Syracuse	"Writing Program Administration"	Louise Phelps & Eileen Schell
Texas A&M	"The English Writing Lab"	Valerie Balester
U of Illinois U-C	"Issues in Writing Program Administration	Catherine Prendergast
U of Kansas	"Writing Program Administration"	Amy Devitt
U of New Hampshire	"Writing Across the Curriculum and Writing Centers: History, Theory, and Practice"	Cinthia Gannett
Washington State	"Administering a Writing Lab"	Lisa Johnson-Shull
Wright State	"The Study of Writing: Writing Center Theory and Practice"	Joe Law

GRADUATE COURSES IN WRITING PROGRAM ADMINISTRATION WITH A WRITING CENTER COMPONENT

For most of the courses in this category, "writing program administration" is used as an umbrella term for various kinds of work in writing programs, writing centers, and writing across the curriculum. In other words, writing center work is (also) writing program work, as the description of the graduate-level WPA course offered at the University of Kansas makes clear:

> This seminar attempts to examine writing program administration as an intellectual activity. Whether directing a first-year composition program, a writing lab, or a writing-across-the-curriculum program, writing program administrations must ground their local, institutional practice in disciplinary knowledge.

More interestingly, perhaps, these courses advance a vision of writing program administration as an intellectual, highly political kind of work,

work embedded within and shaped by layers of disciplinary, institutional, and public contexts. At Syracuse, for example, students are introduced to the "issues, problems, and strategies of writing program administration," to the "complexity of writing programs as communities, including. . .the use of adjunct or part-time labor, mixed constituencies within programs, and relations to English departments." Courses offered at other institutions offer similar descriptions and objectives.

- This seminar will address both theory and praxis of writing program administration for diverse writing programs (first-year composition, professional writing, writing centers, WAC programs) in a variety of institutional contexts. Course readings and seminar discussions and activities will address . . . ethical implications of defining the responsibilities of writing program administrators; rhetorical strategies for documenting writing program administration; [and] institutional policies of characterizing writing program administration as "service," "teaching," or "research." (Rose)

- During this semester we will examine some of the contemporary issues and debates in composition . . . [with a] primary focus on writing program administration. We will look at the role of the Writing Program at the University and the relationship of writing centers to writing programs. We will consider the professionalization of writing and writing programs, particularly the role of contract faculty in sustaining writing programs. . . .Readings concerning Writing Programs, Writing Centers, and Writing Across the Curriculum will necessarily include a variety of issues, such as job roles, training, assessment, relationships between these programs as well as between their administrators and the university administrators, students, and colleagues. . . . [Readings will] give us an idea in both practical and theoretical terms of the diversity of issues, duties, ideas, relationships, and scholarship that WPAs must know and contend with. (Papper)

- This course seeks to prepare graduate students in writing studies and closely related fields for the inevitability of administration. . . . We will be discussing issues such as the politics of remediation, gendered approaches to administration, TA/tutor training, the relationship of administration to research, social action, and professional development. We will be examining extensively the writing program administrator's positioning with respect to the current labor crisis in the academy, manifested in the university's increasing dependence on cheap and temporary labor. (Prendergast)

These courses may not deal with writing center issues exclusively, but they do address writing programs as sytems, viewing writing centers as inherent, important, and equally complex components within these systems.

What we don't see is writing program administration, including writing center work, reduced to a set of skills, devoid of intellectual substance. Instead, these courses work to (re)shape students' ideas about administrative work in rhetoric, to prepare them—as fully as any course can—for the teaching, service, research, and intellectual dimensions of writing program administration, and for the political issues that typically attend these facets of writing program work.

GRADUATE COURSES IN WRITING CENTER THEORY, PRACTICE, AND ADMINISTRATION

The six courses we examined devoted exclusively to writing center work share important features of their counterpart courses in writing program administration. Courses are theoretically and practically grounded, emphasizing the shifting, often contested, theoretical and practical frameworks that have shaped and continue to shape writing center work. Each foregrounds the importance of writing center research, empirical research in particular, while at the same time exploring conflicting perceptions about the value of such work. Each focuses, as conflicts and points of disagreement between the writing center and other communities suggest, on the politics of writing center work, on our attempts to view and talk about ourselves as professionals, while at the same time preparing aspiring members of our community to recognize and challenge attitudes, policies, and cultures that reflect the view that writing center work is neither professional nor professionalized. This last move is what we describe as acculturating students into the paradox of professionalization.

Descriptions taken from the syllabi we collected give us some idea of the range and depth of these courses. For example, "The English Writing Lab" offered at Texas A&M "covers the basic components of writing lab administration, including lab management, tutoring, and the development of learning resources" and offers students opportunities to actually engage in these facets of writing center work. Topics of discussion in this course include the "politics of basic writing, critical pedagogy. . .computers in writing centers, peer tutoring, and collaborative learning." Valerie Balester, who teaches this course almost exclusively, observes that a good deal of class discussion focuses, as well, on professional issues—tenure, promotion, status of writing center directors—especially as literature on these issues has begun to emerge. The graduate-level writing center course, "Administering a Writing Center," offered at Washington State takes on similar issues, in particular the evolution of writing center theories and practices and the professional concerns that attend writing center work. The University of New Hampshire's course, "Writing Across the Curriculum and Writing Centers: History, Theory, and Practice," offers what might be called a more particularized account of writing centers and the work they do, yet it also focuses on the relationship between theory and practice, and on the multiple contexts within which writing centers are situated: "[in this course] we will use a variety of lenses to understand the past events and movements, present theories and practices, and possible futures of writing centers and WAC programs as aspects of large cultural and educational trends as well as local and contextualized narratives."

Requirements in these courses vary—from reading journals, observations/analyses, and "mini projects" to longer, more substantive research projects for conference presentation or publication—and are designed to encourage students to think and act like writing center professionals. The following table lists required activities in order of their frequency (see Table 3).

TABLE 3

Required Assignments in Graduate-Level Writing Center Courses

Activity	*Courses Requiring This Activity*
Research Project	6 out of 6: Florida State, U of New Hampshire, New Mexico State, Texas A&M, Washington State, Wright State
Mini Projects (observations, transcriptions, theory application, interviews, etc.)	4 out of 6: U of New Hampshire, New Mexico State, Florida State, Washington State
Proposal (conference, research)	2 out of 6: Washington State, Wright State
Annotated Bibliography	2 out of 6: U of New Hampshire, Washington State
Book Review	1 out of 6: U of New Hampshire
Profile of a Writing Center	1 out of 6: Wright State
Administrative Project	1 out of 6: New Mexico State
Final Exam	2 out of 6: Texas A&M, Washington State

Two of the courses include a lab component: at Texas A&M, students enrolled in "The English Writing Lab" must work a minimum of six hours a week in the writing center and keep a tutoring journal (listed above) in which they discuss and reflect on their experiences; at Washington State, students are required to work in the writing center a minimum of two hours per week. Other daily and/or weekly requirements include leading discussion and consulting with a writing center tutor about a paper they are writing for class. These course requirements illustrate that writing center professionals must know the scholarly literature that represents a nationally sanctioned view of writing centers, but must also understand the ways in which writing center work is defined by local conditions.

THREE CASE STUDIES: WRIGHT STATE, FLORIDA STATE, NEW MEXICO STATE

In the three brief case studies that follow, we reflect on our own individual graduate-level writing center courses, taking a more sustained look at the way the intentions expressed in syllabi and course descriptions have been translated into practice. In addition to demonstrating the ways in which these courses attempt to define writing center work in terms of both disciplinary knowledge and institutional politics, we also examine the impact of the local institutional contexts in which those courses were offered. While the shape and content of these courses bear witness to the increased professionalization of writing center work, an examination of the institutional context suggests that the professional status of that work—and of those who carry it out—continues to be questioned.

Wright State University

Wright State University differs from the other universities considered here in that it does not offer a PhD in English. It does, however, offer an MA in English with a concentration in composition and rhetoric as one of the options. Students who follow this track tend to remain in the area, many of them teaching in primary or secondary schools or becoming instructors at the community colleges and universities in the vicinity. As even this brief a description suggests, students are likelier to favor the seemingly practical over the kind of explicit "theorizing" described in connection with other courses. In this class, that orientation meant that discussions usually began with issue of practice, then moved to uncover the assumptions underlying those practices.

Otherwise, in its general outline, this course resembles other graduate courses on writing centers. Like Becky and Carrie's courses, for instance, Joe's course devoted early class meetings to examining the history of writing centers, presenting it as an emerging discipline with a distinct identity. The class began with accounts of the origins of writing centers—including some individual accounts of early writing centers as well as Peter Carino's essays (1995, 1996) in "thick description" (Elizabeth Boquet's historical essay was not yet available). Those histories were read in conjunction with what Becky calls "first generation theory." Subsequent sessions dealt with administrative issues before we took up "second generation" theory. Because of the practical orientation of his students, one of his goals was to suggest how "theory" and "practice" impinge on each other within specific institutional contexts, and he arranged the course to reflect the interconnectedness of these concerns. The sequence made it increasingly difficult to discuss any of these topics in isolation from the others.

To emphasize the importance of local exigencies, Joe asked students to investigate how various writing centers reflected (and sometimes resisted) the cultures of which they were part. After looking at the differences evident in the case studies presented in Joyce A. Kinkead and Jeannette G. Harris's *Writing Centers in Context* (1993), students developed a profile of a writing center in the area. After those profiles were completed, a number of writing center directors in the area (including some of those profiled) joined the class for an evening to discuss the nature of their work and how it varied from institution to institution.

Some of the talk was about day-to-day practicalities, such as keeping records and managing a budget, and part of it took up larger issues, such as program assessment. To some degree, those students with experience working in a writing center were already familiar with topics of that sort and were not surprised when they encountered them. What *did* surprise them is the enormous range of "political" complications attending the administration of a writing center. One example will demonstrate how that played out. For one class meeting, the assigned readings included two "historical" pieces—Gary Olson and Evelyn Ashton-Jones's "Writing Center Directors: The Search for Professional Status" (1988) and Jeanne Simpson's "What Lies Ahead for Writing Centers: Position Statement on Professional Concerns" (1985). Also included was the more recent "War, Peace, and Writing Center Administration" by Jeanne Simpson, Steve Braye, and Beth Boquet (1995), a three-way conversation showing that the issues raised in the earlier pieces were still unresolved. By that point in the quarter, most of the class had visited a writing center at another school and talked with the director; in addition, the interim director of the writing center at Wright State attended the class that evening. In the discussion that followed, it was immediately clear that the larger structure of the university was invisible to the students. Once they began to discuss their reading and observations, however, they were surprised, perhaps even alarmed, at what they were discovering. For instance, the question of whether a writing center is housed in an academic department or in some other administrative unit has a tremendous impact on its operation, as does the question of whether the director is classified as faculty or as staff. These questions— even those distinctions that amount to an academic caste system—were new to Joe's students, and these are questions unlikely to be raised in a course that does not focus on administration. Students in such courses will soon be seeking positions in colleges and universities, perhaps asked to be responsible for a writing center or some other program. Those who have had an opportunity to learn how to look at the context in which such programs must operate will be better prepared to expect (and thus deal with) the paradoxical demands they will face.

Florida State University

The graduate course in writing center pedagogy taught at Florida State represents well the paradoxical professional status of writing center work, particularly in the way it negotiates the troubled division between "service" and "scholarship." Florida State prides itself on having one of the first writing centers in the Southeast, founded in the 1960s. From very early on, the writing center was tied directly to the academic mission of the institution, providing for-credit individualized instruction in writing to students who were deemed "at risk," based on SAT and ACT scores, and to students who had difficulty passing the state-mandated College Level Academic Skills Test. What came to be known as the "writing center course" was officially titled "Teaching English as a Guided Study," and served originally not as an introduction to writing center theory and practice but as an official mechanism for providing financial support to graduate teaching assistants as they prepared to teach first-year writing. While students were enrolled in their summer pedagogy course "Teaching College English," they also enrolled in "Teaching English as a Guided Study," which required that they work in the writing center in exchange for a stipend. At that time, working in the writing center meant overseeing students' completion of grammar worksheets. When the first faculty member trained in Rhetoric and Composition was hired at Florida State in the late 1980s, he quickly turned the writing center into a real center for individualized instruction in writing and turned "Teaching English as a Guided Study" into a real graduate course in composition pedagogy. Aside from a few brief discussions about writing centers and the continued requirement that new teaching assistants tutor in the writing center during their summer training, the course did not focus on writing centers as a separate and unique site of writing instruction, but emphasized composition pedagogy more generally. Like many writing centers in the 1970s and 1980s, the Reading/Writing Center at Florida State eventually came to be directed by a graduate student, while "Teaching English as a Guided Study" continued to be taught by Composition faculty who were no longer tied to writing center work.

When Carrie was hired to direct the Reading/Writing Center, she also became the faculty member designated to teach "Teaching English as a Guided Study." Given that the course continued to be required of all TAs during the summer before their first year of teaching at Florida State, Carrie wanted to prepare graduate students to be effective tutors in a very local context. The ultimate shape of the course, which she sub-titled "Teaching for Multiple Literacies," was determined primarily by her analysis of the kinds of work that tutors needed to be prepared to do in this local context. For example, because of the writing center's mandate to teach students deemed at risk based on SAT scores as well as to prepare students who had failed the language portions of the CLAST, Carrie organized one unit around the politics of testing. Other units included attention to cultural and language differences, and to the challenge of working with writing from multiple disciplines and of meeting the needs of graduate students.

At the same time, the course was also influenced by the accumulating body of writing center theory and research, as well as the professional conversations Carrie participated in on the discussion list WCenter and at regional and national writing center conferences. Indeed, although Carrie had specialized in Rhetoric and Composition for her PhD, she had no experience or training in writing center work before she began to direct the Center at Florida State. Becoming a part of a professional community—joining NWCA and WCenter, reading the latest writing center publications—shaped Carrie's sense of what her writing center should be and do, which also shaped her sense of what graduate writing tutors should learn in their required writing center course. For example, Carrie began the course by asking students to read a set of essays that outlined various models for writing centers: Stephen North's "The

Idea of a Writing Center" (1984), Andrea Lunsford's "Collaboration, Control, and the Idea of a Writing Center" (1995), and Marilyn Cooper's "Really Useful Knowledge: A Cultural Studies Agenda for Writing Centers" (1995). These articles helped students see writing centers as sites of research and theory as well as practice and, because these articles situated writing centers in relation to English departments and universities more broadly, helped them see the course as part of their professional training in English.

Although the course units were organized around teaching issues, each unit required scholarly reading and critical response journals in addition to examining student writing and practice conferencing with classmates. This emphasis on the professional was also manifested in the requirement that students complete a ten- to twelve-page paper proposing a theory of literacy learning and teaching. In the paper, students had to include material from their experience, from the course readings, and from their observation of tutorials. (New graduate students were no longer required to provide tutoring while enrolled in their summer training on the grounds that tutors needed some training first—another mark of the professional status of writing center work.)

Such apparent marks of professionalization may be deceptive, however. For instance, the fact that "Teaching English as a Guided Study" was required of all new TAs in English may seem evidence that writing center work is considered professional, as signified by a specialized body of knowledge taught by experts. However, it is important to note that the three credits students earned from taking the course did not count toward their degree unless they were concentrating in Rhetoric and Composition. In other words, the course was required of graduate students, but for most, it didn't "count." It should also be noted that since Carrie has left Florida State, her former faculty position has been converted to a non-tenure-track administrative line, and "Teaching English as a Guided Study" has reverted to its former status as a composition pedagogy course without an emphasis on writing centers. The history of "Teaching English as a Guided Study" illustrates the paradox of writing center professionalization. For those inside the writing center community, a case can be made that writing centers constitute a valid site of specialized knowledge, but such a case has yet to be made convincingly within the university or departments of English or even within the larger Rhetoric and Composition community.

New Mexico State University

The graduate-level writing center course ("Writing Centers: Theory, Practice, and Administration") Becky developed in 1998 at New Mexico State University addresses the complexities of writing center work quite explicitly: it is designed to acculturate aspiring writing center directors into "the profession" by focusing, in part, on the paradoxes of the profession. As Director of the Writing Center and Assistant Professor of English in a department offering both the MA and PhD in Rhetoric, Becky was eager to introduce graduate students to the richness of writing center theory and practice, and to the opportunities writing centers offered for empirical language research. As an Assistant Professor working to integrate her teaching, administrative, and research lives, Becky also wanted to prepare students for the unique demands, complexities, and political dimensions of writing center work, to give them a venue for active problem solving and reflection. Her own interests dovetailed nicely with growing interest among graduate students and faculty in rhetoric and professional communication in developing a core of courses in various areas of writing program work, including writing center and WAC administration.

Students began the acculturation process by becoming familiar and comfortable with the conversations taking place in key areas of writing center studies: historical perspectives, "first-generation" theory, "second-generation" theory, writing center practice, writing center administration, writing center research, and the numerous professional issues that attend writing center work—tenure and promotion, for example. The goal here was to expose students to the range and depth of conversations among the writing center community before moving to discussion of specific local practices, an absolutely necessary move if students were to understand the context-specific nature of writing center work. A good example of this would be the evening the class discussed the shift from "first generation theory"—Bruffee's "Collaborative Learning and the 'Conversation of Mankind'"(1984), North's "The Idea of a Writing Center" (1984)—to "second generation theory"—Cooper's "Really Useful Knowledge: A Cultural Studies Agenda for Writing Centers" (1995), Grimm's *Good Intentions* (1999)—and its relationship to and possibilities for the NMSU Writing Center. Students looked closely at the departmental and institutional contexts within which the NMSU Writing Center is situated and explored the potential and desirability of preparing consultants (and the students with whom they would work) for a more postmodern writing center practice. Simply put, classroom activities and written projects were designed to bring relatively remote disciplinary conversations to life, to encourage students' thinking about these conversations in relation to local realities, and to provide them with opportunities to imagine various ways of responding to various writing center issues in context.

Another example helps to illustrate this movement—from current conversation, to local realities and practices, to extensions or alterations in conversation that might result in material change at both the local and disciplinary levels. Those of who us who direct writing centers know how difficult it can sometimes be to integrate our teaching, research, and administrative responsibilities into a coherent (or somewhat coherent) whole. This is especially difficult when departments have difficulty seeing the local kinds of research writing center directors must do as legitimate, something more than "service." To help students better understand and grapple with the complexity of this issue, Becky asked them to read "Evaluating the Intellectual Work of Writing Program Administration," and Muriel Harris' "Presenting Writing Center Scholarship" (1997). She also distributed copies of the annual evaluation form the department uses to document faculty work, asking students to look closely at the categories—teaching, research, and service—within which different kinds of work might be legitimately placed. Writing center work, which we had discussed throughout the semester as embodying teaching, research, and administration, was relegated to the "service" section of the evaluation form. So-called "local" or "in-house" research—studying patterns of use to determine the need for workshops on working with ESL writers, for example—was difficult to place at all. If it couldn't be considered "research" in the traditional sense, and the evaluation form makes clear that it cannot, what is it? More importantly, what can we, as writing center directors, *do* about this? Publishing the findings of local research—making it relevant to writing center folk outside of our own context—was one of the many options the class explored for addressing this situation. For example, a local survey of consultants' attitudes toward record keeping (an actual study completed by two of the students in this class) might be discussed at a writing center meeting, but it might also be reworked and submitted as an article that other writing center directors would find interesting and useful.

Clearly, graduate level writing center courses like the one Becky developed and taught at New Mexico State serve to "credential" students and, perhaps, make it easier for them to find jobs. More than that, they help to prepare students for the unique and often highly political positions they will find themselves in as writing center directors: they may have a title but no real status; they may be asked to conduct research but find they have little time to actually do it; they may conduct research but find that it has little value; and they may work hard toward promotion and tenure only to find that those who evaluate their work know little, if anything, about it. From Becky's point of view, her responsibility in this kind of course is to expose students to the paradox of professionalization and, in response to this reality, provide opportunities for them to work through issues methodically and strategically. We must prepare students to participate actively in conversations that may affect them and their work in writing centers, but we must help them discover ways to critique, perhaps even transform, these conversations (and realities) as well.

(RE)SHAPING THE PROFESSION

In this essay, we have interpreted the growing number of graduate writing center courses as evidence of the increased professionalization of writing center work. At the same time, a close reading of these courses demonstrates the degree to which the professional status of writing centers continues to be questioned, especially within local institutional contexts. Such is the paradox of professionalization, that while writing center specialists can now point to an extensive body of scholarship as a sign of the status of their work, much of that scholarship addresses the problem of not being treated as status equals in the academy. Exposing graduate students to this literature, and to the institutional politics and local contexts that motivate such scholarship, will prepare these newly minted writing center teachers and administrators to address head-on the gap between writing centers' rightful claim to professional status and the often blatant dismissal of that claim by others in the academic community. Preparing future writing center workers in this way will also, we hope, produce a new generation of scholars with the knowledge and skills to contribute to the continuing professional conversation about the paradox of professionalism. The future (professionalization) of writing centers depends on those willing and able to define their work as both situated within local contexts and also as part of a larger disciplinary project. Graduate writing center courses that make clear this dual obligation go a long way in helping to (re)shape

8

ADMINISTRATION ACROSS THE CURRICULUM
Or Practicing What We Preach

JOSEPHINE A. KOSTER

Writing center administration, a highly complex task as is, has an added complication in that so many new directors plunge in with an almost total lack of preparation.

MURIEL HARRIS

I sometimes fantasize about an inspirational poster with Mickey Harris's intense portrait, arms upraised, and the caption "writing lab directors unite."

JOYCE KINKEAD

When we observe tutoring going on in a writing center, we're likely to hear comments like these: "Well, in a case study you use terms like . . ." or "Now when you're talking about the reverse transcription of this DNA, do you mean that . . . ?" A given of writing center practice and tutor training policy is that our tutors will learn to work with writers across the curriculum, attempt to understand the forms and practices of many specialized areas, and use and manipulate the discourse conventions of those practitioners. While many of our tutors are *not* economics or biology majors, they learn to approximate the language and to appreciate the practices of their clients, in order to project credibility and merit the trust of the writers they are tutoring, and to achieve their joint communication objectives. Using the strategy of "speaking the other's language" leads to successful communication and collaboration between tutor and client.

But what we preach to our tutors does not always carry comfortably over into our own practices. A frequent topic of conversation for writing center administrators (hereafter WCAs) is our wars with the administrators, bureaucrats, bean counters, what have you who control our academic worlds. We report what "they" have done to us—how "they" cut our budgets, reduce our space, and misunderstand our missions and our very real contributions to our institutions. A common theme of these conversations is that administrators fail to understand *our* rhetoric, *our* discipline, *our* practices, *our* values. Beth Boquet speaks for this position when she talks of "the judgments of administrators who may understand little about the idea of a writing center" (Simpson et al. 1995, 23). Jeanne Simpson and Barry Maid (2001) characterize this oppositional position concisely:

> The bonding work of the writing-center community has, unfortunately, also resulted in a shared and frequently articulated hostility toward administration. The community perceives administration as the enemy and frames the lack of administrators' knowledge about writing centers and writing-center pedagogy as at least contemptible and often malevolent. That an economics or biology professor turned provost or dean would have no reason to know anything about writing centers seems not to be a consideration. When more traditional (and familiar) models of writing pedagogy are favored by administrators, the writing-center community may express outrage at the perceived obstructionism. The writing-center community's attempts to provide more accurate information or to offer research-based alternatives often come either too late or are presented defensively. Perceiving a 'marginalization' of writing centers, the community attaches blame to administration for failure to be supportive or interested or understanding. (127)

But as St. Augustine once observed, not the least part of finding the answer is asking the right questions. We might also ask, *should* administrators use our form of discourse? Or might we benefit by appropriating elements of *their* discourse? Should we as writing center administrators practice what we preach to our tutors? In this chapter I would like to suggest that if we apply the tools of audience analysis we would use in a tutorial consultation, we might identify why "they" just don't understand.

After twenty-five years spent working with bureaucracies in business, industry, and education, I've concluded that administration of any organization is an example of chaos mathematics, the study of complex systems in motion. Chaos theory attempts to describe those systems. In a very real sense, academic administrators are chaos theorists. They are constantly trying to describe, control, and direct large numbers of dynamic systems—entities like departments, programs, football teams, what have you—whose personnel, budget, space, and other requirements never are the same from one moment to the next. The formulae central administrators (hereafter CAs) create to manage these systems are necessarily complicated—and must take into account what chaos theorists classify as attraction, repulsion, and neutrality—the effects systems have on another. If the resources allotted for student support one year must go to replacing outdated computers, then other valuable student support services like a writing center will probably suffer—the two budget goals are repulsed by each other. On the other hand, if the reading center and the writing center decide that they can share a receptionist, the salary money saved by eliminating duplication might buy more computers for the two centers to share, providing more services—budget attraction. Most of us are only used to looking at administration from our center-focused vantage point, rather than looking at the entire dynamic system to which we belong. Rhetorically, our viewpoint may be described by Young, Becker, and Pike's (1970) theory of tagmemics—we're able to see the particles, but it's harder to pick up the waves and the fields.

If we only look at our own subsystem, or express our needs and demands in the language of our subsystem, we will likely set ourselves up for miscommunication at best and failure at worst. As Mickey Harris pointed out in her keynote address at the 1999 National Writing Centers Association conference in Bloomington, we must overcome our resistance and listen to our CAs' perspectives even when we disagree with them, just as we ask our tutors to do with their clients. She argues that

> We need to face some realities as to what can be changed and what perceptions will always need to be worked on. Administrators have their worlds and their frames of reference that aren't ours. If they think quantitatively, have a higher regard for credit-bearing courses than student services, consider budget-limiting to be more important than expanding services that students need, then we need to recognize their realities. That will always be their agenda and many administrators are selected because they can attend well to achieving such goals. We can try to modify their perspectives, but we are always going to be faced with talking to a constantly changing group of people who manage the budget, prefer figures and graphs to anecdotal evidence, have mission statements to guide them, have streams of faculty on campus clamoring for larger pieces of their shrinking pies, and have state legislatures and boards of trustees to answer to. (1999)

Neal Lerner (1997) reminds us that the administrators Harris talks about "often want numbers, digits, results" (2). One problem for many WCAs is that we essentialize other disciplines' perspectives as being primarily positivistic. The emphasis on "numbers, digits, results" and needs that CAs can interpret raises in many of us the old fears of having centers regarded as purely remedial, even mechanistic sites. Our conceptual and theoretical frames have taught us to beware of systems that rely on such hard-and-fast measures of outcomes. We recognize that writing cannot be reduced to the answers on a standardized test, and that writing problems cannot be solved by a thirty-minute visit to a fix-it shop. When CAs ask for measures of our effectiveness, we rightly say, "Our discipline doesn't express judgments that way." Yet there may be ways in which we can use the language of other disciplines to articulate our own methods of determining effectiveness and needs if we take an "administration across the curriculum" perspective to dealing with central administration.

For instance, consider the complaint articulated by Boquet (Simpson et al. 1995) that administrators don't understand what we do, haven't read the works of North and others that define our theoretical positions. This is probably true. It's likely that they haven't read the theoretical positions that govern what our colleagues in nursing or music or social work do, either. What administrators read is the information *we* send *them*. Mostly that's in the form of periodic reports; that's how CAs usually acquire information. Typically, the reports we write present our information to CAs in the best possible light from *our* rhetorical perspective, even though that might not be the most effective way to express both our successes and needs. As Jeanne Simpson tells Steve Braye in the trialogue "War, Peace, and Writing Center Administration" (1995), when a WCA writes a glowing report of his or her successes, the message is that "You are doing a great job with meager resources. And since you've proved that you can do that, there is no incentive for the dean/provost to give you more resources. You need to do a great job and also prove that you are about to collapse. Or define other goals that cannot be met without more resources" (165). Typically, too, we present this information in the text-dense prose that is most comfortable to us as humanists, rather than in the graphics- and bullet-list-laden reporting style of administration. We rarely think of how the readers of these reports are accustomed to finding, interpreting, and deciphering the information we present.

We often fail to realize that the language we use to make those proofs and define those goals for our institutions is crucial. CAs have a professional duty to look at the big picture and listen for particular key phrases and terms that define that picture for them. Take 'quality,' for instance. In the humanities, we have a very open definition of quality; as Plato asks in the *Phaedrus*, "What is good and what is not good? Do we need anyone to teach us these things?" In the language of business that so many CAs are familiar with, "quality" has a very specific definition. It means delivering the best service to customers in the most effective, efficient, error-free way. David Schwalm (1995), Provost at Arizona State University West (another writing program administrator turned CA), highlights some of the key phrases to which administrative audiences respond positively:

> [Administrators] tend to value projects that are student-centered. We like projects that encourage retention, since losing students is expensive and state legislators are on our case. We *have* to be concerned about costs. We favor solutions over problems. We like proposals that reflect an understanding of the institution at large. We also like projects that help to overcome the vertical organization of the institution, reduce duplication, and allow for recombinations of existing resources. (62)

Schwalm's statement is full of the buzzwords of the ivory tower administrator: *student-centered, solution, retention,* and so on. This linguistic code shifting, so obvious when we tutor or coach our tutors to work with writers in other disciplines, often escapes us when we deal with administrators. It behooves us rhetorically to construct our arguments on grounds that match the concerns and perspectives of our administrative audiences. As Simpson (1995) says, "Central Administration is interested in information that addresses the issues that concern it. These are things like accreditation, accountability (assessment), staffing plans, space allocation, and personnel dollars. Those are the nuts-and-bolts concerns, the daily assignment of administration. It is crucial to understand that" (49). I was reminded of this myself not long ago when talking to the outgoing and incoming provosts of a respected liberal arts college who had hired me to evaluate their writing center. At one point, I characterized the training of its tutors as "belletristic." The outgoing provost, a Victorian literature specialist, nodded sagely. The incoming provost, a nationally known geologist, asked me what the term meant and why I apparently thought it was a short-coming. I had taken for granted that all of my administrative audience would understand the term; the misunderstanding reminded me that I had to be more audience-focused in communicating my concerns to them.

One place where many WCAs have confronted the language of another discipline is the mission statement, a business tool meant to drive an organization's policies and actions. In recent years, many of us have developed such documents, usually in response to administrative prompting. Since our perspective is the framework of humanistic inquiry, usually with an expressivist or social-constructionist bent, we try to write sweeping mission statements that usually sound something like this: "The Writing Center will provide a nurturing and supportive environment in which all writers are encouraged to develop their full potential for communicating in a wide range of voices and forms through working with their peers in a collaborative setting." For us, that is a rhetorically sound mission, and it describes what we do very well. But for a central administrator it's a nightmare. How do you assess qualities like "nurturing and supportive"? "full potential"? "encouragement"? In the rhetoric of quality management, a mission statement describes an organization's goals and desires in concrete, measurable ways. How many writing center mission statements include sentences like "We aim to serve at least 35% of the student body this year" or "We intend to provide at least one hundred twenty hours of tutoring services a week"? Administrators favor statements like these, because they can be measured; they can determine how many students are served or how many hours the center is open. Moreover, if the institution accepts such a mission statement, the writing center director can then go to the dean or provost at the appropriate time in the budget cycle and say, "To meet our agreed-upon mission of tutoring 120 hours a week, we need to run three sessions concurrently. That means I need another 50 square feet of space, another table and four chairs, and $900 of additional salary money. Where can we find it?" (Using the rhetoric of quality management works both ways; if your central administration wants to have you achieve your articulated mission, it has to give you the tools to do so. Conversely, if you want the tools, you need to show they're necessary through your mission statement.) Understanding and using appropriate budgeting language in the appropriate rhetorical situations can help diminish the perception some WCAs have that the "distribution of funding support within an institution is unpredictable at best, capricious at worst" (Simpson 1995, 48).

Bob Barnett has recently demonstrated how centers can use their rhetorical analysis skills on other management documents to lobby effectively for resources to meet their needs. In "Redefining Our Existence: An Argument for Short- and Long-Term Goals and Objectives" (1997), Barnett shows how his center analyzed the University of Michigan-Flint's Academic Plan for language that would support the center's "top priority—helping students become better writers" (124). Using these results, the center phrased its list of short- and long-term priorities in the language the institution valued so that it could better make the argument for a larger slice of institutional resources and better publicize its efforts to students and faculty on campus. Barnett argues that positioning the center rhetorically as part of the institution's most valued activities—in his case retention and collaboration—allowed his center to "continue making progress toward what I see as our ultimate goal—to bring writing to the center of the university curriculum" (133).

Another illustrative argument for how, indeed, we can make such political cases in language appropriate to our audiences is Joyce Kinkead and Jeanne Simpson's "Administrative Audience: A Rhetorical Problem" (2000), where they patiently explain both the meanings and importance of key administrative terms such as student retention, time-to-degree, student attrition, student credit hours (SCH), full-time equivalents (FTE), productivity, assessment, accreditation, and cost-to-benefit ratios as they apply to writing center work. Kinkead and Simpson argue, correctly in my opinion, that

> Ultimately, all academic issues boil down to budget decisions, and if the goal is to encourage a beneficial decision, the first step is to use the language of budgets. Understanding this terminology will help a WPA [writing program administrator] to see how the economics of the institution work. . . . Administrators use these terms frequently. Their meanings are well-understood and so embedded that, as with a nation's currency, everyone is expected to know how to use them and how they relate to each other. (74–75)

Muriel Harris (1997) likewise argues, in her valuable discussion of how to present writing center scholarship to administrators, that in institutions where accountability is an issue, using outcomes-based language in writing center communication "does permit the director to talk in language other administrators will easily recognize" (97). She also points out that center directors might look to participation in and presentations to organizations of educational administrators, not just writing center or composition specialists, as ways of gaining fluency in such discourses.

Rhetorically, the process these experienced WCA/administrators describe is not difficult, and most of us could, I suspect, theorize it comfortably from our rhetorical, comp-theory, and literary perspectives. How many WCAs, though, feel comfortable talking about the quality of center services in the language of quality management? About budget requirements in terms of demonstrated cost effectiveness? About creating compatibility between organizational goals and human values in the language of organizational behavior, or about staffing and funding decisions in terms of sustainable results or process re-engineering? For these are the kinds of terms our CAs are likely to use. Most recent CAs, if they come from academic backgrounds, have come from either the schools of business or from the quantitative sciences, according to a recent study; educational institutions are increasingly seeking business-oriented leadership and fewer humanists now occupy the highest rungs of CA (Mangan 1998, A43). There is, of course, considerable resistance among humanities-trained faculty to think and speak in these more businesslike terms, and with good reason; they are terms from fields we distrust because they are so different from our own enterprises. In *Management Fads in Higher Education: Where They Come From, What They Do, Why They Fail*, Robert Birnbaum (2000) notes that "Institutions of higher education . . . . function in a trust market in which people do not know exactly what they are buying and may not discover its value for years. . . . Compared to business firms, colleges and universities have multiple and conflicting goals and intangible outcomes" (215-16). To think of dealing with our more number- and product-oriented colleagues and supervisors in a business-like way can seem a betrayal of that trust market, and the goals and outcomes for which we stand.

But if our *rhetorical* approach to our administrators is cast in the conceptual frames of their disciplines, are we not more likely to attract these busy people's attention and gain their trust? Rhetorically, this seems like such a simple decision: it doesn't mean changing what we do or what we value, the nature of *our* trust market, but how we *talk* about it. We tell our tutors and our tutoring clients this all the time. Yet how many writing center administrators have been prepared to do this before accepting their positions, or have learned to do so once on it? Linda Houston (1999) perceptively points out that "Very little is written on the funding of Writing Labs and the politics of them. . . . In all situations, one must be clever in order to secure funding and navigate the politics for a program that meets the needs of the students but is not a required part of a technical program. How do you do that as a Writing Lab Coordinator?" (119).

To look at this issue more closely, I surveyed sixty attendees at the WCenter networking breakfast at the 1998 CCCC conference in Chicago. Eighty percent of the respondents were center directors. Admittedly, this was a convenience sample and may not represent the field as a whole, but given that many of the Executive Board members of the then-NWCA were there, that many active, experienced, and well-known practitioners in our field were there, I believe that the results they reported have considerable significance for us as administrative practitioners. The results of this survey point to some surprising, perhaps even disturbing trends among center directors.

Thirty-five percent of the respondents had PhDs, over 36% had MAs or were ABD, and another eight percent had other doctorates. Only one of the sixty had a degree in any kind of administrative area (educational administration). I asked if the respondents had taken formal coursework or a workshop in, or had other training in, a variety of fields: 72% had preparation in rhetorical theory, 85% in composition and pedagogy, and 56% each in linguistics and in educational methods. Since many centers are housed in and draw their personnel from English departments, this was to be expected; as Steve Braye wryly remarks, "most of us who direct . . . WCs came out of English depts and are comfortable with the career development notions they represent" (Simpson, Braye, and Boquet 157). But on the administrative preparation side, it was a different story: in my survey, only 20% had preparation in management, 10% in accounting, just under 12% in business administration, 16% in educational administration, 20% in organizational psychology, and 10% in marketing.

Similar results came when I looked at the major works respondents had read. First, I selected a small number of well-known books and articles in writing center theory. Almost 82% of the respondents had read North's "The Idea of a Writing Center" (1984) and 80% had read Mickey Harris's book on tutoring (1982). More than 71% had read Mullin and Wallace's theoretical collection *Intersections* (1994). A respectable 40% of respondents had read Marilyn Cooper's "Really Useful Knowledge" (1995). But only five percent had read Richard and

Barbara Smith Gephardt's *Academic Advancement in Composition Studies* (1997), which deals with skills for dealing successfully with administrators. On the business side, of the three best-selling business books of 1997, 40% of respondents had read Steven Covey's *The Seven Habits of Highly Effective People* (1989), but only 23.3% had read Tom Peters's classic *In Search of Excellence* (1982), a book widely admired by CAs. Thirty percent of my respondents had read some book on quality management (including Peters's), but only about 11% had read a book on marketing communications. (However, 26.6% had read the third best-seller, Scott Adam's *The Dilbert Principle* [1996]; at least the cartoons get around.)

These results suggest that the writing center people I surveyed are well- and even superbly qualified to train tutors and articulate the theoretical stances and concerns of writing centers, but they lack familiarity with the kinds of discourse and conceptual frames that administrators often work in—either from formal training or from informal self-education. They don't read the literature, they don't seek out the training, and this puts them at a distinct disadvantage in making their cases to central administration. It is hard to explain in economic terms the value of your service when you don't speak economics, after all. When only ten percent of a widely experienced group of WCAs has training in either accounting or marketing, is it any wonder that we see so many inquiries on electronic discussion lists like "I need to market my center—should I give out pencils?" or "Help! They're cutting my budget! How do I get it back?"

Work like Bob Barnett's (1997) with the language of institutional mission statements, the examples in Kinkead and Simpson (2000) and in Harris's 1997 essay, Neal Lerner's critique of center assessment methods (2001), the perceptive analyses of typical writing center prose by Pete Carino (2002): these begin to model the kinds of rhetorical practices that WCAs can use instead of speaking and writing, in Carino's terms, "like outlaws plotting subversively in an out-of-the-way tavern" (92) or, perhaps even more rhetorically ineffectively, the discourses of victimization when talking about our interactions with administration. As Ray Wallace wrote in "Text Linguistics: External Entries into 'Our' Community" (1994):

> We complain about our budgets, about our low status in our departments, and about how even our own composition colleagues outside our centers don't understand us! We are becoming our own worst enemies in the profes-

sion—if all we can do is complain about how badly we are treated, how no one sees our worth in the composing process, and how we never are given enough resources to do our job, then we clearly are not doing enough to sell ourselves to the external forces who control much of our destiny. . . . We must reach out to other communities in our profession, and such outreach is done by reflection about our own claims and those of other communities. (71)

Such outreach is extremely consistent with a commonly held view of the writing center as source for innovation in our institutional settings, yet perhaps that viewpoint is one of the reasons why we seem to resist so strongly speaking as insiders to instigate such events. Unless we see writing center administration as a rhetorical act, unless we theorize it, interrogate it, and practice it as such, and until we value doing so, we handicap ourselves and the centers we represent.

It might well be argued that the voices Wallace (1994), Simpson (1995), and Maid (1999) describe represent a vocal minority in our world. On the other hand, how many graduate programs in rhetoric and composition, or in English, allow—let alone encourage—students who want to be WPAs or WCAs to reach out to those other communities, and, for instance, take courses in the graduate schools of management or education to prepare themselves for such a career? (Balester and McDonald's recent article [2001] on the training of WPAs and WCAs shows how unusual such training opportunities are.) How many of us get a chance to learn the languages of these other communities? How many of us have taken the steps to educate ourselves to appreciate those other communities' points of view, and negotiate how their discourses might match with our own?

This means, of course, abandoning the expressivist discourse of "WCA as oppressed individual," and turning instead to seeing ourselves as part of not only a system but also an ongoing negotiation. A hard turn but, I think, a necessary one, and one our rhetorical skills prepare us to make. Karen Rodis (2001) notes that

We have been talking for many years now, and misperceptions persist. Moreover, to believe that enlightening the boss will bring an end to these inequities implies that the responsibility for these inequities, as well as the power to correct them, lies primarily with the boss. This implication is dangerous to writing centers in that it renders us powerless: the responsibility and the power lie elsewhere; the best we can do is to convince the powers that be to shine on us. In fact, it is empowering to writing centers and to those who work there to realize that much of the fault for these inequities—and therefore, much of the power to remedy them—lies with us. (177)

One way we can begin to apply "administration across the curriculum" strategies is to collaborate, as we do in tutor training, to help bridge the gaps in our own knowledge by enlisting the expertise of colleagues in other disciplines. For instance, Neal Lerner (1997) points out, "resources abound for us to engage in self-study. Math and statistics colleagues can help with the numbers, behavioral science faculty can help with the surveys, and offices of institutional research can point to the relevant literature"(3). We encourage our tutors to help train each other; an excellent example is Beth Rapp Young's "Using Heuristics from Other Disciplines in the Writing Center" (2001), where she describes how tutors in nursing and engineering demonstrated the methods of inquiry in their disciplines for other tutors and used these methods to help develop tutoring strategies. Why can we not learn in like manner from our colleagues, and use our shared results to better make our cases to CAs?

Additionally, as we ask our tutors to do with clients, we can also try to understand the viewpoints of our administrative audiences, to see our negotiations with other segments of our organizational communities as a complex but essentially rhetorical situation. This seems much harder for WCAs to do. Most react to such a call the same way Luke reacted to Darth Vader's invitation to join him on the Dark Side of the Force: taking up our lightsabers and preparing to fight to the death. Again, focusing on the rhetorical nature of such acts can help us take the essential step toward negotiating the distances that often exist between centers and other institutional priorities. As Steve Braye says,

> I [need to] strive to understand [the administration's] decision-making process, present ideas to them in terms and/or contexts they can understand (budget numbers mean budget numbers, not narratives), and raise their awareness of issues relating to writing and the center. I should never assume that administrative rejection is a rejection of my ideas, but that competing issues are more important or are argued more effectively. . . . I also don't lose battles, but some victories are deferred due to institutional needs. . . . I also demonstrate that I use monies and time successfully in the best interests of the college, but that we have only begun to tap our potential. We should take

what we are granted and use it to serve our students in a way consistent with the·philosophies of the center and the campus. (Simpson, Braye, and Boquet 168–169)

Note that this position does not require that we agree with positivistic reductions of the Center to a page of pie charts or cost-benefit analyses, but rather that we present *our ideas and our positions* in "texts and/or contexts they can understand." As Barry Maid's (1999) Theory of Organizational Chaos asserts, "power is not something which can be given or assigned. It must be taken and used. . . . People who find themselves in conflict or not 'in' the power structure serve their own needs best when they find the chinks in the organization" and take advantage of them (210).

Some, of course, would argue that even this rhetorical repositioning means that centers are participating in their own marginalization or capitulating to the institution. As Beth Boquet (2000) so concisely states it, "To perceive ourselves as being 'allowed' to exist by some external force as long as we prove ourselves 'worthy' is to live with the constant threat of extinction" (23). As much as I admire Boquet's work, I cannot agree with her position here. Centers *are* allowed to exist by an external force, the organizations to which they belong. Atomistic thinking— believing that the centers exist alone on the pinnacle of Truth, or at the center of some isolated world of humanistic belief and inquiry always under attack from the Philistines at the gates—is understandable in theory but not very helpful in practice. We are, for better or worse, part of the institutions that house us. We must learn to represent ourselves as effective parts of those institutions if we accept the challenge of administrating centers. That is our best chance not only to perpetuate what we do well, but also to transform the institutions themselves. If we fail to translate our center-focused anecdotes and instincts into the kinds of persuasion our CAs recognize, we should not be surprised if our efforts fall short. If, on the other hand, we learn to express our importance in the language of our own institutional culture, we improve our chances for success. By changing from the discourse of victimization or opposition to the discourse of administration—that is to say, by understanding and appropriating the rhetorical practices of our administrative audiences—we increase the likelihood that our audiences will understand us, and through understanding respond positively to us. That is what we tell the writers we tutor; that is what we teach our tutors to work on:

establishing common ground and creating ethos by using the language of the audience. We need to do this ourselves.

This appropriation of discourse strategies from administration does not mean that we should change over to a number-crunching perspective, or only judge our successes by quantitative figures; far from it. The trust market works both ways. Even if we must sometimes describe our work in the language of quantitative assessments, there is still space for us to describe the quality of our work as well. But as George Eliot wryly observed, "We have all got to remain calm and call things by the same names other people call them by." When I argue that we must practice what we preach as writing center administrators, I mean that we must remember that directing a writing center is not only a pedagogical, political, and theoretical act, it is a rhetorical one as well. We lose nothing by learning about and employing the conventions, disciplinary practices, and linguistic expectations of administrators, just as we have lost nothing by learning about the conventions, disciplinary practices, and linguistic expectations of literary theorists, educational philosophers, cognitive psychologists, and yes, even chaos mathematicians.

The Council of Writing Program Administrators has already conceded this point, beginning to run workshops at conferences and in the summer to train writing specialists in the discourses and practices of administration. It is time for the IWCA to make an organized effort to help writing center specialists develop these professional skills as well. We should be arguing for allowing graduate students in composition and rhetoric and literature to gain the experience and training in other disciplines that will let them succeed, eventually, as WCAs. They should have the opportunity to take courses in organizational psychology, educational administration, finance, and the like, so that they are prepared to do the best possible jobs when they assume administrative responsibilities. We should be mentoring new WCAs, helping demystify the processes of finance, marketing, and management. We should be discussing the books and trends that our administrators are reading and responding to, so that we know what language we'll be hearing next. We should share examples and methods of making center cases to administration so that other members of our community can learn from our successful (and even unsuccessful) strategies; the new Writing Centers Research Project at the University of Louisville may help in this regard. In short, we should do for ourselves as WCAs what we do for our tutors:

make sure the tools are available to give us the best possible chance to negotiate understanding with our audiences.

Making our case in the language our CAs expect does not mean that we give up any of the advantages of being on the margin, nor that we concede our independence, our humanistic perspectives, our ability to inspire change, or our student-centered focus. Rather, it means that we gain the rhetorical advantages of being able to support, explain, and defend our work in terms that our audiences can't pretend *not* to understand. It means that we use the Force rather than be used by others who wield it better than we do. If we practice as administrators what we preach as tutors, we—and our centers—stand only to benefit.

9

AN IDEAL WRITING CENTER
Re-Imagining Space and Design

Leslie Hadfield

Joyce Kinkead

Tom C. Peterson

Stephanie H. Ray

Sarah S. Preston

We shape our buildings; thereafter, they shape us.

Winston Churchill

The belief that architecture can stimulate health, wealth, and happiness lies at the base of the fascination with *feng shui,* the 3,000-year-old Chinese practice of placing objects, walls, and people in harmony. Some teachers claim that classrooms that have been given the *feng shui* treatment produce students who are "pumped about learning" (May 2000, A10). Others find that clearing clutter, making a place "light and cheery," and adding plants makes common sense; there's no "magic in it" (A10). In Ben Jonson's *The Alchemist* (1610), magic is invoked in the design of a new shop when its owner consults with the pseudo-scientist and astrologist. The salesman certainly believes magic can trick his customers into buying more:

> I am a young beginner, and am building
> Of a new shop, and't like your worship, just
> At corner of a street—here's the plot on't—
> Which way I should make my door, by necromancy,
> And where my shelves, and which should be for boxes,
> And which for pots. I would be glad to thrive, sir.
> And I was wished to your worship by a gentleman,

One Captain Face, that says you know men's planets,
And their good angels, and their bad.

(Ben Jonson, *The Alchemist*, 1.3.10–16)

Invoking magic in a store design improves trade? The look and feel of architectural spaces does influence its occupants and visitors. As Winston Churchill philosophized, "We shape our buildings; thereafter, they shape us." On one campus, a new liberal arts building received architectural awards, but its occupants termed it the "death star" for its inhospitable structure. Although an imaginative architectural place, its concrete form and substance do not foster creativity.

Learning can take place anywhere, from the storefront buildings of a tribal college to a grassy quad during springtime. In fact, we expect imagination to thrive in unimaginative spaces.[1] Terry Vaughan, architect and teacher, "believes in the importance of connecting people, places, and landscape, . . . that teaching and learning are more effective in places of particular character and clear position within the university" (1991, 15). Keeping that philosophy in mind, if the opportunity presents itself to enhance or build an ideal learning space—in this case, an ideal writing center—what are the considerations? What are the needed resources? To whom do we turn for consultation? On many campuses, expertise resides in campus planners, support staff, and design faculty.

To think about the spaces where tutoring occurs, we assembled an interdisciplinary research team: three undergraduates (a writing tutor and two interior design students) and two faculty members (a professor of English and a professor of interior design). The undergraduates led the research project with guidance from the faculty mentors. While the vocabularies of our different disciplines produced a certain language barrier, we learned that what we had in common was a sense of *process*.

PEDAGOGY AND DESIGN

When charting unfamiliar territory, we turn to that which has been written on the subject. Unfortunately, there is a paucity of literature on the pedagogical building or learning space. A good deal exists on designing elementary school rooms (remember the "pod" concept?), but the challenge of creating imaginative college classroom spaces gets short shrift. Even when we do find some useful information about college classrooms and construction, a space such as a writing center—which is neither classroom nor office—is not addressed.[2] We reviewed the concepts of effective working and learning spaces before we turned to the particular task of designing a tutorial center.

Architect and academic Josef Stagg (1991) divides architects into two categories: formalist (which emphasizes the visual) and behaviorist (which emphasizes human behavior). The formalists controlled corporate America for a number of years, favoring designs that won awards but did not provide comfort to employees stuck in mind-numbing, cookie-cutter cubicles. Architectural behaviorists focus more on "environmentally and behaviorally oriented approaches to design" (20). They note that task performance and job satisfaction are affected by ambient conditions (e.g., uncomfortable room temperature, stuffy air quality, lack of natural light, loud colors, surrounding noise) and room size, presence and arrangement of furniture and equipment (21). Behaviorists lead in "creating diverse, vital spaces that foster creativity and serendipity" (Gladwell 2000, 60), and their corporate *campuses* may very well provide the model that will eventually arrive—ironically arrive, we might add—on college campuses. In the corporate world, workplace design has as its goal creating spaces that offer happy and productive work lives to employees and invite interaction among disparate groups of people. An office that follows this tack might very well look more like a village or feel more like a neighborhood.

The architectural philosophy of Christopher Alexander of the University of California, Berkeley Center for Environmental Structure, articulated in a three-volume series, resonated with our research team. He endorses the concept of organic architecture based on piecemeal growth and participatory decision-making. *The Oregon Experiment* (1975), although somewhat dated, provides key concepts for thinking about what a campus looks like. Based on the idea that people "should design for themselves their own houses, streets, and communities," the book espouses principles adopted by the University of Oregon as it replaced its traditional planning with what were almost 30 years ago—and probably still are—radical concepts about process and outcomes. "Everyone helps to shape the parts of the environment that he knows best" (38) according to Alexander. People who use the spaces "must own them psychologically" (41). Universities are places that "are created and modified by the people who pass through them[;] the university will gradually be shaped by an accumulation of actual human experience and, as such, will be a place fit for other, newer human experiences—a place far fitter than any impersonal and inflexible environment could ever be" (49).

The three volumes by Alexander and his colleagues demonstrate that structures can be imaginative, healthy, and inspiring. Besides *The Oregon Experiment*, Alexander's first volume, *A Timeless Way of Building* (1979), laid the foundation for his architectural theory while volume two in the series, *A Pattern Language* (1977), defined an architectural language to enact that theory. Of some 250 patterns developed, Alexander found 18 "special patterns to solve . . . problems . . . peculiar to universities." These particular patterns focus on the concepts of an open university, student housing distribution, living learning circles, department space, local administration, classroom distribution, student workplaces, real learning in cafes, and department hearths. These are coupled with overarching principles of positive outdoor space, arcades, wings of light, south facing outdoors, tree places, access to water, and activity nodes (105–106). Alexander's concept of "wings of light," making use of natural illumination, becomes important to writing center design since so much close reading occurs there.

Alexander proposes including students, staff, and faculty members in discussion of physical design. Would that it were so. Typical to campuses, but antithetical to Alexander's principles, is the "master plan" that charts the next 20 years. It is the rare faculty member who actually knows what committee or office on campus determines the physical space that surrounds him or her. The American Association of University Professors (AAUP) envisions a "faculty role whenever *academic quality is at stake*" (9, emphasis added) to represent teachers' and students' perspectives. As a special issue of *Academe* on "The Pedagogical Building" (1991) notes: "good rooms will not necessarily make us good teachers, but bad rooms will assuredly make us bad ones." If faculty members participated on the planning committee for a humanities building would seats have been bolted in place in classrooms? We think not.

The effects of architectural decisions greet teachers daily. Why is a lectern fixed before the screen so that films are difficult to see, or why are classroom doors positioned in such a way that tardy students must necessarily disrupt the class? Terry Wilson Vaughan (1991) maintains that "good architecture can inspire a new understanding of teaching" and influence curricula, an observation made after her academic program was moved among a number of university sites, "some magnificent, some faceless" (12). Some spaces promoted synergy between two studio classes and their faculty, and student projects were the best they ever had been, she asserts. Harvey J. Kaye reminds us that it's not just our classrooms but also our offices that reflect faculty members' "intellectual traditions" and serve as "vessels of self-expression." Yes, there is "pedagogical significance" in offices that are monotonous "institutional spaces" until shaped by the desire to turn them "into exhibition spaces that materially substantiate our arguments and tales" (B16).

A writing center is a curious mix of office and classroom, but metaphors of home are also often used to describe writing centers with the proverbial coffee pot offering a welcoming cup. Muriel Harris highlighted the welcoming cup in her chapter in Kinkead and Harris (1993a) that described the writing center she built at Purdue (4). Yes, home and hominess are important, if intangible. According to architectural theorists, space and design decisions should result in a space where people enjoy spending time and where they are happy, productive, creative, and social. Those are certainly worthy goals for a writing center.

We move now from the overarching principles of university and workplace design to the specific task of designing an effective writing center, drawing on the participatory process delineated by Alexander and the expertise of our Design Program team members.

THE DESIGN PROCESS

For our project, we assumed a new building at Alchemy University, which has a student population of 10,000. Other assumptions: the writing center employs sufficient tutors to assure that four to six tutors are available in the center at any given time; a director, assistant director, and full time receptionist are on staff. The main activity of AU's center is one-to-one tutoring, but areas for group conferences and study are needed, too. The final supposition is that a computer lab should be adjacent to the center for flexibility between word processing and tutoring.

The research team interviewed those who use and work in a center. For designers, the term for research and data collection is *programming*, a systematic approach to gathering, analyzing, and interpreting specific quantitative and qualitative project requirements. (See the appendix for specific questions to be asked.) Following this stage, the designers developed a number of *space* plans, working with their informants in an iterative way to arrive at a design that architecturally enhances and functionally contributes to the mission of the center. The physical environment is especially important in peer tutoring. For some students, seeking help is anxiety provoking. Our goal was to create a non-threatening, comfortable environment that generates—rather than inhibits—conversation. We took these concepts and issues into consideration as we debated the plan for our writing center, adding what we know about design that makes for an inviting learning space. Not surprisingly, all three groups—tutors, students, and staff—share common ideas about what makes an ideal writing center.

THE SPACE PLAN

The environment that we developed for an ideal writing center is calm, non-threatening, and easily understood. (See Figures 1 and 2.) The overall square footage of our center is 4,813, the main area totaling 2,788 and the computer lab 2,025. At the entrance of the writing center is an information center, a visual that serves as an introduction even if the center is closed. Bulletin boards outside the entrance demystify tutoring for the first-time visitor by offering explanations as well as photographs of actual sessions. As the students walk in, they immediately see a reception desk where they can sign in and be welcomed. Cross (2000) points out that in environmental psychology, people have a "general response to a room and will be unsure at first in a new space. Even air movement affects the occupants."

The designers on our team echoed this theory by reminding us that the question always in the mind of a first-time visitor to any space is "How will I be welcomed and is this a situation where I'll find myself embarrassed?" Seeing into a space begins to obviate a sense of dread.

The room is comfortable, with familiar eight-foot ceilings; light, calming colors; soft carpet; plants, and soft lighting—provided by cove lighting and a skylight. Daylight is considered more inviting and conducivè to a positive work environment, but ambient, task, and accent light sources are also used for specific areas. The indirect cove lighting, using warm, fluorescent lamps, makes a horizontal line throughout the room, which has a calming effect, bounces off the ceiling, and eliminates shadows. A waiting area features durable yet comfortable sofa and chairs covered in soft green fabrics, green being a universally accepted and reassuring color. The green chosen here is a *cool* color, but almost any color can be perceived as calming if presented in the proper value

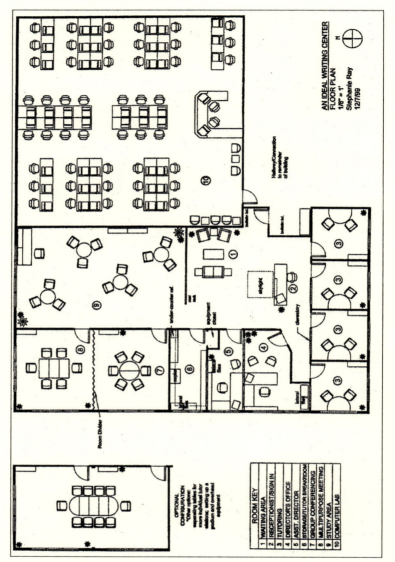

Figure 1. Space plan for the writing center. Design by Stephanie H. Ray.

and level of intensity. The table and shelves are made from light wood, which warms the room.

A moveable room divider separates the waiting area and the group study area and can be removed to extend the room for workshops or meetings. While in place, it gives the study area privacy. Tutors expressed concern about noise levels during their interviews, which led the designers to include an acoustics plan, taking into account natural and electronic solutions. Speech privacy and intelligibility can be accomplished simply by recognizing that thick, porous, and soft materials absorb more sound than do materials that are thin, dense, and hard. *White noise,* a subtle, electronically-produced background noise, is used to mask conversational level dialogue.

Across from the study area, along the west wall, a group conference room and a multipurpose meeting room are closed off from the rest of the center by a wall to lower the noise level. This room could be the site of the tutor-development seminar. Inside, an accordion-type divider separates the group conference section from the multipurpose section. It can be opened to join the two rooms. The round table in the group conference room can be split and added to the ends of the rectangular tables in the multipurpose room to create a large race-track-shaped conference table. This also allows room for a podium and computer technology used in presentations such as an overhead projector and a flat screen video system. These rooms, like the waiting area, have soothing colors and soft lighting.

A small workroom, which serves as a storage place and a tutor station, with lateral files and a copier, separates the group areas from the director's office. This room provides a sound barrier between the louder group areas and the quieter tutoring area. The tutors asked for a place to "dump our backpacks" while the director said, "don't clutter up the workroom." The types of storage required and the pieces of equipment to be accommodated drive the size and configuration of this area. It may be the one space that requires a plumbing plan if a sink is included for receptions and lunches.

The director requested an office that is central; she can see the tutoring rooms through the office door. The trade-off between oversight and privacy is a difficult one. A director needs access, influence, and control, according to Smith (1994, 40) but also engages in confidential conversations regarding the administration of the center. A new role—fundraiser and steward to donors—means the director may also use the writing center as a space for receptions. A staff member that must be all, see all, and hear all challenges even good design. For the director, who is in the center for long hours, we must never forget the importance of windows to her well-being. Likewise, the *task* chair, mounted on a pedestal base with casters, must be comfortable.

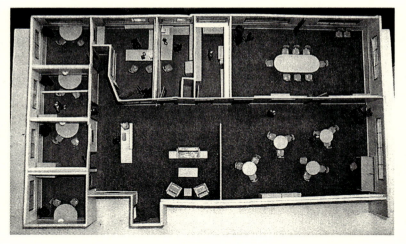

Figure 2. Photograph of model. Model by Stephanie H. Ray and Sarah S. Preston.

The tutoring rooms, positioned along the south wall behind the receptionist, have the same encouraging colors and soft lighting. While round tables are standard, in these small rooms, a half-round table is placed against the sidewall and has two *pull-up* or *guest* chairs. The surfaces of the table and the simple fabric designs eliminate distractions and strain and make it easier for students to focus on their papers during a conference. A window on the south wall, which allows the warmest light in for most of the day, and sconces above the table that bring the light closer to the students' level and reduce shadows, create a bright but not harsh environment. Our designers considered surface mountings, pendants, indirect, and down-lights before deciding on the sconces. A designer uses specific lighting language, beginning with the type of light or *lamp*. While most people would describe a lamp as an item to set on a table, technically, a *lamp* is a *light bulb*, which comes in three basic types: *incandescent, fluorescent,* and *high-intensity discharge.* The electrical plan includes lighting but also wiring, data ports, and switches. The volubility of technology dictates planning for sufficient power outlets as well as data ports and, possibly, docking stations. Wireless connectivity may be a possibility. The space is designed to accommodate tutorials based on hard copy or computer screen copy. Each tutoring room also includes standard reference materials organized for quick and easy retrieval. Finally, the tutors said, "please don't forget plants and art," aesthetic additions to the rooms.

This non-threatening environment enhances writing center conferences by helping the students feel more relaxed and welcome. The design conveys to students that the writing center is a place where they can receive help without the pressure that comes with a classroom environment.

Our research revealed yet another value that is included in our plan: *green design*. Because we are aware of the environmental consequences of our design choices and our daily behaviors we have included elements to minimize "negative environmental impact" ("Green" 2001, 5). These elements include efficient, reliable heating and cooling systems as well as policies for our use of natural resources such as paper.

BUILDING VERSUS REMODELING

While the construction of an ideal writing center may not be within reach for every campus, the components that enhance the center can be implemented in remodeling. Plants, artwork, furniture, colors, and lighting are all factors that can easily be changed or added to improve a writing center. A campus' deferred maintenance budget may be available for such changes. Resources in time, money, and effort are, of course, major issues in any plan for building or remodeling space. Surprisingly, the current cost of building new space or remodeling old is nearly equal. Some campuses employ "organizational experts" to assess efficiency of existing space and make suggestions for improved flow of traffic and human interactions. Space has been called "the organization's second most expensive resource" (Becker and Steele 1995), and yet the literature on the architecture of effective learning environments is precious little.

The environment where interaction between and among people occurs is crucial as it affects the way people feel and, therefore, the way people interact. A well-designed writing center has an identity that speaks implicitly to its patrons. It's not alchemy. It is instead the collaboration of experts—those in design and those in writing—who come together in a participatory, iterative process to plan and structure an environment for learning.

APPENDIX

The term for research and data collection in architecture and interior design is *programming*, a systematic approach to gathering, analyzing, and interpreting specific quantitative and qualitative project requirements. The better the response to a designer's questions, the better the overall outcome of a project. An initial conversation between the client and the designer/architect might include information on flaws, problems, and situations of the current setting, but the staff should be prepared to address the following, which will be useful in the development of the project *program*.

1. Usable square footage requirements: from existing or new construction and how this will be allocated, i.e., by user group or support function.
2. Current and projected user requirements, keeping in mind long-range planning to avoid underestimating future needs.
3. Adjacency requirements: who needs to be next to whom and what.
4. Job classifications of those using the space: director, assistant director, tutors. (Some campuses will have square footage amounts assigned to particular ranks or positions.)
5. Work surface area: how many and what are their ideal sizes?
6. Machine use: list all types of equipment to be used (e.g., computers, printers, copiers).
7. Workstation area: how much space is ideal for the task to be performed, offering specific dimensions if possible.
8. Conference requirements: number to accommodate, which indicates number of chairs needed—with or without arms—and type of chairs.
9. Storage: how much storage and of what type.
10. Configuration: include any ideas about where work areas should be located and if it's important to face a certain direction.
11. Lighting: consider ambient (general) lighting, task lighting, and accent lighting. The latter is often left out but can provide a significant boost to the aesthetic quality of the environment.
12. Accessories: what types of objects will be added that will be functional (e.g., tack boards) or aesthetic (e.g., artwork, plants) and how many.
13. Safety/ADA: compliance with fire codes and with regulations regarding Americans with Disabilities Act.
14. Institutional image, branding, or look that may include specified character, detailing, and symbolic values.

10

MENTORING IN ELECTRONIC SPACES
Using Resources to Sustain Relationships

JAMES A. INMAN
DONNA N. SEWELL

Electronic media influence more and more of contemporary writing center theory and practice, whether offering new tutoring options, stimulating outreach and other professional connections, or providing new genres and forms for scholarship. Books like *Wiring the Writing Center* (Hobson 1998) and *Taking Flight with OWLs: Examining Electronic Writing Center Work* (Inman and Sewell 2002) have identified specific aspects of electronic media's influence, as has the CD-ROM *The OWL Construction and Maintenance Guide* (Inman and Gardner 2002). Leading journals like *Writing Center Journal, Writing Lab Newsletter, Computers and Composition*, and *Kairos: A Journal of Rhetoric, Technology, and Pedagogy* (http://english.ttu.edu/kairos) have also featured publications about the increasing influence of electronic media on writing center theory and practice.

Electronic media enable writing center professionals to stay connected to each other. Such interactive media as electronic mail (email), electronic lists (e-lists), and MOOs have enabled several important forums.[1] Perhaps most prominent is WCenter, an e-list created by Lady Falls Brown and Fred Kemp at Texas Tech University and now moderated and maintained solely by Brown.[2] In operation since 1991, it provides a popular discussion forum for writing center professionals, and its active participant base includes many prominent individuals in the writing center community, all of whom contribute regularly. Reflecting this popularity, as well as the importance of the e-list as a forum for professional exchange, citation of WCenter posts has been evident for some time in publications (Brown 2000; "Conversations"). Another important electronic forum is PeerCentered, created by Clinton Gardner in 1998.[3] Initially held mostly in The Virtual Writing Center (a

MOO at Salt Lake Community College), PeerCentered sessions enabled writing center professionals to discuss theoretical and practical issues in real time. Now, Gardner has shifted PeerCentered to an asynchronous blogging community, where individuals share ideas as their time allows. His choice reflects not just the changing nature of technology options, but also the material conditions around writing center work; professionals struggled to commit to a specific time every week, so the asynchronous format has proven more popular. Both forums, WCenter and PeerCentered, help us consider the possibilities of electronic media for connecting writing center professionals in new and important ways.

The issue is more than opportunity, however. Contemporary writing center theory and practice compel us to learn about how to connect with other professionals as effectively as possible through electronic media. After all, the writing center community has now become global, with the relatively recent change of the National Writing Centers Association to the International Writing Centers Association, as well as the emergence of the European Writing Centers Association and new initiatives in such countries as South Africa. Budgets simply do not allow everyone to travel globally and to connect with each other in person, but we can utilize electronic media to reach out, and we need to do more of this sort of work. If we are truly an international organization, then the same support systems and professional initiatives that are available in national contexts should be available around the world, including opportunities for writing center professionals to sustain each other in ways like mentoring. New and veteran writing center professionals need each other's support and guidance, but we cannot just magically begin this work. We also need training—detailed knowledge about how to mentor across great distances by using resources like electronic media. Thus far, the writing center community has simply done what it can, and the results have been useful, but we need to know and do much more.

We begin below with a definition of *mentoring*, followed by a corresponding definition of *electronic mentoring*. We then apply this definition to WCenter practices, using the resulting knowledge to craft recommendations for future mentoring practices. We study the past and the present in this chapter to present information valuable for the future. For too long now, writing center professionals have had limited or no guidance about how to utilize electronic media effectively in reaching out to colleagues for purposes like mentoring. This chapter fills that gap and, we hope, meets the compelling need for such specific guidance. In so doing, we hope it becomes part of a roadmap for the future success of the writing center community—a truly global writing center community, where electronic media help us span great distances to work closely together and guide each other to professional success.

DEFINING ELECTRONIC MENTORING

Mentoring is a contested term. Simultaneously, it suggests identifying an earnest commitment to the development of colleagues, and imposing values onto those colleagues. This section surveys definitions and implications of mentoring before offering our own definition of electronic mentoring.

Mentoring has been defined as a form of teaching. The idea of mentoring appears in Homer's *Odyssey*, which includes a half-God, half-man figure named Mentor, who guides Telemachus. In the American colonial period, mentoring linked to apprenticeship. Learners sought out "masters" of a skill or trade and then worked under them, eventually becoming masters themselves, forging ahead on their own. Recent discussions of mentoring have constructed mentors as professional guides, helping protégés develop and follow maps to professional success. Theresa Enos and Richard C. Gebhardt both wrote chapters on mentoring in *Academic Advancement in Composition Studies: Scholarship, Publication, Promotion, Tenure* (Gebhardt and Gebhardt 1997), with Gebhardt's chapter in particular emphasizing that administrators must foster mentoring relationships. Likewise, several essays in Gary A. Olson and Todd W. Taylor's *Publishing in Rhetoric and Composition* (1997) explore the way publication can operate in a mentoring fashion, in which experienced writers develop collaborative relationships with less-experienced writers and develop projects together.

Critics of mentoring have identified potentially problematic elements of mentoring relationships. In the *Odyssey* example cited above, the idea that Mentor is half-God clearly suggests his superiority over those humans with whom he worked. The American colonial "master" model demonstrates the same hierarchical relationship. In the Olson and Taylor collection (1997), Janice Lauer critiques traditional, hierarchical mentoring, wondering why graduate students cannot extend that role and become mentors themselves, or why more genuinely collaborative relationships are not imagined between mentor and protégé. Such reality goes directly to voice (who gets to speak as a mentor) and to authority (whose voice counts and why). Indeed, mentoring can perpetuate injustice and oppression instead of empowerment.

Considerations of "electronic mentoring" have attracted attention both to the way mentoring has been defined traditionally and its potential to be problematic for mentor and protégé alike. Discussions about electronic mentoring occurred during the first "Town Hall" forum at the 2000 Computers and Writing conference in Fort Worth, Texas; the theme for the forum was "Graduate Student(s) Matter(s)!" Ten scholars presented position statements, all published together in issue 5.2 of Kairos. Rebecca Rickly (2000) cites work by Theresa Enos to identify the social realities of mentoring in the academy: "Mentoring, in practice, grows out of a master/apprentice model, a model that invokes patriarchal and hierarchical power issues. Such a model indeed fits nicely into an academic institution, with its stratified power structures and hierarchical organization." Bill Condon (2000) suggests, however, that different opportunities exist for those working with electronic media, adding also a layer of responsibility for those who have been mentored to become mentors themselves:

> I'm arguing that those of us already active in the field have a duty to cheer on those just entering it. As we fulfill that duty, we almost instantly create new colleagues whose work helps ease our paths at the same time as we ease theirs. I'm also arguing that in other fields, graduate students represent the future of the field; in ours, graduate students have always represented the present as well—starting with a graduate student named Hugh Burns, whose dissertation about computer-assisted Topoi basically founded the field.

Condon's (2000) and Rickly's (2000) perspectives represent a sensible take on the nature of mentoring. Condon is right that electronic media sometimes change the equation—perhaps not completely redefining the hierarchical social system associated typically with mentoring in the academy, but at least opening spaces wherein those who would otherwise be protégés by default (graduate students, for instance) can become mentors themselves. Yet Rickly is right that we need to remember at all times the problematic potential of mentoring relationships, asking ourselves who leads and why, and thinking together about redefining mentoring to reflect less innate hierarchy.

Rickly's, Condon's, and indeed all perspectives on electronic mentoring prove relative to the access conditions associated with the electronic media utilized in any mentoring interaction. That is, because access conditions are never equal and rarely equitable, mentoring interactions are necessarily never technologically equal themselves. The difference may be as seemingly straightforward as that in which one participant in a mentoring interaction has a new computer and broadband Internet access, while another participant has an older computer and dial-in access. However, as scholars like Cynthia L. Selfe and Charles Moran have noted in a series of publications, matters may also be more complex. Neighborhoods, particularly in inner-city and rural environments, do not always have the telecommunications infrastructure needed; in fact, a number of neighborhoods in the United States do not have phone service, a reality that often surprises individuals accustomed to positive access conditions. Globally, access problems are amplified as third-world nations in particular do not often possess a strong telecommunications infrastructure. Simply put, access must be addressed in any careful and responsible examination of electronic mentoring, because it's important not just who's able to participate actively, but also who's limited and who's unable to participate at all.

In crafting our own definition of "electronic mentoring" for this chapter, we take our cue from scholars like Rickly and Condon, attempting to keep the positive possibilities of mentoring relationships without losing sight of their problematic implications. We also remember to keep the material conditions around such mentoring practices strongly in mind. Thus, we ultimately define electronic mentors for the writing center community as online colleagues who collaborate with others, successfully meeting the material challenges around and between them, to help these colleagues see both themselves and their evolving professional identities, as well as the broader profession around them. Electronic mentors may be seasoned writing center faculty, staff, and administrators, but they may also be students, colleagues in industry, and others with important experiences and ideas to share. Correspondingly, we define electronic mentoring in the following way: offering responsible professional support and guidance to colleagues across institutional positions and contexts through the use of electronic media, working proactively to mediate challenging material conditions around the use of these media. We invite readers to imagine electronic mentoring as a truly global endeavor, and to see such work as innately valuable for the emerging global writing center community, connecting all of us in new and important ways that are sure to further the community's future.

WCENTER: AN ELECTRONIC WRITING CENTER COMMUNITY

Building on the definition of electronic mentoring above, and our earlier discussion of the writing center community's compelling need for knowledge about how it is best done, we now look specifically at WCenter, the e-list maintained by Brown. We focus on the attention WCenter has received as an important electronic forum for forging connections among writing center professionals, then provide results from a survey of subscribers we conducted, as well as a case study of WCenter interaction.

WCenter functions as a wonderful resource for writing center professionals,[4] in part because of the people who subscribe. Theresa Ammirati (2000) posts to WCenter a specific example of how Muriel Harris became her mentor when Ammirati began creating a writing center at her institution:

> She sent me materials, answered my panicky questions over the phone, lent tremendous moral and physical support—so that even twenty years (and two other directors in the last five years) later, I see the results of her professional and personal kindness and concern in our very successful operation. Through the years, having actually met Mickey in person only once or twice, I think of her as a mentor and a support, in short, an exemplar.

Harris generously invested time and effort into helping Ammirati. Also, most of this mentoring occurred at a distance. While telephone and postal mail served as the primary means of mentoring in this instance, technology such as WCenter can increase the possibilities of such support. Ammirati's anecdote, then, provides a perspective on long-distance mentoring as we look at WCenter's potential.

WCenter first received a great deal of scholarly attention at a panel for the 1998 Conference on College Composition and Communication in Chicago, Illinois. Lady Falls Brown posted a summary of that session ("Session H.17") to WCenter on April 7, 1998. Brown states that she focused on the history of WCenter, Bobbie Silk analyzed the way WCenter discourages dissent, Paula Gillespie examined WCenter's use as a research tool, Jeanne Simpson explored WCenter's role in her life and her role as advisor to members with questions about administration,

Stephen Newmann wondered whether WCenter should count as professional activity, Jo Koster Tarvers suggested research on the typical newbie experience, and Muriel Harris explored reasons people lurk. Our chapter focuses on an important question Brown notes as being from Jeanne Simpson: "How can the mentoring role on WCenter be sustained and protected?" We also consider what counts as sound electronic mentoring, and ponder the potentially problematic implications mentoring might bring. In other words, does WCenter support electronic mentoring? If so, how? If not, why not? Which practices should continue, and which should be re-examined?

Part of what allows for the possibility of electronic mentoring is the welcoming and generous ethos of WCenter, described in a post by Simone Gers (1998): "I enjoy the friendly banter and camaraderie. These aspects of the list suggest to this neophyte that the group is friendly and open to new voices." Paula Gillespie (2002) claims a connection between WCenter's atmosphere and its creation of a community:

> As I look over the earliest logs of WCenter in the archives, I'm struck by the clowning, the fellowship, the good-natured community established there, and indeed these qualities are the reasons that many busy administrators do *not* subscribe: it's too much for some people, and they tell us so as they unsubscribe. But in that clowning, there is a sense of community-building that makes it easy to contribute, easy to ask and sometimes answer questions. (41)

An initial attempt, then, to answer Simpson's question suggests that WCenter continue to create a friendly environment, open to newcomers, free for the most part from the crankiness sometimes found on other academic e-lists. The sense of community that develops out of that friendliness keeps people returning to WCenter. Without such an ethos, mentoring relationships may not develop.

Survey Responses

To determine further how members of WCenter understand electronic mentoring, Inman (2001) posted a questionnaire to the list. He wanted to obtain specific commentary about such mentoring beyond the sorts of regular-posting list messages we cited above. Only seven participants responded to this questionnaire initially, so Inman randomly sampled WCenter subscribers who had posted to the list in 2001 in order to gather email addresses; he then reposted the questionnaire to those fifty-two participants. Fourteen of the fifty-two recipients responded from twelve states and the District of Columbia.[5] These participants represent private and public institutions; liberal arts colleges, community colleges, comprehensive colleges, and research I institutions; religiously affiliated institutions and corporate educational institutions. It's fair to say, then, that the participants also represent a host of different access conditions, including both high-tech and low-tech hardware and software, cable and dial-in Internet connectivity, and more. The WCenter posts cited in this section are specific responses to the survey Inman conducted.

Most respondents accept that informal mentoring occurs online via the many requests for help and advice that occurs in this electronic environment. A writing center director may post a question about staffing a center, preparing annual reports, or using faculty notification forms, and within a few days the director may receive public responses to the post in addition to responses sent via private email. This kind of exchange sets up WCenter as an information resource. Lauren Fitzgerald (2001) suggests that the advice alone can move toward mentoring: "I see lots of advice, and some of that advice seems to gel into a kind of mentoring for its recipients, particularly when everyone responding to the original post refers to the sender by name, really talks to him/her, and addresses his/her problem specifically." While cautious about labeling this practice *mentoring* because of its transitory nature, this type of exchange creates a sense of community, reassuring the poster that others share his or her concerns. Gillespie (2002) compares WCenter to other academic forums:

> It can sound like a conference session with a good give and take, but it has two unique qualities: Those who need to know can determine the shape the discussion will take, because there is no need to mask insecurity behind a show of professionalism. We can say, "We are just starting out and need help." Imagine saying that at a CCCC session. The WCenter session can be more attuned to audience and purpose than a conference session, because the audience will speak up and make its needs known.[6]

Those participants who receive public responses sometimes receive the kind of detailed and personal responses that, at least, border on electronic mentoring despite the temporary nature of the relationship.

WCenter also functions as more than an information resource. In his response to the survey, Kurt Bouman (2001) notes that he has engaged in "backchannel conversations" about his work: "This mentoring has been important in keeping me professionally focused and involved, and it makes me feel like a more full and/or substantial member of the comp/rhet community." Lauren Fitzgerald (2001) reports similar experiences to Bouman and values the informal and formal mentoring: "A couple of people took me aside, in offlist discussions, to help me out individually." WCenter creates a potential for electronic mentoring, even when that mentoring does not occur publicly. Those participants who post for advice sometimes receive more sustained career guidance and support delivered through personal email. Without WCenter, though, such opportunities for interaction would be much more limited.

In her response, Katie Fischer (2001) notes the way her own relationship to WCenter members has changed. Originally, she looked for mentors on WCenter, but now she views its participants more as colleagues. Fischer's response indicates a growth in expertise that occurs with time in the field. This changing relationship is apparent in the responses of others as well; Mary Wislocki (2001) states, "Mentoring is an idea that I'm trying to grow into in as many ways as I can." Wislocki's response reminds us of the responsibility involved in helping others, the need to support the WCenter community by assisting those who request assistance.

Aware of the problematic implications of mentoring, Dean Hinnen (2001) notes that "mentoring" isn't quite the right word for what happens on WCenter as "the exchanges have tended to be more 'conversations of equals' than mentoring, per se." Hinnen explains his perspective more fully:

> I do think a certain amount of "mentoring" takes place on lists such as WCenter and WPA-L. However, even the more knowledgeable potential "mentors" on these lists usually refrain from adopting rhetorical positions as "mentors," and instead project an "ethos of equality," as it were, in their mentoring role. It seems to me that the breaking down of the mentor/protégé relationship, which seems to occur naturally on these lists, makes it easier for novices to seek advice. This mentoring in public spaces does, however, require more subtlety than the traditional mentor/protégé role in a face-to-face environment.

Sabrina Peters-Whitehead (2001) also focuses on the "collaborative, non-hierarchical mentoring experience" of WCenter "in which all members of WCenter mentor each other without any designation of certain people being the mentors and others being the 'mentees.'" WCenter, then, manages to provide electronic mentoring to subscribers in a relatively egalitarian manner, allowing those with questions to ask them and those with responses to post them. While members may become authorities in certain areas (such as Jeanne Simpson's expertise on upper-level administration), any member may respond to anyone's post. Because we do not have any better terminology for this collegial mentoring, we continue to use the term *mentoring* for now, despite agreeing with Hinnen (2001) about the practice of mentoring on WCenter.

Jo Koster's (2001) response suggests new directions for WCenter based on her experience on the Chaucer list: "The Chaucer MetaPage at UNC-CH . . . has some 'Chaucer Meta-Mentors'—three experienced scholars who have agreed to two-year terms as online mentors, and visitors to the page can email the mentors directly with specific questions. . . . I wonder again if we couldn't set something like this up." While this suggestion may look like a movement away from the current egalitarian nature of the list, we think it deserves careful consideration. Having designated electronic mentors should not subtract from the daily questions, responses, and discussions that keep the e-list busy. Instead, it may allow for more sustained and in-depth electronic mentoring that is not as common currently via email or e-list.

Case Study

To bring this discussion into specific relief, we turn to one WCenter thread that began on January 17, 2003, when Lauren Fitzgerald posted a question about whether or not faculty tutors should work with their own students in the writing center. This post kicked off a thread, in which twenty-one speakers posted thirty-four messages. This thread began on a Friday, making the response even more amazing, since many WCenter subscribers anticipated a long weekend with the Martin Luther King, Jr. holiday approaching.

This topic resonated with WCenter members, prompting a flurry of posts examining varied angles. While initial responses talked directly to Fitzgerald, soon posters moved beyond a discussion of her particular situation and the wording of a policy for her writing center into a discussion of the assumptions undergirding positions for and against tutoring one's own students. Eleven of the respondents explicitly or implicitly agreed with Fitzgerald's policy against working with one's own students, two disagreed, and seven took no stand. The numbers provide context for the discussion, but the discussion, not the numbers, intrigues us. This section examines public interaction on WCenter to see how it relates to the notion of electronic mentoring.

Although direct responses suggest the establishment of a relationship between two individuals, failure to name the original poster doesn't indicate lack of concern in the question. Instead, later respondents focus on follow-up posts. W. Gary Griswold (2003) writes, "For me it seems simple (though of course there may [be] complexities I don't know about): if the faculty work with their own students during their time in the writing center, they are doing what should be done during their office hours, and thus are essentially being paid twice for the same thing." Greg Dyer (2003) responds to Griswold's post, noting that the context of his center means tutors aren't being paid twice because they volunteer. Both Griswold and Dyer stay close to the issues raised by Fitzgerald, even though Dyer never mentions Fitzgerald in his post. Fitzgerald and many other readers still benefit from this discussion. Does the benefit rise to the level of electronic mentoring? Perhaps not, but the resource of WCenter allows for the potential of mentoring.

We need research into long-term mentoring relationships conducted mainly via electronic resources, but gathering such data proves difficult. Although we don't have the email and transcripts to document other cases, both authors of this chapter have participated in online mentoring. Donna Sewell began attending Tuesday Café, gaining several online mentors, most notably Tari Fanderclai and Sharon Cogdill. While Sewell learned a great deal about incorporating synchronous computer technology into her classes, relationships developed, rather than simply resources. Those relationships began completely online and, like many mentoring relationships, moved beyond their initial purpose (helping Sewell teach in an electronic environment) into professional career advice, discussions of promotion and tenure, and friendship. We call for more research into this area, for long-term data collection into mentoring relationships that occur mostly online. Such research has begun with teacher apprentices, with students teaching while being mentored at a distance by university professors, but we want to know about relationships that begin through electronic lists of varied kinds.

FOR THE FUTURE: RECOMMENDATIONS

Given the global and increasingly high-tech ethos of the contemporary writing center community, electronic media provide valuable options, like WCenter and PeerCentered, for supporting relationships that help us improve as professionals. Our research indicates that though members of the writing center community have been doing some effective electronic mentoring thus far, we can all improve, bringing more of our professional energy to this important activity. We conclude this chapter with specific recommendations for doing just that.

We recommend the following actions to support the continued emergence of effective electronic mentoring practices:

- Electronic mentors and mentees should learn about technology access conditions in their institutional and organizational contexts, and develop detailed agreements for acknowledging and proactively addressing any possible access complications.
- Electronic mentors and mentees should learn about the general institutional and organizational contexts associated with their professional lives, so conversations can focus on the specific needs of each individual in the mentoring relationship, rather than relying on generalities.
- Electronic mentors and mentees should have experience with and be able to employ a range of electronic media in support of their electronic mentoring relationship, and they should interact both within and outside of electronic communities, like WCenter and PeerCentered.
- Electronic mentors and mentees should understand the vulnerability that is innately a component of every mentoring relationship, and strive to maintain an "ethos of equality" (Hinnen 2001), thinking about each other's institutional and organizational positions, as well as each other's professional identities.
- Electronic mentors and mentees should serve as professional advocates for more support for such relationships, working to secure formal recognition of the importance of these relationships in institutional and organizational contexts, as well as in professional organizations.

Emerging from our research, these recommendations serve as a foundation for electronic mentoring in contemporary writing center theory and practice.

In true writing center spirit, we close with an invitation for conversation. That is, we've learned a great deal about electronic mentoring and its vital role in the future of the writing center community through our research, but we realize that there's much more to learn, and we hope you'll join us in that pursuit. We invite you specifically to conduct your own studies, sharing best practices and mentoring strategies with everyone, so that we can all grow and become the best electronic mentors we can be. Today's global and increasingly high-tech writing center community compels our most determined efforts.

NOTES

NOTES TO INTRODUCTION (Michael A. Pemberton and Joyce Kinkead)

1. This essay draws on a previously published article in *The Writing Center Journal*, "The National Writing Centers Association as Mooring: A Personal History of the First Decade," 16.2 (spring 1996):131–141.

2. In fact, Harris has sometimes described herself as "the writing center *yenta.*"

NOTES TO CHAPTER 1 (Michael A. Pemberton)

1. The next issue (May 1977, 1.2:1) included an announcement that "a list of established writing labs" would be compiled by Helen Naugle, but this data was maintained and distributed separately from the list of *WLN* subscribers that appeared in subsequent issues. Naugle reported in October 1977 (2.2) that she had compiled a list of 283 lab addresses.

2. Of necessity, the *Newsletter* had to defer this function to a separate *Writing Lab Directory*, first compiled from the results of a survey printed in the February 1984 (8.6) issue. An announcement for the *Directory's* publication appeared in the September 1984 (9.1) issue, and by April 1985 it was already in its third printing.

3. In Gary Olson's report on the first Southeastern WCA conference (June 1981, 5.10), he also makes a public call for the creation of a national writing center association and says he has contacted representatives of the East Central WCA to pursue this goal (6).

4. Meaning, the last seven years covered by the Index, volume 18.1 (September 1993) through volume 24.9 (May 2000). This statistic may be slightly misleading, since the *Newsletter* has had more pages (16) since May 1988 (12.9) than it did previously, but the articles published in recent times have been lengthier, overall, than earlier ones, so I suspect matters balance out.

5. The May 1988 (12.9) and June 1988 (12.10) issues were the first to reach 16 pages in length, though these issues were stapled in the corner like

the ones that preceded them. The move to a 16-page booklet format (which has been maintained to the present time) was prompted, in part, by the need to fill a standard printing "signature."

NOTES TO CHAPTER 3 (Neal Lerner)

1. McCracken (1979) tells us that it is the tutor who is making that initial "diagnosis" of student error, for one of the benefits of her system is that "lab staff members who are trained in careful diagnosis of writing problems become superior tutors" (2).
2. While published studies are few, the number conducted is likely quite large. When I gave a talk on this subject at the 2000 International Writing Centers Association conference in Baltimore and asked my audience how many had conducted such studies, nearly all the hands in the room went up. The fact that so few of these studies see the light of publication is perhaps an indication of our uneasiness with statistical methodologies.
3. FYC average represents a student's mean grade from the two-semester composition sequence. Students' grades were fairly consistent from one semester to the next, and the difference between these two grades was not statistically significant for the four years I calculated.
4. For two additional published statistical studies, each with its own set of flaws, see Roberts (1988); Waldo (1987). For a more thorough critique of my own study, see Lerner (2001).
5. Number of faculty surveys returned was 28 or roughly 28% of the total full-time faculty during the 2000–01 academic year.
6. The claim of "writing center as safe house" is a long-standing one as demonstrated by the following comment from a 1951 CCCC workshop on "Organization and Use of a Writing Laboratory": "The writing laboratory should be what the classroom often is not—natural, realistic, and friendly" (18).
7. For an example of one attempt to describe the writing center environment, see Connolly, DeJarlais, Gillam, and Micciche (1998).
8. I am grateful for the help of my colleagues Lila Foye and Xiangqian Chang in performing these statistical analyses.
9. My test of statistical significance indicates that there was a five percent or less probability that the differences between these mean scores were due to chance alone. That is the usual accepted level of "error" in studies such as these (Johanek 2000, 107).

10. To account for students who made a single writing center visit per course requirement, I also ran the analysis for two groups: 1) students who had visited the writing center two or more times and 2) those who had visited once or not at all. The former group's expository writing grades and first-year GPA were significantly higher than the latter. It is also interesting to note that when dividing the two groups up this way, the one-or-no-visits group had a mean SAT Verbal that was significantly larger than the two-or-more-visits group!

11. Regression equation adjusted R^2 = .29; P value for each variable: SAT Verbal = .016, SAT Math = 1.15×10^{-10}, High School GPA = 1.42×10^{-12}, Writing Center Visits = 1.12×10^{-8}.

12. For the 2000-01 academic year CIRP results, see Sax, Astin, Korn, and Mahoney (2000).

NOTES TO CHAPTER 4 (Harvey Kail)

1. An earlier version of this reading was published in "Narratives of Knowledge: Story and Pedagogy in Four Composition Texts," Rhetoric Review 6(2):179–189 (1988).

NOTES TO CHAPTER 6 (Michele Eodice)

I am grateful to the editors of this collection, and to Muriel Harris who inspired this volume, for providing the reason to finally write about what I have been doing at my institution and what I believe about collaboration and writing center work. In addition, thanks to my trusted readers, Kami Day, Emily Donnelli, Anne Ellen Geller, and Jon Olson. And just talking with my friends Beth Boquet, Kirk Branch, and Michael Spooner helped me greatly.

1. I take this part of my title from the Muriel Harris (1992a) article title and notion that *Collaboration is not Collaboration is not Collaboration.*

2. From the transcript of a workshop on collaboration and collaborative academic writers, CCCC Minneapolis, 2000.

3. A definition of "alchemy" from Merriam-Webster online, http://www.m-w.com/cgi-bin/dictionary.

4. Ibid.

5. See *(First Person)²: A Study of Co-Authoring in the Academy* by Kami Day and Michele Eodice (Logan: Utah State University Press, 2001) for a book-length example of the effort.

6. From a very good exploration by Laura Micciche of disappointment, work, and emotion, see "More than a Feeling: Disappointment and WPA Work," *College English*, 64(4):432–458 (2002).

7. To promote a move beyond the trope of marginality, I looked at Lil Brannon and Stephen North's essay, "The Uses of Margins," *Writing Center Journal* 20(2):7–12 (2000), where they describe a "rhetoric of marginality," but also ask directors to "find ways to build alliances within the university." Thanks go to Beth Boquet for pointing me toward a very good essay by Ian Frazier that takes up the value of margins ("A Lovely Sort of Lower Purpose," *Outside Magazine*, May 1998). See also Wendell Berry on "margins of divergent possibility" in his discussions of agricultural margins for farmers (*The Unsettling of America: Culture and Agriculture*, 1977, San Francisco: Sierra Club Books, 1977).

8. Written in my rushed handwriting on a yellow post-it note over my desk is something Sharon Crowley wrote on a WPA listserv message. It is her definition of *kairos*, and describes a quality I see as essential to and essentially found in writing center work: "prepare, wait, and exploit the moment." When I copied this down years ago I did not take note of the date of her post.

9. I learned the idea of "leaning in" from taking an Aikido class. This martial art asks us to literally "lean in" to the opponent in order to best utilize the energy of both parties, without getting off balance—off center. From: http://www.aikidoonline.com:

> The essence of all Aikido technique is the use of total body movements to create spherical motion around a stable, energized center. Students train themselves to capture the opponent's action and redirect it with techniques of martial efficiency and power. At the same time, they become aware of the tendency to overreact to opposition, and learn to remain centered under all conditions.

10. I take this term from a book by Howard Gardner, Mihaly Csikszentmihalyi, and William Damon called *Good Work: When Excellence and Ethics Meet* (2001).

> Doing good work feels good. Few things in life are as enjoyable as when we concentrate on a difficult task . . . ; these highly enjoyable moments occur more often on the job than in leisure time. (5)

11. "We Gotta Get Out Of This Place" by Eric Burdon and the Animals (1965) (Lyrics for Barry Weil and Cynthia Martin):
    We gotta get out of this place
    If it's the last thing we ever do.

We gotta get out of this place
'Cause girl, there's a better life for me and you.

12. You might have missed my IWCA 2002 presentation about *memes* in writing center work. ("Of Memes and Themes." 6th. Conference of the International Writing Centers Association, Savannah, GA. April 2002.) This is, so far, an unpublished presentation.

13. I found these thoughts in a review of the book, *The Boundaryless Organization: Breaking the Chains of Organizational Structure* (Ashkenas et al. 1995). One tenet of boundarylessness: "Solutions to problems should encompass everyone, whether inside or outside of the organization." Included in a description of what the engineering school at the University of Georgia has implemented:

> This unconventional approach to organizing a major discipline is unique and may be the first of its kind at a research university in the United States. It employs principles of entrepreneurship, boundarylessness, networking and life-long learning to create a learning organization that is responsive to unpredictability and adoptive of opportunity. (*Electronic News* 1996 [www.ebase10.com/glossary.htm#boundary])

14. www.socwel.ku.edu/strengths/index.html. See also: Donald Clifton and Chip Anderson's *Strengths Quest* (2001) for more on working with students from a strengths perspective.

15. Cindy Pierard (at the time, head of instruction for Watson Library at Kansas University) and I wrote "Surfing for Scholarship: Promoting More Effective Student Research," *National Teaching and Learning Forum* 11(3) [www.ctl.mnscu.edu/ntlf/surfing.htm].

16. A post written by Neal Lerner on WCenter listserv 1 Nov 2002 takes up this idea as well:

> I'm haunted by Steve North's words from "Idea of a Writing Center" when he proposes that we make "writing centers the centers of consciousness about writing on campuses, a kind of physical locus for the ideas and ideals of college or university or high school commitment to writing." I'd even substitute "teaching and learning" for "writing" in that sentence. The question is how could we achieve that ideal, and one answer is, I believe, through a sustained program of research in which the writing center is the "laboratory" of sorts. And I also think that a clear and consistent methodology would emerge from such a research program, one particular to writing center contexts and one that would be important to any person in the field. We'd learn lots of interesting things about our work, and we'd be trading in the currency that's valued in higher ed. It's not "acceptance" I'm necessarily

looking for here; its resources, capital, and the power to improve the teaching and learning that goes on in our institutions.

17. You won't find me using war metaphors to describe our "struggle" in writing center work, so admittedly the term "smart mob" seems a bit strong to me. But used by Howard Rheingold, the author of *Smart Mobs: The Next Social Revolution* (2003), it evokes the weight, the press, needed to make my point. Jennifer Lee attributes the exponential growth of antiwar protests across the world to the development and use of "smart mob" organizational strategies:

> Military theorists are fond of saying that future warfare will revolve around social and communication networks. Antiwar groups have found that this is true for their work as well. (Week in Review, *New York Times*, 23 February 2003, 3)

NOTES TO CHAPTER 9 (Leslie Hadfield et al.)

1. Wendy Bishop called our attention to this phenomenon in her 2000 call for proposals for CCCC.
2. Physical layouts of writing centers are included in Kinkead and Harris' *Writing Centers in Context* (1993), but they offer designs without much reflection on pedagogical implications.

NOTES TO CHAPTER 10 (James A. Inman and Donna N. Sewell)

1. We should define the technologies mentioned.
   An *electronic list* (e-list) is a discussion forum wherein participants send messages to a single email address and then those messages are distributed to all subscribers. E-lists are sometimes referenced as listservs, though that term is technology-specific. Listserv and majordomo are two of the most popular technologies that enable e-lists.
   A *MOO* is a text-based virtual reality world, in which users can chat with others in real time and design their own objects and places. MOO itself is an acronym for MUD Object-Oriented, and MUD is an acronym for Multi-User Domain, Multi-User Dimension, or Multi-User Dungeon. The "Dungeon" reference hints to the beginning of MOO as a technology; it was created in the late 1970s in Britain by players of fantasy role-playing games like *Dungeons and Dragons*, who wanted to design fantasy

worlds online and to play with others from around the world. MOOs are not all alike. Two prominent technological foundations for MOOs currently are enCore, a Web-based system designed by Cynthia Haynes and Jan Rune Holmevik, and Jay's House Core, a system that requires a telnet or client connection and is designed by Jay Carlson. Popular educational MOOs include Connections (http://web.nwe.ufl.edu/~tari/connections), led by Tari Fanderclai, and LinguaMOO (http://lingua.utdallas.edu), led by Haynes and Holmevik.

2. For more information about WCenter, visit the e-list's official home page at http://english.ttu.edu/wcenter.

3. For more information about PeerCentered, visit the forum's official home page at http://www.slcc.edu/wc/peercentered.

4. For more discussion of WCenter as information resource and as community, see Donna N. Sewell, "What's in a Name? Defining Electronic Community" (forthcoming).

5. Nancy K. Baym (2001) notes that low responses rates are typical in electronic mail. Because of this low response rate, we do not offer these responses as representing the views of most WCenter subscribers.

6. Of course, we do not know to what extent the audience will speak up in an electronic list, given the percentages of list subscribers who lurk without ever posting.

REFERENCES

Adams, Scott. 1996. *The Dilbert Principle: A Cubicle's-Eye View of Bosses, Meetings, Management Fads & Other Workplace Afflictions.* New York: Harper Business.

Administration. 1994. *Composition Studies/Freshman English News* 22.1:65–95.

Alexander, Christopher. 1979. *A Timeless Way of Building.* New York: Oxford University Press.

Alexander, Christopher, Sara Ishikawa, and Murray Silverstein. 1977. *A Pattern Language: Towns, Buildings, Construction.* New York: Oxford University Press.

Alexander, Christopher, Murray Silverstein, Shlomo Angel, Sara Ishikawa, Denny Abrahms. 1975. *The Oregon Experiment.* New York: Oxford University Press.

Almasy, Rudolph and David England. 1979. Future Teachers as Real Teachers: English Education Students in the Writing Laboratory. *English Education* 10:155–162.

Ammirati, Theresa. 9 April 2001. Re: Exemplar Mickey. Online posting. WCenter. <http://lyris.acs.ttu.edu/>.

Arkin, Marian and Barbara Shollar. 1982. *The Tutor Book.* New York: Longman.

Ashkenas, Ronald N., Dave Ulrich, Todd Jick, and Steve Kerr. 1995. *The Boundaryless Organization: Breaking the Chains of Organizational Structure.* San Francisco: Jossey-Bass.

Astin, Alexander W. 1993. *Assessment for Excellence: The Philosophy and Practice of Assessment and Evaluation in Higher Education.* Phoenix: Oryx Press.

Balester, Valerie. 16 May 2001. Interview by the author.

Balester, Valerie, and James C. McDonald. 2001. A View of Status and Working Conditions: Relations between Writing Program and Writing Center Directors. *Writing Program Administrator* 24.3:59–82.

Ballard, Kim, and Rick Anderson. 1989. The Writing Lab Newsletter: A History of Collaboration. *Composition Chronicle* 2.1:5, 7–8.

Barefoot, Betsy. 15 September 2000. "On-Line Jeopardy." Policy Center on the First Year of College. <www/brevard/edu/fyc/FYA_contributions/barefoot.htm>.

Barnett, Robert W. 1997. Redefining Our Existence: An Argument for Short- and Long-Term Goals and Objectives. *The Writing Center Journal* 17.2:123–133.

Barnett, Robert W. and Jacob S. Blumner, eds. 2001. *The Allyn and Bacon Guide to Writing Center Theory and Practice.* Needham, MA: Allyn & Bacon.

Barton, David and Mary Hamilton. 1998. *Local Literacies: Reading and Writing in One Community.* London: Routledge.

Barton, David, Mary Hamilton and Roz Ivanic. 2000. *Situated Literacies: Reading and Writing in Context*. London: Routledge.

Baxter Magolda, Marcia B. 1999. *Creating Contexts for Learning and Self-Authorship: Constructive-Developmental Pedagogy*. Nashville: Vanderbilt University Press.

Baym, Nancy K. 2001. The Performance of Humor in Computer-Mediated Communication. *Journal of Computer-Mediated Communication* 1.2 (1995). 20 March 2001 <http://www.ascusc.org/jcmc/vol1/issue2/baym.html>.

Beck, E.C. 1939. Composition-Teaching in a State Teachers College. *English Journal* 28:593-597.

Becker, Franklin, and Fritz Steele. 1995. *Workplace by Design: Mapping the High-Performance Workscape*. San Francisco: Jossey-Bass Management Series.

Behm, Richard. 1989. Ethical Issues in Peer Tutoring: A Defense of Collaborative Learning. *Writing Center Journal* 10:3–12.

Bell, James H. 2000. When Hard Questions Are Asked: Evaluating Writing Centers. *The Writing Center Journal* 21.1:7–28.

Birnbaum, Robert. 2000. *Management Fads in Higher Education: Where They Come From, What They Do, Why They Fail*. San Francisco: Jossey-Bass.

Bizzell, Patricia, Bruce Herzberg, and Nedra Reynolds. 2000. *The Bedford Bibliography for Teachers of Writing*. Boston: Bedford/St. Martin's Press.

Bokser, Julie. 2000. Dilemmas of Collaboration for the Tutor with Work Experience. *Writing Lab Newsletter* 24.9:5–9.

Boquet, Elizabeth H. 1999. "Our Little Secret": A History of Writing Centers, Pre- to Post-Open Admissions. *College Composition and Communication* 50.3:463–482.

Boquet, Elizabeth H. 2000. Intellectual Tug-of-War: Snapshots of Life in the Center. In *Stories from the Center: Connecting Narrative and Theory in the Writing Center*, edited by Lynn Craigue Briggs and Meg Woolbright. Urbana, IL: NCTE.

Boquet, Elizabeth H. 2002. *Noise from the Writing Center*. Logan: Utah State University Press.

Bouman, Kurt. 2001. Re: Electronic Mentoring: Request for Responses. Email to the authors. 26 March 2001.

Boyer, Ernest L. 1990. *Scholarship Reconsidered: Priorities of the Professoriate*. San Francisco: Jossey-Bass.

Brannon, Lil and Steven M. North. 2000. The Uses of the Margins. *The Writing Center Journal* 20.2:7–12.

Brooks, Jeff. 1991. Minimalist Tutoring: Making the Student Do All the Work. *Writing Lab Newsletter* 19.2:1–4. Reprinted in *The St. Martin's Sourcebook for Writing Tutors*, edited by Christina Murphy and Steve Sherwood, 1995. New York: St. Martin's Press.

Brown, Lady Falls. 2000. OWLs in Theory and Practice: A Director's Perspective. In *Taking Flight with OWLs: Examining Electronic Writing Center Work*, edited by James A. Inman and Donna N. Sewell. Mahwah, NJ: Erlbaum.

Brown, Lady Falls. 7 April 1998. Session H.17 at CCCC. Online posting. WCenter. 14 April 2001 <http://www.ttu.edu/wcenter/9804/msg00059.html>.

Brown, Stuart C. Rebecca Jackson, and Theresa Enos. 2000. The Arrival of Rhetoric in the Twenty-First Century: The 1999 Survey of Doctoral Programs in Rhetoric. *Rhetoric Review.* 18.2:233–242.

Bruffee, Kenneth. 1973. Collaborative Learning: Some Practical Models. *College English* 34:635–643.

Bruffee, Kenneth. 1978. The Brooklyn Plan: Attaining Intellectual Growth Through Peer Group Tutoring. *Liberal Education* 64:447–468.

Bruffee, Kenneth. 1983a. *Elegaic Romance: Cultural Change and the Loss of the Hero in Modern Fiction.* Ithaca: Cornell University Press.

Bruffee, Kenneth. 1983b. Peer Tutoring and the "Conversation of Mankind." In *Writing Center Theory and Administration,* edited by Gary A. Olson. Urbana, IL: NCTE.

Bruffee, Kenneth. 1972. *A Short Course in Writing: Composition, Collaborative Learning, and Constructive Reading.* Cambridge, MA: Winthrop Publishers.

Bruffee, Kenneth A. 1984. Collaborative Learning and the "Conversation of Mankind." *College English.* 46.7:635–652.

Campbell, Joseph. 1956. *The Hero with a Thousand Faces.* Cleveland: Meridian Books.

Capossela, Toni-Lee. 1998. *The Harcourt Brace Guide to Peer Tutoring.* Fort Worth: Harcourt, Brace.

Carino, Peter. 1995. Early Writing Centers: Toward a History. *Writing Center Journal* 15.2:103–115.

Carino, Peter. 1996. Open Admissions and the Construction of Writing Center History: A Tale of Three Models. *Writing Center Journal* 17.1:30–48.

Carino, Peter. 2002. Reading Our Own Words: Rhetorical Analysis and the Institutional Discourse of Writing Centers. In *Writing Center Research: Extending the Conversation,* edited by Paula Gillespie, Alice Gillam, Lady Falls Brown, and Byron Stay. Mahwah, NJ: Erlbaum.

Clark, Irene Lurkis. 1988. Preparing Future Composition Teachers in the Writing Center. *College Composition and Communication* 39:347–350.

Clark, Irene Lurkis. 1990. Maintaining Chaos in the Writing Center: A Critical Perspective on Writing Center Dogma. *The Writing Center Journal* 11.1:81–95.

Clark, Irene Lurkis. 1995. *Writing in the Center: Teaching in a Writing Center Setting.* Dubuque: Kendall/Hunt. 3rd ed., 1998.

Clark, Irene Lurkis. n.d. Non-Directive Tutoring: A Retrospective.

Clark, Irene Lurkis and Dave Healy. 1996. Are Writing Centers Ethical? *Writing Program Administration* 20.1/2:32–48.

Clark, Beverly Lyon. 1985. *Talking About Writing: A Guide for Teacher and Tutor Conferences.* Ann Arbor: University of Michigan Press.

Clifton, Donald O. and Edward "Chip" Anderson. 2001. *StrengthsQuest: Discover and Develop Your Strengths in Academics, Career, and Beyond.* Washington, DC: Gallup Organization.

Cogie, Jane. 2001. Peer Tutoring: Keeping the Contradiction Productive. In *The Politics of Writing Centers*, edited by Jane Nelson and Kathy Evertz. Portsmouth, NH: Boynton/Cook Heinemann.

Condon, Bill. 2000. It's STILL Not Far to the Frontier: Encouraging Students to Become Active Professionals in C&W. *Kairos: A Journal for Teachers of Writing in Webbed Environments* 5.2. 3 Apr. 2001 <http://english.ttu.edu/kairos/5.2/binder.html?features/townhall1/th1.html>.

Connolly, Colleen, Amy DeJarlais, Alice Gillam, and Laura Micciche. 1998. Erika and the Fish Lamps: Writing and Reading the Local Scene. In *Weaving Knowledge Together: Writing Centers and Collaboration*, edited by Carol Peterson Haviland, Maria Notarangelo, Lene Whitley-Putz, and Thia Wolf. Emmitsburg, MD: NWCA Press.

Connors, Robert J. 1984. Journals in Composition Studies. *College English* 46:348–365.

Conversations: Excerpted E-List Dialogues. 1998. *Kairos: A Journal for Teachers of Writing in Webbed Environments* 3.1. 3 April 2001 <http://english.ttu.edu/kairos/3.1/ news/conversations/start.html>.

Cooper, Marilyn. 1995. Really Useful Knowledge: A Cultural Studies Agenda for Writing Centers. In *Landmark Essays on Writing Centers*, edited by Christina Murphy, Joe Law, and Steve Sherwood. Davis, CA: Hermagoras Press.

Cope, Bill and Mary Kalantzis. 2000. *Multiliteracies: Literacy Learning and the Design of Social Futures*. London: Routledge.

Corbett, Edward P. J., Nancy Myers, and Gary Tate, eds. 2000. *The Writing Teacher's Sourcebook*. New York: Oxford University Press.

Covey, Stephen R. 1989. *The Seven Habits of Highly Effective People: Restoring the Character Ethic*. New York: Simon and Schuster.

Crisp, Sally. 1992. Assertive Collaboration in the Writing Center: Discovering Autonomy Through Community. *The Writing Lab Newsletter* 16.3(March):11–16.

Cross, Heather. 2000. More than a Place for the Coffeepot: Writing Center Environments, Multiple Intelligences, and Environmental Psychology. Paper presented at the annual convention of the CCCC, March, Minneapolis.

Cuseo, Joseph B. 17 June 2000. Assessment of the First-Year Experience: Six Significant Questions. Online posting. Policy Center on the First Year of College. 12 June 2001 <http://www/brevard/edu/fyc/FYA_contributions/CuseoRemarks.htm>.

Davis, Kevin. 1995. Life Outside the Boundary: History and Direction in the Writing Center. *The Writing Lab Newsletter* 20.2:5–7.

Deasy, C. M. and T. Lasswell. 1999. *Designing Places for People: A Handbook on Human Behavior for Architects, Designers, and Facility Managers*. New York: Whitney Library of Design.

DeCiccio, Al. 1989. Literacy and Authority as Threats to Peer Tutoring: A Commentary Inspired by the Fifth Annual Conference for Peer Tutors in Writing. *The Writing Lab Newsletter* 13.10:11–13.

Dukes, Thomas. 1981. The Writing Center as Crisis Center: Suggestions for the Interview. *The Writing Lab Newsletter* 5.9:4–6.

Dyer, Greg. 17 January 2003. Re: Why Can't Faculty Tutors Tutor Their Own Students? Online posting. WCenter. 3 April 2003 <http://lyris.acs.ttu.edu>.

Ede, Lisa, and Andrea Lunsford. 2000. Some Millennial Thoughts about the Future of Writing Centers. *The Writing Center Journal* 20.2:33–37.

Eggers, Tilly. 1979. Evaluation and Instruction. *The Writing Lab Newsletter* 4.4:4–5.

Enos, Theresa. 1997. Mentoring–and (Wo)mentoring–in Composition Studies. In *Academic Advancement in Composition Studies: Scholarship, Publication, Promotion, Tenure*, edited by Richard C. Gebhardt and Barbara Genelle Smith Gebhardt. Mahwah, NJ: L. Erlbaum.

Enriquez, David, Carol Peterson Haviland, Candace Olson, and Dian Pizurie. 1998. To Define Ourselves or to be Defined. In *Weaving Knowledge Together: Writing Centers and Collaboration*, edited by Carol Peterson Haviland, Maria Notarangelo, Lene Whitley-Putz, and Tia Wolf. Emmitsberg, MD: NWCA Press.

Eodice, Michele. 2002. Of Memes and Themes. Paper presented at 6th Conference of the International Writing Centers Association, April, in Savannah, Georgia.

Ferruci, Stephen A. 2001. Composition's Professionalism and the Writing Center Director: Rethinking the Director as a Teacher. *The Writing Instructor*. 16 September 2001. Available at <http://www.writinginstructor.com/essays/ferruci.html>.

Fischer, Katie. 20 March 2001. E-Mentoring. Email to the authors.

Fishman, Judith. 1980. The Writing Center—What Is Its Center? *The Writing Lab Newsletter* 5.1:1–4.

Fitch, Sarah. November 1999. E-mail interview.

Fitzgerald, Lauren. 25 March 2001. Email to the authors.

Fitzgerald, Lauren. 17 January 2003. Why Can't Faculty Tutors Tutor Their Own Students? Online posting. WCenter. 3 April 2003 <http://lyris.acs.ttu.edu>.

Flower, Linda. 1981. *Problem-Solving Strategies for Writing*. New York: Harcourt Brace Jovanovich.

Flower, Linda, John R. Hayes, and Heidi Swarts. 1980. *Revising Functional Documents: The Scenario Principle*. Pittsburge: Carnegie-Mellon University.

Foster, Rebecca. 26 March 2001. Re: Electronic Mentoring: Request for Responses. Email to the authors.

Gardner, Howard, Mihaly Csikszentmihalyi, and William Damon. 2001. *Good Work: When Excellence and Ethics Meet*. New York: Basic Books.

Gebhardt, Richard C. 1997. Mentor and Evaluator: The Chair's Role in Promotion and Tenure Review. In *Academic Advancement in Composition Studies: Scholarship, Publication, Promotion, Tenure*, edited by Richard C. Gebhardt and Barbara Genelle Smith Gebhardt. Mahwah, NJ: L. Erlbaum.

Gebhardt, Richard C., and Barbara Genelle Smith Gebhardt, eds. 1997. *Academic Advancement in Composition Studies: Scholarship, Publication, Promotion, Tenure.* Mahwah, NJ: L. Erlbaum.

Gee, James Paul. 2000. The New Literacy Studies: From "Socially Situated" to the Work of the Social. In *Local Literacies: Reading and Writing in One Community,* edited by David Barton, Mary Hamilton, and Roz Ivanic. London: Routledge.

Geller, Anne Ellen. 25 April 2000. Re: WC Mentors. Online posting. WCenter. 9 April 2001 <http://lyris.acs.ttu.edu>.

Gers, Simone. 10 April 1998. Re: Session H.17 at CCCC. Online posting. WCenter. 14 April 2001 <http://www.ttu.edu/wcenter/9804/msg00153.html>.

Gillam, Alice M. 1994. Collaborative Learning Theory and Peer Tutoring Practice. In *Intersections: Theory-Practice in the Writing Center,* edited by Joan A. Mullin and Ray Wallace. Urbana: NCTE.

Gillam, Alice M., Susan Calloway, and Katherine Hennessy Wikoff. 1994. The Role of Authority and The Authority of Roles in Peer Writing Tutorials. *The Journal of Teaching Writing* 12.2:161–198.

Gillespie, Paula. 2002. Beyond the House of Lore: WCenter as Research Site. In *Writing Center Research: Extending the Conversation,* edited by Paula Gillespie, Alice Gillam, Lady Falls Brown, and Byron Stay. Mahwah, NJ: L. Erlbaum.

Gillespie, Paula and Neal Lerner. 2000. *The Allyn and Bacon Guide to Peer Tutoring.* Boston: Allyn and Bacon.

Gladwell, Malcolm. 2000. Designs for Working. *The New Yorker,* 11 December, 60–70.

Goldsby, Jackie. 1981. *Peer Tutoring in Basic Writing: A Tutor's Journal.* Berkeley: University of California–Berkeley, Bay Area Writing Project.

Green Building Design: Practicing What You Teach. 2001. *Administrator* 20.1 (January).

Grimm, Nancy Maloney. 1996. Rearticulating the Work of the Writing Center. *College Composition and Communication* 47:523–548.

Grimm, Nancy Maloney. 1999. *Good Intentions: Writing Center Work for Postmodern Times.* Portsmouth, NH: Boynton/Cook Heinemann.

Griswold, W. Gary. 17 January 2003. Re: Why Can't Faculty Tutors Tutor Their Own Students? Online posting. WCenter. 3 Apr. 2003 <http://lyris.acs.ttu.edu>.

H&H Publishing. 1987. *Learning and Study Strategies Inventory (LASSI).* Clearwater, FL: H&H Publishing.

Hadfield, Natalie. November 1999. E-mail interview.

Harris, Jeanette. 2001. Reaffirming, Reflecting, Reforming: Writing Center Scholarship Comes of Age. *College English* 63:662–668.

Harris, Muriel. 1977. We Are Launched! *The Writing Lab Newsletter* 1.1:1.

Harris, Muriel. 1979. CCCC's conference report. *The Writing Lab Newsletter* 3.9:1–2.

Harris, Muriel, ed. 1982. *Tutoring Writing: A Sourcebook for Writing Labs.* Glenview, IL: Scott, Foresman.

Harris, Muriel. 1986. *Teaching One to One: The Writing Conference.* Urbana: NCTE.

Harris, Muriel. 1988. . . . from the editor . . . *The Writing Lab Newsletter* 12.10:1–2.

Harris, Muriel. 1991. Solutions and Trade-Offs in Writing Center Administration. *The Writing Center Journal* 12.1:63–79.

Harris, Muriel. 1992a. Collaboration Is Not Collaboration Is Not Collaboration: Writing Center Tutorials vs. Peer-Response Groups. *College Composition and Communication* 43:369–383.

Harris, Muriel. 1992b. OH NO. . . A Price Increase? *The Writing Lab Newsletter* 16.6:14.

Harris, Muriel. 1993a. A Multiservice Writing Lab in a Multiversity: The Purdue University Writing Lab. In *Writing Centers in Context: Twelve Case Studies*, edited by Joyce A. Kinkead and Jeanette G. Harris. Urbana: NCTE.

Harris, Muriel. 1993b. . . . from the editor . . . *The Writing Lab Newsletter* 18.1:1.

Harris, Muriel. 1995. Talking in the Middle: Why Writers Need Writing Tutors. *College English* 57.1:27–42.

Harris, Muriel. 1997. Presenting Writing Center Scholarship: Issues for Faculty and Personnel Committees. In *Academic Advancement in Composition Studies: Scholarship, Publications, Promotion, Tenure,* edited by Richard C. Gebhardt and Barbara Genelle Smith Gebhardt. Mahwah, NJ: Erlbaum.

Harris, Muriel. 1999. Where *Should* We Go? Writing Centers and Navigating the New Century. National and East Central Writing Centers Associations Conference, April 15, Indiana Union, Bloomington.

Harris, Muriel. 2000. Preparing to Sit at the Head Table: Maintaining Writing Center Viability in the Twenty-First Century. *The Writing Center Journal* 20.2:13–21

Harris, Muriel. 2001. Centering in on Professional Choices. *College Composition and Communication* 52:429–440.

Harris, Muriel. 17 April 2001. Personal interview.

Harris, Muriel. 2003. *Prentice Hall Reference Guide to Grammar and Usage,* 5th ed. Upper Saddle River, NJ: Prentice Hall.

Harris, Muriel. Forthcoming. *Writing Center Administration: Making Local, Institutional Knowledge in Our Writing Centers.*

Haswell, Richard H. 1991. *Gaining Ground in College Writing: Tales of Development and Interpretation.* Dallas: Southern Methodist University Press.

Haviland, Carol Peterson, and Denise Stephenson. 2002. Writing Centers, Writing Programs, and WPAs: Roles by Any Other Names? In *The Writing Program Administrator's Resource: A Guide to Reflective Institutional Practice,* edited by Stuart Brown and Theresa Enos. Mahwah, NJ: Erlbaum.

Hawkins, Thom. 1980. Intimacy and Audience: The Relationship Between Revision and the Social Dimension of Peer Tutoring. *College English* 42:64–68.

Hawkins, Thom and Phyllis Brooks. 1981. *Improving Writing Skills.* New Directions for College Learning Assistance, No. 3. San Francisco: Jossey-Bass.

Hawthorne, Joan. 2001. Researching the Conference: What Do We Learn from Discourse Analysis? Paper presented at Conference on College Composition and Communication.

Hayes, John R. 1981. *The Complete Problem Solver.* Philadelphia: Franklin Institute Press.

Hemmeter, Thomas. 1990. The "Smack of Difference": The Language of Writing Center Discourse. *The Writing Center Journal* 11.1:35–48.

Hesse, Doug. 1999. Preface. In *Administrative Problem Solving for Writing Programs and Writing Centers,* edited by Linda Myers-Breslin. Urbana, IL: NCTE.

Higher Education Research Institute. 2000. *The Cooperative Institutional Research Program (CIRP).* Los Angeles: Higher Education Research Institute, UCLA Graduate School of Education.

Hill, James S. 1978a. The Writing Lab: An Anecdote. *The Writing Lab Newsletter* 2.7:3.

Hill, James S. 1978b. The Writing Lab as Supplement to Freshman English. *The Writing Lab Newsletter* 2.9:1.

Hills, Matt. 2002. *Fan Cultures.* London: Routledge.

Hinnen, Dean. 1 April 2001. Survey on Mentoring. Email to the authors.

Hobson, Eric, ed. 1998. *Wiring the Writing Center.* Logan: Utah State University Press.

Houston, Linda S. 1999. Budgeting and Politics: Keeping the Writing Center Alive. In *Administrative Problem-Solving for Writing Programs and Writing Centers: Scenarios in Effective Program Management,* edited by Linda Myers-Breslin. Urbana, IL: NCTE.

Inman, James A. 20 March 2001. Electronic Mentoring: Request for Responses. Online posting. WCenter. 21 March 2001 <http://lyris.acs.ttu.edu/>.

Inman, James A., and Clinton Gardner, eds. 2002. *The OWL Construction and Maintenance Guide.* Emmitsburg, MD: IWCA Press.

Inman, James A., and Donna N. Sewell, eds. 2000. *Taking Flight with OWLs: Examining Electronic Writing Center Work.* Mahwah, NJ: L. Erlbaum.

James, William. [1899] 1958. *Talks to Teachers on Psychology, and to Students on Some of Life's Ideals.* New York: Norton.

Johanek, Cindy. 2000. *Composing Research: A Contextualist Paradigm for Rhetoric and Composition.* Logan: Utah State University Press.

Jones, Frederic H. 1993. *The Concise Dictionary of Interior Design.* Los Altos, CA: Crisp.

Jones, Kathryn. 2000. Becoming Just Another Alphanumeric Code: Farmers' Encounters with the Literacy and Discourse Practices of Agricultural Bureaucracy at the Livestock Auction. In *Situated Literacies: Reading and Writing in Context,* edited by David Barton, Mary Hamilton, and Roz Ivanic. London: Routledge.

Kail, Harvey. 2000. Writing Center Work: An Ongoing Challenge. *The Writing Center Journal* 20.2:25–28.

Kalantzis, Mary and Bill Cope. 2000. Changing the Role of Schools. In *Multiliteracies: Literacy Learning and the Design of Social Futures*, edited by Bill Cope and Mary Kalantzis. London: Routledge.

Karlen, Mark. 1993. *Space Planning Basics*. New York: Van Nostrand Reinhold.

Kaufer, Davis S. and Brian S. Butter. 1996. *Rhetoric and the Arts of Design*. Mahwah, NJ: L. Erlbaum.

Kaye, Harvey J. 2002. It's Not Just an Office, It's a Vessel of Self-Expression. *The Chronicle of Higher Education*, 8 February, B16.

Kennedy, Mick. 1997. Expressionism and Social Constructionism in the Writing Center: How Do They Benefit Students? *The Writing Lab Newsletter* 22.3:5–8.

King, Mary. 1983. Teaching for Cognitive Growth. *The Writing Lab Newsletter* 7.7:7–9.

King, Mary. 1982. A Writing Lab Profile. *The Writing Lab Newsletter* 6.8:6–8.

Kinkead, Joyce A. 2001. The National Writing Centers Association as Mooring: A Personal History of the First Decade. *The Writing Center Journal* 16.2(1996):131–143. Reprinted in *The Allyn and Bacon Guide to Writing Center Theory and Practice*, edited by Robert W. Barnett and Jacob S. Blumner. Needham, MA: Allyn & Bacon.

Kinkead, Joyce A., and Jean Simpson. 2000. Administrative Audience: A Rhetorical Problem. *Writing Program Administration* 23.3:71–84.

Kinkead, Joyce A. and Jeanette G. Harris, eds. 1993. *Writing Centers in Context: Twelve Case Studies*. Urbana, IL: NCTE.

Kinkead, Joyce A. and Jeanette G. Harris. 2000. What's Next for Writing Centers? *The Writing Center Journal* 20.2:23–24.

Kolodny, Annette. 1998. *Failing the Future: A Dean Looks at Higher Education in the Twenty-First Century*. Durham, NC: Duke University Press.

Koster, Josephine A. 21 March 2001. Re: Mentoring. Email to the authors.

Lamb, Mary. 1981. Evaluation Procedures for Writing Centers: Defining Ourselves Through Accountability. In *Improving Writing Skills*, edited by Thom Hawkins and Phyllis Brooks. New Directions for College Learning Assistance, No. 3. San Francisco: Josey-Bass.

Lauer, Janice. 1997. Graduate Students as Active Members of the Profession: Some Questions of Mentoring. In *Publishing in Rhetoric and Composition*, edited by Gary A. Olson and Todd W. Taylor. Albany: SUNY Press.

Lerner, Neal. 1997. Counting Beans and Making Beans Count. *The Writing Lab Newsletter* 22.1:1–4.

Lerner, Neal. 1998. Research in the Writing Center. In *The Writing Center Resource Manual*, edited by Bobbie Bayliss Silk. Emmitsburg, MD: NWCA Press.

Lerner, Neal. 2001. Counting Beans Wisely. *The Writing Lab Newsletter* 26.1:1–4.

Leverenz, Carrie Shively. 2001. Graduate Students in the Writing Center: Confronting the Cult of (Non)Expertise. In *The Politics of Writing Centers*, edited by Jane Nelson and Kathy Evertz. Portsmouth, NH: Boynton/Cook Heinemann.

Lunsford, Andrea. 1995. Collaboration, Control, and the Idea of a Writing Center. In *Landmark Essays on Writing Centers*, edited by Christina Murphy and Joe Law. Davis, CA: Hermagoras Press.

Lunsford, Karen J., and Bertram C. Bruce. 2001. Collaboratories: Working Together on the Web. *Journal of Adolescent and Adult Literacy* 45:52–58.

Maid, Barry M. 1999. How WPAs Can Learn to Use Power to Their Own Advantage. In *Administrative Problem-Solving for Writing Programs and Writing Centers: Scenarios in Effective Program Management*, edited by Linda Myers-Breslin. Urbana, IL: NCTE.

Mangan, Katherine S. 1998. Boardroom Expertise. *The Chronicle of Higher Education*, 27 March, A43.

May, Heather. 2000. Is It a Bad Chi Day? More People Turning to Feng Shui for Help. *Salt Lake Tribune*, 9 April 2000, A-1, A10.

McCracken, Nancy. 1979. Evaluation/Accountability for the Writing Lab. *The Writing Lab Newsletter* 3.6:1–2.

Meyer, Emily and Louise Z. Smith. 1987. *The Practical Tutor*. New York: Oxford University Press.

Miller, Richard. 1998. *As if Learning Mattered: Reforming Higher Education*. Ithaca, NY: Cornell University Press.

Miller, Richard. 1999. Let's Do the Numbers: Comp Droids and the Prophets of Doom. *Profession*. 96–105. New York: MLA.

Muir, Gale and Sally Blake. 2002. *Foundations of collaboration*. Available at <www.ucet.ufl.edu/ProgramService/essay6.htm>.

Mullin, Joan. 22 March 2001. Re: CCCC Impressions, Relevance of WC Work. Online posting. WCenter. 9 April 2001 <http://lyris.acs.ttu.edu/>.

Mullin, Joan. 2002. Learning to Fly: Lessons from Twenty Years of *WCJ* Scholarship. Unpublished essay.

Murphy, Christina, Joe Law, and Steve Sherwood. 1995. *Landmark Essays on Writing Centers*. Davis, CA: Hermagoras Press.

Murphy, Christina, Joe Law, and Steve Sherwood. 1996. *Writing Centers: An Annotated Bibliography*. Westport, CT: Greenwood Press.

Nelson, Jane, and Kathy Evertz, eds. 2001. *The Politics of Writing Centers*. Portsmouth, NH: Boynton/Cook Heinemann.

Neuleib, Janice. 1980. Proving We Did It. *The Writing Lab Newsletter* 4.7:2–4.

Neuleib, Janice. 1982. Evaluating a Writing Lab. In *Tutoring Writing: A Sourcebook for Writing Labs*, edited by Muriel Harris. Glenview, IL: Scott, Foresman.

Neuleib, Janice. 1984. Research in the Writing Center: What to Do and Where to Go to Become Research Oriented. *The Writing Lab Newsletter* 9.4:10–13.

New London Group. 2000. A Pedagogy of Multiliteracies: Designing Social Futures. In *Multiliteracies: Literacy Learning and the Design of Social Futures*, edited by Bill Cope and Mary Kalantzis.

Newmann, Stephen. 1999. Demonstrating Effectiveness. *The Writing Lab Newsletter* 23.8:8–9.

North, Stephen. 1981. Us 'n' Howie: The Shape of Our Ignorance. *The Writing Lab Newsletter* 6.1:3–7.

North, Stephen. 1984. The Idea of A Writing Center. *College English* 46:433–446.

Olson, Gary, and Evelyn Ashton-Jones. 1988. Writing Center Directors: The Search for Professional Status. *WPA* 12.1/2:19–28.

Olson, Gary A., and Todd W. Taylor, eds. 1997. *Publishing in Rhetoric and Composition.* Albany: SUNY Press.

Olson, Jon, Dawn J. Moyer, and Adelia Falda. 2001. Student-Centered Assessment Research in the Writing Center. In *Writing Center Research: Extending the Conversation,* edited by Paula Gillespie, Alice Gillam, Lady Falls Brown, and Byron L. Stay. Mahwah, NJ: L. Erlbaum.

Optiz, Jane Z. 1978. Saint John's WRITING WORKSHOP: A Summary of the First Semester Report. *The Writing Lab Newsletter* 2.9:2–3.

Organization and Use of a Writing Laboratory: Report of Workshop No. 9. 1951. *College Composition and Communication* 2:17–18.

Pace, C. Robert and George D. Kuh. 1998. *College Student Experiences Questionnaire,* 4th ed. Bloomington: Indiana University.

Palmeri, Jason. 2000. Transgressive Hybridity: Reflections on the Authority of the Peer Writing Tutor. *Writing Lab Newsletter* 25.1:9–11.

Panero, J., and M. Zelnik. 1979. *Human Dimensions & Interior Space.* New York: Whitney Library of Design.

Pardoe, Simon. 2000. Respect and the Pursuit of "Symmetry" in Researching Literacy and Student Writing. In *Situated Literacies: Reading and Writing in Context,* edited by David Barton, Mary Hamilton, and Roz Ivanic. London: Routledge.

The Pedagogical Building. 1991. *Academe* 77.4:9.

Perdue, Virginia and Deborah James. 1990. Teaching in the Center. *Writing Lab Newsletter* 14.10:7–8.

Perkins, Lorraine. 1977. An Approach to Organization. *The Writing Lab Newsletter* 2.4:2.

Peters, Thomas J. and Robert H. Waterman, 1982. *In Search of Excellence: Lessons from America's Best–Run Companies.* New York: Harper & Row.

Peters-Whitehead, Sabrina. 3 April 2001. Re: Electronic Mentoring: Request for Responses. Email to the authors.

Peterson, Andrea. 10 October 1999. Interview with the author.

Petit, Angela. 2001. Removeable Feasts: The Writing Center as Carnival. *Composition Forum.* 12:40–58.

Rayfield, J. 1994. *The Office Interior Design Guide.* New York: John Wiley & Sons.

Reigstad, Thomas J. and Donald A. McAndrew. 1984. *Training Tutors for Writing Conferences.* Urbana: ERIC/NCTE.

Review of *The Boundaryless Organization. Electronic News* 42(2100):40 (1996).

Rheingold, Howard. 2003. *Smart Mobs: The Next Social Revolution.* Cambridge, MA: Perseus.

Rickly, Rebecca. 2000. Mentoring, (Wo)Mentoring, and Helping Students to Take Responsibility for Their Own Education. *Kairos: A Journal for Teachers of*

Writing in Webbed Environments 5.2 (2000). 3 Apr. 2001 <http://english.ttu.edu/kairos/5.2/ binder.html?features/townhall1/ th1.html>.

Riewoldt, Otto and Jennifer Hudson. 1997. *Intelligent Spaces: Architecture for the Information Age*. Translated by Susan Mackervoy. London: Laurence King.

Riley, Terrence. 1994. The Unpromising Future of Writing Centers. *The Writing Center Journal* 15:20–34.

Roberts, David H. 1988. A Study of Writing Center Effectiveness. *The Writing Center Journal* 9.1:53–60.

Rodis, Karen. 2001. Mending the Damaged Path: How to Avoid Conflict of Expectation When Setting up a Writing Center. In *The Allyn and Bacon Guide to Writing Center Theory and Practice*, edited by Robert W. Barnett and Jacob S. Blumner. Needham, MA: Allyn & Bacon.

Rohan, Liz. 2002. Hostesses of Literacy: Librarians, Writing Teachers, Writing Centers, and a Historical Quest for Ethos. *Composition Studies* 30:61–77.

Rosner, Mary, Beth Boehm, and Debra Journet. 1999. *History, Reflection, and Narrative: The Professionalization of Composition, 1963–1983*. Stamford, CT: Ablex.

Ryan, Leigh. 1994. *The Bedford Guide for Writing Tutors*. Boston: Bedford Books.

Sadlon, John. 1980. The Effect of a Skills Center Upon the Writing Improvement of Freshmen Composition Students. *The Writing Lab Newsletter* 5.3:1–3.

Sax, Linda J., Alexander W. Astin, William S. Korn, and Kathryn M. Mahoney. 2000. *The American Freshman: National Norms for Fall 2000*. Los Angeles: Higher Education Research Institute.

Scanzello, Angela. 1981. The Writing Center in an Identity Crisis. *The Writing Lab Newsletter* 6.4:6–8.

Schwalm, David E. 1995. E Pluribus Unum: An Administrator Rounds Up Mavericks and Money. In *Writing Center Perspectives*, edited by Byron L. Stay, Christina Murphy, and Eric Hobson. Emmitsburg, MD: NWCA Press.

Sewell, Donna N. 2002. What's in a Name? Defining Electronic Community. In *Electronic Collaboration in the Humanities: Issues and Options*, edited by James A. Inman, Cheryl Reed, and Peter Sands. Mahwah, NJ: L. Erlbaum.

Shamoon, Linda K. and Deborah H. Burns. 1995. A Critique of Pure Tutoring. *The Writing Center Journal* 15.2:134–151.

Silver, Marcia, with contributions by Kenneth A. Bruffee, Judy Fishman, and Judith T. Matsunobu. 1978. Training and Using Peer Tutors. *College English* 40:442–449.

Simpson, Jeanne. 1985. What Lies Ahead for Writing Centers: Position Statement on Professional Concerns. *The Writing Center Journal* 5.2/6.1:35–39.

Simpson, Jeanne. 1995. Perceptions, Realities, and Possibilities: Central Administration and Writing Centers. In *Writing Center Perspectives*, edited by

Byron L. Stay, Christina Murphy, and Eric Hobson. Emmitsburg, MD: NWCA Press.

Simpson, Jeanne, and Barry Maid. 2001. Lining Up Ducks or Herding Cats? The Politics of Writing Center Accreditation. In *The Politics of Writing Centers*, edited by Jane Nelson and Kathy Evertz. Portsmouth, NH: Boynton/Cook Heinemann.

Simpson, Jeanne, Steve Braye, and Beth Boquet. 1995. War, Peace, and Writing Center Administration. In *Landmark Essays on Writing Centers*, edited by Christina Murphy and Joe Law. Davis, CA: Hermagoras Press.

Sledd, James. 2000. Return to Service. *Composition Studies* 28:41–58.

Smith, Phyl, and Lynn Kearney. 1994. *Creating Workplaces Where People Can Think.* San Francisco: Jossey-Bass Management Series.

Sosnoski, James J. 1994. *Token Professionals and Master Critics: A Critique of Orthodoxy in Literary Studies.* Albany: SUNY Press.

Sperling, Melanie. 1991. Dialogues of Deliberation: Conversation in the Teacher-Student Writing Conference. *Written Communication* 8.2:131–162.

Spooner, Michael. 1993. Circles and Centers: Some Thoughts on the Writing Center and Academic Book Publishing. *Writing Lab Newsletter* 17.10:1–3.

Sprott, Walter J. H. [1958] 1970. *Human Groups.* Pelican Psychology Series. Hammondsworth, Middlesex: Penguin Books.

Stagg, Josef. 1991. Form & Function: The Enderis Hall "Parti." *Academe*, 77.4:17–21.

Street, Brian V. 1984. *Literacy in Theory and Practice.* Cambridge: Cambridge University Press.

Steward, Joyce S. and Mary K. Croft. 1982. *The Writing Laboratory: Organization, Management, and Methods.* Glenview, IL: Scott, Foresman.

Stull, William. 1982. The Writing Lab's Three Constituencies. *The Writing Lab Newsletter* 6.5:1–4.

Trimbur, John. 1987. Peer Tutoring: A Contradiction in Terms? *The Writing Center Journal* 7.2:21–28.

Trimbur, John. 1992. Literacy Networks: Toward Cultural Studies of Writing and Tutoring. *The Writing Center Journal* 12:174–179.

Trimbur, John. 2000. Multiliteracies, Social Futures, and Writing Centers. *The Writing Center Journal* 20.2:29–31.

Upcraft, M. Lee and John H. Schuh. 26 May 2000. Assessing the First-Year Student Experience: A Framework. Online posting. Policy Center on the First Year of College. 12 June 2001 <http://www/brevard/edu/fyc/FYA_contributions/UpcraftRemarks.htm>.

Upton, James. 1999. Brain-Compatible Learning: The Writing Center Connection. *The Writing Lab Newsletter* 23.10:11–12.

Van Gennep, Arnold. 1960. *The Rites of Passage.* Translated by Monika B. Vizedorn and Gabrielle L. Caffee. Chicago: University of Chicago Press. Originally published as Les Rites du Passage (Paris. E. Nourry, 1909).

Vaughan, Terry Wilson. 1991. Good Teaching Rooms: A Campus Resource. *Academe* 77.4 :11–15.

Vukelich, Carol and LuAnn D. Leverson. 1987. Two Young Writers: The Relationship Between Text Revisions and Teacher/Student Conferences. In *Research in Literacy: Merging Perspectives,* edited by John E. Readence and R. Scott Baldwin. Thirty-Sixth Yearbook of the National Reading Conference. Rochester: National Reading Conference.

Waldo, Mark L. 1987. More Than "First-Aid": A Report on the Effectiveness of Writing Center Intervention in the Writing Process. *Issues in College Learning Centers* 5:12–22.

Wallace, Ray. 1994. Text Linguistics: External Entries into "Our" Community. In *Intersections: Theory-Practice in the Writing Center,* edited by Joan A. Mullin and Ray Wallace. Urbana: NCTE.

Wingate, Molly. 2001. Writing Centers as Sites of Academic Culture. *The Writing Center Journal* 21.2:7–20.

Wislocki, Mary. 2 April 2001. Re: Electronic Mentoring: Request for Responses. Email to the authors.

Young, Beth Rapp. 2001. Using Heuristics from Other Disciplines in the Writing Center. *The Writing Lab Newsletter* 25.9:6–8.

Young, Richard Emerson, Alton L. Becker, and Kenneth Lee Pike. 1970. *Rhetoric: Discovery and Change.* New York: Harcourt, Brace & World.

Zelenak, Bonnie, Irv Cockriel, Eric Crump, and Elaine Hocks. 1993. Ideas in Practice: Preparing Composition Teachers in the Writing Center. *Journal of Developmental Education* 17:28–30, 32, 34–35.

INDEX

CONTRIBUTORS

PETER CARINO is Professor of English at Indiana State University, where he directs the writing center and teaches technical writing, rhetorical theory, and American literature. His articles on writing centers have appeared in *WCJ* and *WLN* as well as in several edited collections. He has also published essays on American literature and on baseball in literature and culture.

MICHELE EODICE is the director of the writing center at the University of Kansas. She hails from the East and earned a doctorate from Indiana University of Pennsylvania. With Kami Day, she wrote *(First Person²) : A Study of Co-authoring in the Academy* (USUP 2001). Eodice is an active board member in the IWCA, MWCA, and NCPTW and is currently Associate Editor of Development for the *Writing Center Journal.* Among her interests are collaborative writing, institutional leadership, and speed golf.

NANCY GRIMM is director of the Michigan Technological University Writing Center and an associate professor in the Humanities Department where she teaches graduate and undergraduate courses in literacy studies. She is author of *Good Intentions: Writing Center Work for Postmodern Times,* and she has published essays in *The Writing Center Journal* and *College Composition and Communication.* Her current research examines the role of identity in literacy and learning.

LESLIE HADFIELD, STEPHANIE H. RAY, AND SARAH S. PRESTON are graduates of Utah State University, Leslie completing a degree in English and Stephanie and Sarah majoring in Interior Design. The collaborative project described in their chapter was funded through an Undergraduate Research and Creative Opportunities Grant, undertaken as part of a project in the Rhetoric Associates Program in which Leslie Hadfield was employed.

JAMES A. INMAN is Assistant Professor of English at the University of South Florida in Tampa, Florida, where he directs the writing center and coordinates the major in professional and technical writing. His writing center publications include *Taking Flight with OWLs: Examining Electronic Writing Center Work* (LEA, 2000), *The OWL Construction and Maintenance Guide* (IWCA, 2002), and articles in *Writing Center Journal and Writing Lab Newsletter.* Inman is incoming Vice President of IWCA and current President of the Southeastern Writing Centers Association.

REBECCA JACKSON is an Assistant Professor at Southwest Texas State University, where she teaches undergraduate and graduate courses in rhetoric, composition, and technical communication. Her work has appeared in *Rhetoric Review,* as well as several edited collections, including *Preparing College Teachers of Writing, Strategies for Teaching First-Year Composition,* and *The WPA Resource.* Her current work examines the possibilities of narrative research in writing centers, with a particular focus on students' counternarratives of identity.

HARVEY KAIL is Associate Professor of English at the University of Maine, where he directs the writing center and teaches composition and literature courses. He has been working primarily in writing centers since 1977 and has published on peer-tutor training and collaborative learning in *The Writing Lab Newsletter, The Writing Center Journal, College English, CCC* and *Rhetoric Review.* He lives in Orono, Maine.

JOYCE KINKEAD is Professor of English and Vice Provost for Undergraduate Studies and Research at Utah State University. Her interest in meaningful academic employment and hands-on learning for undergraduates is evidenced in the Rhetoric Associates Program, a tutoring program that also requires students to complete publication-worthy projects. A charter member of the National Writing Centers Association, she served as Executive Secretary (1983-1989) as well as co-editor of *The Writing Center Journal* (1985–1991). Her latest publication is *Valuing and Supporting Undergraduate Research* (Jossey-Bass, 2003).

JOE LAW is the director of the University Writing Center, coordinator of Writing Across the Curriculum and professor of English at Wright State University (Dayton, Ohio). In addition to writing centers and WAC, his research interests include Victorian literature and the interrelations of the arts.

JOSEPHINE A. KOSTER is Associate Professor of English and a recovering writing center director who teaches at Winthrop University in South Carolina. Her checkered career includes stints running writing centers for Bell Labs, the BOC Group, and Winthrop, and terms on the Boards of the Southeastern Writing Center Association and the International Writing Centers Association. She is the author of *Teaching in Progress: Theories, Practices, Scenarios* (3rd ed., Longman).

NEAL LERNER is Lecturer in Writing Across the Curriculum at the Massachusetts Institute of Technology. He is co-editor (with Beth Boquet) of *The Writing Center Journal* and co-author (with Paula Gillespie) of *The Allyn & Bacon Guide to Peer Tutoring, 2nd ed.* He has twice won the IWCA Outstanding Scholarship award, and his current research focuses on the history of teaching both writing and science via "laboratory methods."

CARRIE SHIVELY LEVERENZ is Associate Professor of English and Director of Composition at Texas Christian University. She has published articles in *JAC, Computers and Composition,* and *WPA,* and is currently working on a book entitled, *Doing the Right Thing: Ethical Issues in Institutionalized Writing Intruction.* Beginning in the fall of 2003, she will be co-editor with Ann George of the journal *Composition Studies.*

MICHAEL A. PEMBERTON is Associate Professor of Writing and Linguistics at Georgia Southern University, where he also directs the University Writing Center. He has published widely on writing center, WAC, and technology issues, edited a collection of essays on *The Ethics of Writing Instruction: Issues in Theory and Practice* (Ablex, 2000), and co-authored *Bookmarks: A Guide to Research and Writing, 2nd ed.* (Longman, 2003) with John Ruszkiewicz and Janice Walker. He is currently serving as Past President of IWCA.

TOM C. PETERSON is Professor and Director of Interior Design at Utah State University, where he has been honored with a number of teaching awards, including being selected by the students as the 27th Annual Last Lecturer. During the 2002–03 academic year, he served as director of Honors; he is also on the steering committee for the School of the Arts initiative.

DONNA N. SEWELL directs the Writing Center at Valdosta State University, where she is an Associate Professor of English. She co-edited *Taking Flight with OWLs: Examining Electronic Writing Center Work* with James A. Inman. In addition, she serves on the Executive Board of the International Writing Center Association and serves as Vice-President of the Southeastern Writing Center Association.